RUNNING THROUGH THE NIGHT
– *Ultramarathon adventures in Europe*

DAVID BYRNE

First published in 2019 by David Byrne

Copyright © David Byrne 2019

The right of David Byrne to be identified as the author of this work has been asserted by him in accordance with the Copyright, Designs and Patents Act 1988.

All rights reserved. This book is sold subject to the condition that no part of this book is to be reproduced, in any shape or form. Or by way of trade, stored in a retrieval system or transmitted in any form or by any means, electronic, mechanical, photocopying, recording, be lent, re-sold, hired out or otherwise circulated in any form of binding or cover other than that in which it is published and without a similar condition, including this condition being imposed on the subsequent purchaser, without prior permission of the copyright holder.

Printed in Great Britain by KDP Ltd

Contents

PREFACE ... 5
1 EARLY BEGINNINGS ... 7
2 THE ITRA AND THE UTMB ... 12
3 GATHERING POINTS ... 17
4 CCC 2010 ... 21
5 CCC 2011 ... 31
6 BACK PAIN ... 39
7 LAKELAND100 RECCE 2014 ... 48
8 LAKELAND100 RACE 2014 ... 52
9 TREADMILL INCLINES ... 58
10 UTMR RECCE 2015 ... 64
11 UTMR RACE 2015 ... 83
12 ECOTRAIL OSLO 2016 ... 95
13 TIERRA ARCTIC ULTRA 2016 ... 104
14 TRANSYLVANIA 50 2017 ... 125
15 Ut4M 2017 ... 153
16 SOUTH DE FRANCE 100 2017 ... 179
17 ECOTRAIL PARIS 2018 ... 196
18 TRANSYLVANIA 80 2018 ... 209
19 ZUGSPTIZ ULTRA 2018 ... 220
20 TDS 2018 ... 237
Annex A Results ... 249
Annex B Kit list ... 251
ACKNOWLEDGEMENTS ... 255

DISCLAIMER

This book has been written to give an insight into ultramarathons. Whilst I enjoy competing there are many dangers involved and things can go very badly wrong. Just because something is there doesn't mean it it sensible to do it; operate within your own boundaries of comfort / experience and only enter an event if you feel you can complete it safely.

All the content herein is the authors perceptions, recollections and memories and any errors are unintended and the authors own. None of the events, or persons mentioned, have seen this book, and it in no way represents an endorsement by them.

PREFACE

This story is about finding a pastime that provides an escape from what might be deemed a normal life. It's about choosing a lifestyle and exploring the envelope of personal physical and mental capacity and capability. It's about the realisation of aging and questioning how many years it is possible to do something as the sand falls ever quicker to the bottom of the hour glass. It's about getting off the fireside rug and going out in to the dangers of the cold and the dark.

When around twenty years old we tend to think we have all the time in the world, but when thirty and forty come the perspective of time, and what time means, starts to change and some things just have to be done now before it is too late. The realisation of the passing seasons can be very powerful as it means every day, week, month and year have to count.

There is a balance to be struck between saving for retirement and living life on the way through, balancing financial security against financing memories. Having the luxury of aiming for either is a privilege as many don't have this choice, living life in perpetual poverty due to their circumstances. This other world is all around us on a daily basis and all it takes is a toss of a coin to land on one side or the other.

Whilst this story is about ultrarunning it could really be about anything – take away the actual activity and see the personal satisfaction and feeling of self-worth lying within. It just so happens that this escape is about pushing physical boundaries to new limits and attempting to turn the seemingly impossible in to the possible.

I've done many things in my life; however, my proudest achievements are not my academic or professional ones but those times I spent out on the trails both training and racing. I hope the essence of what I experienced comes through in the chapters that follow and it inspires others to follow their dreams in whatever field that is.

This book will trace the journey from one flagship ultramarathon to another. Welcome to the world of ultrarunning.

1 EARLY BEGINNINGS

The earliest memory I have of endurance athletes was watching Greg LeMond and Miguel Induráin in the Tour de France. I used to watch the 30-minute highlight programme on Channel 4, fascinated with what they, and their fellow competitors, could achieve.

As a teenager I cycled a lot but, unfortunately, one day was in a very bad road traffic accident, suffering a fractured skull and a sub-arachnoid haemorrhage. Part of the bike had a catastrophic failure and I went over the handlebars and skidded along the road stopping at the kerb. I looked left and saw a car coming and tried to lift myself off the road. As my bike lay on its side, with me still on it, I tried to stand up but couldn't. I then reached out to the pavement thinking I could use my hands to pull me off the road however there was no strength there to do this. Barely moving I thought this was the end and shut my eyes thinking my time to die had come, at least it would be quick. My next recollection was trying to get my bike in to the shed at home, several miles away, but not having the strength to do this as I could not lift the bike up the single step. I headed in to the house and stated 'I've crashed my bike' and went to sit down on the couch and could not. I said 'I think I'd rather lie down' and carefully got down on to the floor and became unconscious. It turned out that the car stopped and I had a perfectly lucid conversation with the driver who ran me home – I have absolutely no recollection of the journey or even what they looked like. My parents phoned 999 and an ambulance quickly came and my next recollection was the fresh air as I was taken out of the house in to the ambulance. I was soon in hospital and things went from bad to worse so I was moved to a specialist Intensive Care Unit (ICU) at a hospital 100 miles away. I'd been experiencing bad vision problems and I thought this would be the last time I'd see my home town as I looked out of the ambulance doors as we headed through the night. Looking back through the rain covered rear window, trying to burn every image in to my brain, was an upsetting experience. I spent a few days in the ICU then was released to a ward. In the ICU you realise you are surrounded by people who are in a really bad way, everyone trying to get better. I saw it as a real positive to be moved out of that ward but felt sorry for the injured individuals I left behind. Whilst we were all ill, in hospitals you do have a lot of time so start talking to people in adjacent beds and learn a little about what happened to them. None of us had experienced something pleasant to be there.

In the regular ward I soon got bored so decided to try and work out a way of getting from my fourth-floor ward to outside of the hospital building and back in without being spotted. In any situation it is always possible to create a challenge and an adventure. To picture the scene, imagine a badly bruised tall teenager, wearing pyjamas, who has balance problems so cannot walk straight, and only has one eye that will open, trying to blend in and move around inconspicuously. What played in my favour was that every patient was injured and part of my rehab had been to practice walking in straight lines with a physio, so to the lay observer it would look like I was doing some homework.

My first challenge was to try to get to another floor and this was relatively easy by asking to be let out of the floor I was on as I wanted to practice some walking. The nurse let me out of my floor and walked me up to the next floor and let me in the fifth-floor door so I could practice a length of their room before being let back down. It was a bit annoying to have gained a floor as I was trying get down and out of the building, but I had a plan. When on the practice walks, I'd spotted there was a staff staircase, and this would be where my mini-adventure would take place. The staff staircase door had a swipe activated lock on it and was a little slow to shut after a staff member went through so it was fairly easy to get through then wait in the stairwell until they had disappeared. I then headed down and let myself out in to the glorious fresh air with a push button. I had about 30 seconds outside then worked my way back up in a similar fashion. It was a real mini-adventure and I really enjoyed it!

Whilst at the hospital I saw a beige cardboard folder with my name and date of birth on it and, in big red letters 'Must not be read by patient' stamped on it. Part of me wanted to open it to see what it said as I presumed it would have something like 'chance of full recovery x%' but could not be sure I would not get caught opening it so decided to leave it. Whilst opening it may sound a dishonest thing to do, I think most people, in that situation, would be a little curious.

Within about a week of leaving the ICU I was transferred back to the original hospital and ultimately to home where it took months to recover. The vision problems were resolved after a few months – once the swelling had gone down and I'd had my tear ducts unblocked. Being able to read again, after months of having problems, was a really liberating experience. In these dark times I had my motto of 'my time will come' and, slowly but surely, I recovered. Having a bad head injury is not a nice experience in many ways – there is the constant pain as your brain swells up inside your head and presses against your skull, there is the pain to touch any part of it on the outside (the fracture I had was about 4 inches long) and there is the pain caused by being near anything verging on a bright light as the eyes really hurt. Although it took almost a year, I was lucky to make a full recovery, as many don't. This made me realise how, with a click of the fingers, everything can change, so the time to do something is now.

The accident delayed my university start by one year and I think this time really framed my personality as someone who is determined and will keep trying despite any adversity that comes along. Throughout university I continued to have various health problems but I was able to get back on the bike, so I bought myself a mountain bike. This was my transport (as I didn't own a car) to get around university and I did a little cycling out of term time but not much. Eventually I had to buy a car for work but the car also brought something more – a way of getting my bike to mountain bike races!

I raced for 3-4 years in regional events, never winning but being towards the top of the field. In one particular race I was very much 'in the zone' and realised I had a chance of a podium finish if I was fully committed to the race. At one point I was going down a steep road overtaking a car and suddenly there was a blind bend and I was going too fast to sensibly brake and slip in behind the car so I accelerated overtaking not knowing if I would head straight in to on-coming traffic. Fortunately, there was no vehicle and with a massive rush of adrenaline I pushed on to the end coming 5th, my best ever result in a bike race. I'd had a proper scare though and vowed never to take such a risk on the road again. I was starting to question if bike racing was my forte as whilst I had the power/skill to succeed as a weekend warrior I wasn't comfortable with the risks I'd have to take.

My last ever bike race took place in Swinley Forest in Berkshire. It was a two-lap affair of about 10 miles per lap and the race started on a wide fire track and quickly went in to single track. As we sat on the start grid, about 10 wide and 6 deep, we all knew the trail would narrow in about 200m so we would have to get in single file for a tight right-hand bend. The flag dropped and we were off, all pedalling hell for leather to get ready for that bend. Lots of jostling was going on in the pack as we hammered up the stony path and with a dab of the front brake I slipped in line as we went in to the bend. The track was now undulating and we approached what is known as a 'bomb hole' or crater up ahead. The technique is to carry some speed over the edge to get back up the other side. Like frenzied ants the line zipped down and then up the other side with the person in front only just making it, but continue on we did. The path was now shouldering a hill in an undulating fashion and the person in-front suddenly stopped for no obvious reason. I braked heavily and stopped without going in to them. The person behind me had worse reactions and went straight in to me. I went forward and my front chainring dug in to my right leg, making a mess of blood and cycle oil. Racing is racing so I was quickly up and going again. Coming to a wide field I could see there had been a bad crash and a rider was down, with the marshals quickly going to their aid. I carried on to the second lap and during this I could hear a helicopter land and, when I got back to the crash, I could see the helicopter parked with several medics treating the person. This did not look good for someone out for some Sunday afternoon fun – possibly life changing. The afternoon's events had made me reassess what risks I was willing to take and at the end of the course there was a small jump with a photographer. I got off my bike and walked it. My lens wielding friend called me a coward for not cycling it. I decided I needed to get my racing fix elsewhere so decided to take up running. At least it was possible to stop quickly and a bad accident is less likely to happen.

The trouble was I could not run due to various pains and it took several years to get up to being able to do 30mins on the treadmill at 10kmph. Once I was able to do this, I entered several 10k and half-marathon events but was starting to want something more. It felt to me as if I had some unfulfilled potential and the mysterious world of ultrarunning looked like an interesting one to get to know more about.

2 THE ITRA AND THE UTMB

There are many ultra-runners in history – the most famous possibly being Pheidippides, the Athenian messenger sent to Sparta in 490 BC to seek help against the Persians in the Battle of Marathon. Throughout time many messengers will have travelled great distances through day and night carrying little either to sustain or protect them from the elements. These ancient messengers were the real pioneers of the ultra-world.

Often when training on a long route I put myself in the shoes of the messengers of old. I find it interesting to ask others what they think they would have done had they been around hundreds of years ago – most see themselves in position of power or authority. I feel I'm more of a realist, seeing myself as a messenger. Most of my long-distance training I do by myself in the UK, out in all weathers, day and night. During this solitude my mind wanders to the role of the messenger and I start to look out for ancient river crossings, old inns and the like. It helps to pass the miles. My true calling is moving on my feet.

There has been a lot written elsewhere about the origins of the marathon, and the rise of popularity of it, with many seeing it as the pinnacle of running achievement. Whilst the marathon became hugely popular towards the end of the 20th Century there was also a subculture of ultra-running bubbling in the background.

As with anything there are always those who want a little more, the pioneers who always want to go to that next hill to see the view, reach that headland to see the coast around the corner. These people drove the market for longer distance running events. Initially there were not many such events but over the years more and more have started to address this desire.

As with any sport or activity ultrarunning has governing bodies and acronyms. Many races are accredited by the International

Trail Running Association (ITRA) (http://www.i-tra.org/) who grade races by difficulty and award points for those who successfully complete them. Firstly, there is a points system, of whole numbers between 1 and 6. A 1-pointer could be a 50k run with 500m of height gain compared to a 6-pointer which could be a 170k run with 10000m of ascent/descent. When I was starting out there was a different scheme in operation colloquially known as 'UTMB points' which had a scale running from 1 to 4. A 170k run with 10000m of ascent/descent would be a 4-pointer in the old scheme.

As more and more races joined the calendar it was becoming harder to distinguish the relative difficulty of one to another so the ITRA introduced two other numbers; the mountain rating and the performance index. The first being a whole number between 1 and 13 which was the mountainous rating – 13 being very extreme and the second being a score based on the runner's time to completion known as the performance index or cotation. This second number has nothing to do with final position or the fastest time or anything like that. The performance index helps the runner chose the next race. E.g. my current value is 456 so a race of 350 should be within my grasp, however to succeed in a race of 500 may be very hard or impossible, even with lots of training. Some races are more popular than others and they will ask for a number of points (within the last two years) to allow entry to their event.

There are many good races out there that are not accredited with the ITRA – e.g. the Zugspitz Ultra, so a runner who only focuses on ITRA races will miss out.

Probably the most famous race in the calendar is the Ultra Tour Mont Blanc (UTMB) that takes place in Chamonix at the end of August each year. There are actually five events taking place in 'UTMB week' from beginner level to extreme. The events are listed in Table 1 below. Note that the points required, and even the routes, do change from one year to the next so for any aspiring entrant the latest position should be ascertained from the UTMB website.

	OCC	CCC	TDS	UTMB	PTL
Runners	1200	1900	1600	2300	300
Pts (2018)	6	8	8	15	Experience
Cotation	340	390	390	420	N/A
Pts awarded	4	5	6	6	N/A
Distance	55k	101.5k	121k	170k	300k
Ascent	3500m	6100m	7300m	10000m	25000m
Cut off	14hrs30	26hrs30	33hrs	46hrs30	151hrs30

Table 1: UTMB series events for 2018 (http://utmbmontblanc.com/en/accueil.php)

The UTMB is a significant undertaking so many will aim at the shorter Courmayeur Champex Chamonix (CCC) that follows the second part of the UTMB course. Both the CCC and UTMB go clockwise around the Mont Blanc massif. There is another race, the Sur les Traces des Ducs de Savoie (TDS), which goes anti-clockwise from Courmayeur to Chamonix and is more mountainous than the UTMB. Finally, there is the Petite Trotte à Léon (PTL) which is for runners who want to compete in one of the toughest races out there. This race has teams of 2-3 taking part, the pre-requisite being at least one member must have completed the UTMB.

If a runner completes the UTMB, CCC or TDS and one other Ultra-Trail World Tour (UTWT) (http://www.ultratrail-worldtour.com/) event in the same calendar year they will be given a UTWT ranking. To many this is even more of a motivation to take part.

In race week Chamonix turns in to the nearest thing to heaven on earth for an ultrarunner. Firstly, the town square is covered in stands advertising races and selling race gear. The outdoor shops are all focused on the ultrarunners with their bright displays selling all manner of products. Various kit doubts creep in to the mind – "should the hat that weighs 100g less be bought as it may make a difference to finishing as there will be less weight to carry? Sure 40 euros seems a lot but it could save the camel's back from being broken by a straw." Chamonix itself is now visited by more runners in summer than skiers in winter so running is big business. Everywhere you look there are runners walking around with UTMB carrier bags or little running rucksacks. There are signs everywhere advertising the event. As well as the thousands of runners there are many friends/family and supporters also walking the streets. To an ultrarunner it really feels as if the tribe has been found.

Hearing 'Conquest of Paradise' by Vangelis at the start of one of the races really stirs the soul as the runners stand in anticipation at the start of one of the greatest adventures of their lives. Running, or walking, the last km in to Chamonix is a truly remarkable experience – no matter what time of day or night there are people out cheering and clapping. It's humbling. It's emotive. Those who have experienced this will count it as one of life's highpoints, something to be looked back upon as a fond memory for the rest of their life.

This book charts my progress in European races from the CCC in 2010 through to the TDS in 2018. It doesn't cover every event, just those on the journey that still exist. One of my favourite events ever was the X-NRG 2-day race around the coast of the Isle of Wight and this would have featured but this event no longer takes place. It was a favourite for many reasons – friendly organisers, a great route, daylight and warm! This event was a key stepping stone to many other multi-days I've done – some of which are covered later on this book.

Back in 2010 there was a ballot for both CCC and UTMB, however TDS did not sell out. Fast forward to 2018 and all events were over-subscribed. If a runner is unsuccessful in the draw, and they maintain their points in races they get a coefficient of two when entering the ballot for the same race in the following year i.e. their name is placed in the hat twice. If unsuccessful in the second draw, and provided they maintain their points they are guaranteed a place in the third year. Factor in the need to have points which will typically take a year to get then it can be seen as a long drawn out affair. Finally, the weather can really impact things when out there – the race gets re-timed, rescheduled or abandoned so many runners think it is best to aim for two attempts to get a finish so it can easily turn in to a five to ten-year campaign. For many people the UTMB will take over many years of their life.

With the time it takes to get a place, and the general hype around the event, it is easy to see why so many runners want to be in Chamonix for race weekend each year. There are many other good races at the same time of the year, such as the Ultra Tour Monte Rosa, or the Ultra Trail de 4 Massifs, but nothing comes close to the scale of the UTMB weekend which is where this story will begin and end.

3 GATHERING POINTS

It was around 2005 when I first heard of the four most hallowed letters in the ultrarunning world; U-T-M-B. In the years since there probably hasn't been a day pass by when those letters have not slipped in to my consciousness at all. I heard about it from a friend, Christian, who had completed the very first UTMB when it was 'only' 158.1k and 8650m. He provided advice for my first ever ultra in 2007 which was Trailwalker, a 100km walk on the South Downs Way to raise money for Oxfam, a UK based charity. I led a team of four, of which only Steve and I finished and I thoroughly enjoyed the experience. We had the luxury of a support crew headed up by a friend, Fox, who had been resourceful enough to secure a nice wooden table that went along the route atop the Land Rover he had borrowed so we certainly had good crew support!

Steve and I were always interested in new walking experiences and some others in our circle of friends, notably Hannah and Nicki, were familiar with the Yorkshire 3 Peaks and suggested a weekend in Yorkshire 'doing' it. The Yorkshire 3 Peaks is a popular running/walking route that takes in the summits of Whernside (736m), Ingleborough (723m) and Pen-y-ghent (694m) over a distance of 39k. We set off early from a campsite and walked to a local shop to use a clocking-in machine to stamp a small piece of card. When we returned, we would re-stamp it to get an official time. We got to the end in something like 12 hours and I asked if anyone wanted to go up the first one again for good measure. The group thought I was joking and laughed it off but the trouble was I wasn't however I kept this feeling to myself. I had a lot of energy left in me and thought I had not really pushed myself and that there must be something more out there for me. I actually ended up going several times to 'do' the 3 Peaks and always came away with the feeling there was more to be 'done'.

Next came the national 3 Peaks of Nevis, Scafell Pike and Snowdon raising money for charity. This was a really easy event for the walker as it was really about doing 3-4 hrs walk per hill with plenty of rest in-between. It was far more of an undertaking for those doing the driving. In our team we even had a Border Collie, Holly, along for good measure, who, whilst she didn't seem to enjoy the wet Lake District, did enjoy sitting on me and keeping me warm in the minibus.

I started to investigate other events and Fox sent me a link to something called the Lakeland 100 which was a 100-mile race around the Lake District. I instantly felt excited but also knew this was a big step up from Trailwalker. They also ran a Lakeland 50 race so I entered that in 2009. Now in entering this I saw it came with 'two UTMB points' for those who finished it not really thinking they would be of any use to me – still it was nice to enter something that gave away points. Originally, we talked about both entering with the possibility of entering the 100 mile the following year but, as it happened, I entered alone. In the following years I would enter a 50-mile event with Fox and another friend PJ, we three circumnavigated Jersey in a day. In the years since I've walked with both over a variety of distances. At the time of writing PJ is having a resurgence of interest in distance walking and in 2018 we did two very long 'post work walks' together of around 100k. We head out around 17:00 and walk through the night finishing lunch time Saturday at a rail station wherever our walk has taken us.

July 2009 came and I thoroughly enjoyed the Lakeland 50 - my first fifty-miler. The race started at midday and I finished in the small hours having spent a large part of the night running with Jimmy, who I would meet again in 2010. Finishing earned me two points so now I needed only another two to get to the Alps!

In the Lakeland 50 I met lots of people who were collecting points who filled my head with all sorts of ideas. It seemed that many who were taking part in the Lakeland 100 would be going on to tackle the UTMB about a month later. Those in the Lakeland 50 had their

3 GATHERING POINTS

hearts set on CCC. Then there was something in between called TDS that everyone accepted was very tough and no one there was entering. In the years that followed I tended to only hear bad news stories about the TDS and how hard it was – in an odd way this seemed to make it more appealing to attempt.

Like many people I'd started Internet dating and had met a few people over the summer months. The trouble was they all seemed to be only interested in running so I decided I'd actively try and find someone, 'E' who had other pursuits. I found someone who listed 'reading' as a pastime – apart from Dickens I've never had any real interest in fiction so this struck me as someone who had genuinely different interests to me so it was worth a punt. We started to exchange small talk via e-mails and over the space of a few weeks getting to know each other a little more. The next thing was to meet up but it was getting critically close to my next 50-mile race, the Caesar's Camp Endurance Run (CCER). This was the race that would get me enough points to race in the Alps in 2010! I was focused on the race and thought if I met E the weekend before the race, and we got on, E would probably want to meet up race weekend and that would be no good – I'd either have to choose one or the other and this would not do. I took the approach that it was best to meet the weekend after the race – sure there was a risk E would walk away and that might be my loss but I'd trained hard for this! CCER went well and I put down my first sub-12hr, finishing in 11:29. The next weekend I met E for the first time, with bad plantar fasciitis in both feet, and we've been together since, so my strategy paid off. True to E's original pitch there has been little to no running, or running chat, but we have done an awful lot of walking which is possibly my influence. In return I've learnt to ski and through some races have found new places to visit in winter time to take on the slopes.

By now I had enough points for either the short CCC or the longer TDS so had to decide which race to do. I chatted it through with PJ who suggested that I enter the easier CCC in 2010 then the harder TDS in 2011. When you are young(ish) you think you have all the time in the world so this seemed a reasonable idea so I entered the ballot for CCC and waited for the result. In the middle of January 2010, I found I had been successful so all I needed to do was to start training and book flights and accommodation.

As things turned out I've mixed opinions if I did the correct thing as, in the years since, I've had several near misses and flirts with TDS and would not get to stand on the start line until 2018.

4 CCC 2010

An attempt at CCC in 2010 was now on so it was time to start thinking about training. For about a year I'd been religiously plodding at 10-12 kmph on the flat chatting to my treadmill buddies for about 30 minutes every morning - this approach enabled me to do sub 2hr half-marathons but I knew this was not going to be good enough for CCC.

From talking to other runners at the Lakeland50 I'd learnt that for CCC training for downhill was equally as important as uphill but decided to ignore this for financial reasons. I lived in a flat part of the country so any hill training would have to be on a treadmill in the gym. Sessions lasted anywhere from 20 minutes to several hours and as things progressed the entire route was attempted over six sessions. If the real route was an ascent it would be matched on the treadmill e.g. if the course climbed 500m over 10k I'd put the treadmill at 5% and do 10k. Any level section on the real route would be with the treadmill level and any descent would be with the treadmill level as there was no other option. This approach was also useful to learn about hydration as on a two-hour session, even with drinking a litre of water, it was possible to drop 2kg in weight. Adding a rucksack with weight presented further challenges. The first time I tried this I turned up with an empty rucksack and put a bundle of running mags that were lying around the gym in it. At the end of the session I felt quite guilty when I found the edges had turned to a damp sweaty pulp so I had no option to bin them and deny others their reading material. I tried running with tins of baked beans and these really started to dig in so it wasn't very long before I dropped the whole idea of running with a weighted rucksack. On these long training runs night time TV was my gym friend as I pounded the treadmill at 5 AM alone until people started to arrive around 6. More typically I'd be in 6ish and do 30-45 mins in the company of others with my maps propped up on the controls area of the treadmill whilst I mentally told myself what each transition in gradient meant i.e. where I was. I've never seen anyone else run on a treadmill with maps so I naturally got some interest from the curious. A number of gym buddies got interested in what I was doing, notably Nick B and Dave M; chatting about progress helped in the build-up to the race. I find having treadmill buddies really helps as it doesn't matter who is the fastest as you can both push each other on to achieve greater things – Nick B and I ran huge distances next to each other for years and had some great chats along the way. Dave M is a far more focused runner who can run fast for long periods; his ability to talk is inversely proportional to his speed!

The months passed by and in August E and I headed out to Chamonix for the biggest race of my life. It was our first trip away anywhere and would be a test of many things in many respects. On the plane going out I met Jimmy who I'd raced with during the night in the Lakeland 50 the year before. Jimmy had a place in the UTMB having been timed out at Courmayeur (about half way round) the year before. Sadly, the same would happen in 2010. I've met a number of people like Jimmy who keep trying, and not succeeding, at the same event; each time coming back for one last go. I admire the drive and determination and at that time wondered if I would ever get to that point with something. Would I get the itch I just kept having to scratch? Would something ever creep under my skin so deep? The nearest I got over the years has been TDS and I didn't stand on the start line until 2018!

We landed at Geneva airport then caught one of the many shuttle buses to Chamonix. Seeing Mont Blanc for the first time is spectacular, the mountain majestically rising skyward in the distance to the right of the road. Chamonix was abuzz with race fever and after dropping our bags in the B&B we headed in to the centre of town.

There was a temporary expo in the public square with all sorts of exotic races being advertised by their organisers. Caught up with the excitement I picked up a number of leaflets and, with hindsight, wish I had entered some of them at the time e.g. Libya looked really interesting in 2010. The only fly in the ointment being I'd just taken on a large mortgage so any expensive race was unaffordable!

Next thing to do was to go to kit check in the big sports hall. For anyone who has not done this before give yourself a few hours as everything moves slowly but, eventually, you get a tag on your bag, tag on your wrist, get given your race number and pick up your bus ticket to get to the Courmayeur the next morning. The dream was upon me – the big day would be tomorrow. The seriousness of the venture always kicks in when tagged, like a tag around the wrist prior to being anaesthetized at a hospital telling you that something important is imminent.

Being cautious about what to eat, and having a thing for tinned mackerel, we sat on our B&B balcony whilst I ate bread, cheese and fish. I've no memory of what E ate but it was probably the same (possibly without the fish) – at that point we had not known each other that long so went along with each other's dietary quirks. E eventually came out declaring less of a love for tinned fish than I.

Next morning, we were up very early for the bus and I was full of excitement as we headed through the Mont Blanc tunnel. The road winds out of Chamonix and slowly but surely climbs to the tunnel portal for the road through to Italy. It's the longest tunnel I'd ever been in and I was amazed at the various signs and rescue areas on the way through. The road drops out high on the Italian side then works its way down the mountain to the small town of Courmayeur that sits nestled between the mountains.

We got dropped off somewhere in the town and no-one knew where to go. We first followed some signs over the river and got to the UTMB resting hall. We then doubled back and eventually found the start which is in the centre of the village near a large plastic dinosaur. The clock was now ticking and in this final few minutes I passed a few items of clothing to E and I went through our plan again of meeting in Champex, Trient and Vallorcine. I passed my camera to someone who took a picture of E and I at the start line then after a quick 'good luck' from E I headed in to the start pen. I think it is really only when standing in the start pen of a big event you realise the enormity of what you are taking on and how you are challenging yourself and failure is a very real possibility. More and more people entered the start pen and I positioned myself about ¾ of the way to the back. The announcer gave various messages, mostly in French, and the tension grew within the pack. Everyone had worked so hard to get to this point and the moment of reckoning was about to come. The race build-up featured some very emotive rousing music by Vangelis and as the race was about to start the heavens opened. As we set off, I stayed on the right of the course to give E a quick wave and managed to spot her (in part due to the bright red Peter Storm coat) in the crowds and that was it – the adventure had officially started. Everyone was running and lots had their walking poles fully extended getting in the way and catching ankles – I never know why people start with extended poles. I know some don't collapse, and that is different, but if they can collapse surely it is in the best interests of everyone to do so? The pack ran through the streets of Courmayeur before almost doubling back on itself to come back through the town and head for the mountains.

It was still early days in my running career and this time I was wearing my NF Rucky Chucky shoes in a vibrant red. The only reason I had these was I'd seen an advert in some magazine which showed that someone called Lizzy Hawker had worn them in some record-breaking run in Nepal. I thought they must be good shoes if Lizzy, whoever she was, could run a huge distance in them. I'd upgraded other gear to an Osprey Talon 15 rucksack (£60) and a Sprayway Gore-Tex Paclite coat (£40 in a sale). Below this I had my trusty blue Gore-Tex cycling top (sold as a jumper but is really a long-sleeved top) that I'd bought for £90 in 1998. At the time I was cycling everywhere to save money so thought having a warm underlayer was a sound investment and a treat. This top has proved excellent value for money as is still fully functional 20 years later. On my legs I had a pair of Nike running shorts and some 1000-mile socks. I was not even aware of calfguards or quadguards at this point so my leg hair was very free to blow in the wind.

Once everyone was properly soaked the rain started to ease off and about 5k in it had almost stopped. This first hill was hard and I stopped to take my coat off and about 100 people shot past whilst I fumbled to get it in to my bag without slipping off the trail. Along with others I got lots of nettle stings on this hill. I'm certainly not masochistic but there was something about being in the herd and all getting stung together that bonded us and was part of the adventure.

It wasn't long before we were at the first Check Point (CP) at Bertone (1991m) and, anecdotally, I was aware there can be lots of pushing and shoving here and it can be hard to get water or food. When I got there, I found it to be busy but everyone was pleasant and polite. I drank about 400ml of water and finished off a Torq bar. It wasn't long before it was time to head off on an elevated shoulder path that looked down on the valley below. The view from this section is mesmerizing – looking down to Courmayeur (1220m) far below in the valley, and up to the Mont Blanc massif looming intimidatingly under the glowering sky.

I had walking poles that twisted to lock and for some reason I could not lock one of them out so from here on in I only had one pole I could use and the other sat in my bag. The upshot of this was my right bicep was getting more and more painful as the day progressed. The consequence of having a pole in my bag was, at one point, I found the bag to be half open as the faulty pole was trying to make a break for freedom but fortunately everything was still in there when checked.

The path continued on along a wide ridge line then headed to the right to get off this hill before doubling back to the Bonatti CP (2025m) - the race course no longer includes this section instead taking a different route out of Courmayeur. At Bonatti I had some salty soup and three cups of cola – so far I'd had 800ml of fluids at the CPs. I only know this detail as post-race I'd made some notes to learn from for future events. I've found making notes a useful part of training typically scribbling about a page of A4 the day after a race writing down what worked well and what needs tweaking.

The next descent seemed quite long heading down in to the valley and the next CP at Arnouzaz (1769m). Here the CP was a long tent that was situated at the end of the road in the valley – a number of supporters were out to see their family members probably taking about 20 minutes to get from Courmayeur by car compared to our six hours by foot. I ate two small cereal bars, four salty crackers, a few biscuits, three pieces of dark chocolate and ½ of a small Bakewell tart. There was a lot on offer here and I was spoilt for choice enjoying the various snacks before re-filling my water and setting off with one litre; I could carry two litres but I thought saving a kg in weight was sensible for the big hill to come. Race reports are often conflicting when describing what is available to eat/drink but at any of the UTMB races supplies are plentiful wherever the runner is in the field.

In all my treadmill training one hill I'd really been focused on was the route up the Grand col Ferret (2537m). I knew this was the high point of the course and would mark the point the route left Italy and entered Switzerland. In advance I'd told myself I would keep going and not stop until the top no matter how slow I was going. The path sets off and, after a few hundred metres of ascent, levels out at a mountain chalet and gives some respite before the main hill begins. It is a relentless slog, with no flat sections, that just keeps on going and going. On this hill I managed to polish off three snacks on the way up and at the top I was out of water. Not good. I thought about trying to find a river to fill up from but as there was nothing obvious decided against this. I'd taken a chance setting off on this hill with only one litre of water (to save one kg of weight) and I was going to be paying the price for this decision by being dehydrated until the next CP.

At the top I had a secret wish to go off to the side a bit to a nearby viewpoint but didn't and pushed on down the other side. My calves were a bit crampy on this stage. I sort of ran down the other side as it was a wide track but it was really starting to hurt my legs – they had never been challenged like this. My treadmill training had clearly helped with going up the hills but I'd not really done any training going down the hills so my legs were suffering. In my post-race notes I wrote 'need downhill practice' knowing this would be easier said than done living in a flat part of the country.

The next section was relatively flat following a river and passing through the CPs of La Peule (2071m) and La Foully (1592m). At La Foully my notes say '3 cups of coke, 1 cup salty soup. Took 15 mins in tent. Wasted time. 800ml'. At this point I was starting to get tired and I knew I had half of the course still to go but was well ahead of 'cut off' pace so, at the time, the 15 minutes probably seemed reasonable but with my hindsight spectacles on it did not! Beyond La Foully the course drops to Praz de Fort (1151m) and at this point I knew daylight was closing in but I wanted to get to Champex (1470m) before I needed my head torch. It's 'only' 300m up-hill but when tired this is a lot. What made this worse was that in my head I thought the ascent was 300ft and so the hill seemed way too long! There were also large sculptures of mushrooms that messed with my head when judging distances on this section.

There was still some daylight in Champex when I met E. I had a banana, a Mars Bar and took on 1.75 litres of water. Meeting people at CPs is always interesting as there are a lot of things to be done. Firstly, not to cause offence to your supporter by taking any of your woes and grumbles out on them – after all they have been waiting for ages and are probably very bored. Next it is important to spend a little time asking how their day has been - this has to be balanced with your goal of spending the least time possible at a CP. I've found spending up to 10 mins is a reasonable compromise so I tend to go with that. After a quick chat we agreed to meet up further down the course and so it was time to tackle the infamous Bovine in the dark. I'd heard a lot about Bovine but I would now not really see it as the light faded very quickly and then it was dark – just a string of head torches disappearing up the mountain and in to the sky. The path here is very blocky and I started to get lower back pain that would be present until the end of the race. As we climbed upwards, we came to a river and there was a feeling of 'what now' as it was not clear how to cross it. Some looked for a bridge. Some tried to balance on rocks. I decided to wade on in and get wet as I didn't want to fall on the rocks in the dark. The weather was now getting worse and worse and we were getting in to a storm. The path levelled off and we were now on an exposed whaleback of a summit and the wind was getting stronger and stronger to the point where getting blown off was starting to become a real possibility. I was in a group of about seven and without talking about it we realised what we had to do. We got in to a human conga line bending forward on to the rucksack on the back of the person in front. For about five minutes our human caterpillar crossed this most windswept of locations, the town of Martigny glistening in the valley far, far below. At the start of the descent was a tiny tent across the course that contained a marshal and four plastic school chairs that had been tied down. I took my bag off and changed my gloves realising I was very cold as my hands struggled to function. It probably only took two minutes to change my gloves but in this short period I could feel the cold tentacles of the wind grasping my ribs like a boa constrictor so I knew I had to get moving quickly as I didn't want to go hypothermic on the mountain. Fortunately, the path started to drop down and we were soon in the dark woods before eventually reaching Trient in the middle of the night. The tent here had two parts – the main part had food/shelter, etc. and was for runners only. The small outer part, which was very cold and had rain coming in the front, was for runners with their supporters but the supporters were only allowed in if the runner was there. What this meant was that E was sheltering outside in the rain under an overhanging roof with many others. We quickly got in to the cold tent and I took on some more food that E was carrying. I went in to the main tent and filled up my bladder with 1.75 litres of water and it was time for off. Seeing E, and the others, standing cold in the middle of the night did make me think what they go through – each time a headtorch comes in wishing it is their runner – not knowing how long they will have to wait, standing there in the cold.

The next hill is the steepest on the course but at this point I knew I'd cracked it if I could finish so just plugged on up with my single walking pole. The top was very windy and I was seeing people fall and picking up small injuries. On the way down there was a large drop on the left of the trail and a strong gust caught me and blew me to the side, fortunately not in to the dark abyss below. At this point I thought things were getting really dangerous so decided to withdraw at the next CP at Vallorcine. For the final 500m I decided to push as hard as I could to take a few places purely for personal pride. As I got to the CP, I met E and told her I wanted to withdraw for safety reasons and E told me the race was being stopped due to the weather. I didn't really take this in at first so E had to repeat it a few times. On the one hand I felt relief as I was safe and out of danger, on the other I'd come so far and not finished. If I'd been about half an hour earlier, they would have let me through to the finish but the weather changes quickly and the organisers definitely did the right thing. E reassured me my decision was sound as if they thought it to be unsafe it probably was. It was about 04:00 and we both needed to get back to Chamonix along with several hundred others. We spent a bit of time in the large dry mess tent then were told the bus would be up at the road. It was about a five-minute walk to the road and we waited there along with a large group of very wet, short, Italian men wearing ponchos clutching their retracted walking poles like drumsticks. A bus arrived and indicated left to go down to the tent. The drumstick ensemble had an alternate view and they pulled the wipers forward so the driver could not see anything in the torrential rain. They then took their walking poles and like angry bees started to 'clack-clack' the outside of the bus to encourage the driver to open the doors holding their poles above their heads so they were 'clack-clacking' in the drivers eyeline. The driver edged a little forward to go down to the tent but the bees were having none of it click-clacking their drumsticks. In the end the driver gave up on getting to the tent and it was a free for all to jam on the bus. The seats quickly filled then every available standing space was taken as we sardined ourselves in. I was sardined next to E close to the side door and the one saving grace of being so tightly packed was there was some warmth, albeit with a damp musty smell from the occupants of the bus. It was a short drive to Chamonix and when the bus pulled in the side door opened. A woman who had been near the door fell out and collapsed on the ground between the bus and the pavement. She was lucky not to have been injured but soon got up and was OK. We all then headed to the race finish nearby to get our finishers fleeces. I'd covered 81k with 4675m in 19:25 which wasn't bad, all things considered.

It had rained for most of the day and was not reckoned by anyone to have been a 'hot' year. Despite taking on 9.5 litres of water I'd only urinated twice and it had been somewhere between honey and brown ale so this was a learning point for the future.

All in it had been a good first attempt at CCC that had only stopped due to the weather. It had been a test bed for personal training ideas on the treadmill. On the one hand the treadmill inclines worked well, on the other the lack of downhill running experience was an issue. Over the course of the day weak core muscles caused pain and this would be a recurring theme in future events.

When we got back to the hotel, around 06:00, we were both tired and my notes of the race end with 'Dry clothes immediately at hotel when down – don't throw in corner!'.

The next day my legs were wrecked. They were stiff and barely able to bend and taking the tiny slope to the crystal museum in Chamonix was at my limit. In the following days around Chamonix there was the steady trickle of runners completing both UTMB and PTL coming through the town always being cheered by strangers.

Prior to the race I wondered if, having completed CCC in 2010, I'd have the desire to come back for UTMB in 2011. At the end of the race I knew this was not going to happen as I'd have to now come back for CCC in 2011. I also had this itch called TDS that I could not help but keep scratching. This itch would last for years.

5 CCC 2011

The 2010 foray to Chamonix for CCC had been a baptism of fire into mountain ultras. The effort required to go both up, and down, was far greater than I'd expected. It was really clear that to make it more pleasurable more hill training would be required.

In the months following the 2010 race I kept asking myself the question where could I have gone quicker. This question kept surfacing, as I knew had I been 30 minutes quicker I would not have been stopped at the CP and I would have been able to continue to complete the full distance. Had this happened instead of wanting to enter CCC again I may have had my sights set on TDS or UTMB in 2011. Like getting an unexpectedly low mark at school in an exam, the fact that I didn't get to the end would always sit on my running record. Of course, it makes no real difference in any sense and stopping for a valid reason is a reasonable thing to do however it would be a little axe that would chip away at my insides that would keep chipping away until I'd completed a full CCC. My thoughts came back to doing more training should I get in to the race again and it was not long before it was time to enter the ballot and in Jan 2011, I found I had a place in CCC for that year. This gave about six months of training, time to get myself prepared.

I'd already entered the Lakeland 50, the race being at the end of July, and would use this as a final tune-up of both myself, and my equipment. There was still more I needed to do out in the real world away from the gym so in May E and I headed to North Wales and went up Tryfan which was fun. In the mist we got badly lost just below the summit and ended up back at the same point about 20 minutes after seeing it having done a complete circle on the mountain– a real lesson in spatial disorientation.

In July the Lakeland 50 came and went in 12.5hrs. I've since completed the race many times as it is enjoyable for so many reasons. It is well organised, the route is scenic, the CPs are friendly and it has a real sense of achievement. However, this time I had a fall a few miles from the end on the rocky descent from the final pass landing on my backside/lower back. When I got to the end, I had a medic look at it as I was cut and a bit bruised and they thought that someone should probably look at it when I got back home as thought it would need physio treatment.

A few weeks later I was doing some basic renovation on the house and moved a UPVC door (and frame) in one lift and something in my lower back hurt.

Finally, I ended up falling out of bed and my legs flipped over my head as my back landed on the floor – I remember announcing 'that was not good'.

A combination of the three events above would cause problems to this day.

I knew my lower back was sore, abnormally sore, but did not know why. I'd set my heart on doing UTMB in 2012 so figured all I had to do was to see CCC through in 2011 and continue to endure the pain until Aug 2012 then stop as I thought my body really needed a rest. I thought 13 months reasonable as if I stopped now, I feared I would never start racing again. At this point it can be seen I was very much sucked in to the mythology of the UTMB and had a need to succeed – it had gripped me in some way. I'd also gone off the idea of TDS as had heard horror stories about the 'big hill' and the rope down the other side and I just didn't think I had the skills to succeed.

In August 2011 all I could really do was rest until we headed out to CCC, this time there was a real question mark hanging over my health as could I cope with the pain? It was a bit like someone had a blunt axe and they were slowly pushing it harder and harder in to my back pushing right in the nerves. Many times, I thought all I needed was a large mallet to whack the area really hard as this may give some sort of relief and realign things as I didn't feel I had full mobility. Sometimes I thought if I bit my tongue really hard, I may bite through and this may hurt more and thus give some relief in the back as I would be unable to feel the pain down there. Both of these may seem extreme thoughts but anyone who has had significant pain would be able to relate to this. I started seeing doctors around this time to try and diagnose the problem and the collective wisdom was a tight piriformis. It would be over a year before the correct diagnosis was made.

Pushing all this to the side I headed out to Chamonix for CCC 2011 to give it my best shot.

After last year E&I agreed that we would meet at Champex and Chamonix as there was little point in hanging around Vallorcine in the cold in the small hours.

For this year I had a few kit changes – I'd bought some new Black Diamond walking poles that had clip grips instead of twist grips so would be easier to use when cold. My old NF Rucky Chucky shoes had worn out so I was now with a cheaper shoe, the NF Voza. I actually had a new pair of Rucky Chucky shoes but decided to go with the Voza as they were lighter – with hindsight an error of judgement as the Voza did not grip well. I've still got the new pair of Rucky Chucky shoes sitting unworn in their box. In an odd way I cannot break them out as their brother did me proud in CCC 2010 so for some unexplainable (to myself) reason they sit hidden away in a box years later. A bit like a trophy sitting in the back of a dark cupboard.

On the start line the organisers advised that there was bad weather coming so to get over the major pass, the Ferret, as soon as possible and that the course would be on a different route that would be marked when we got there. There was no indication of length or height gain or number of CPs.

I looked around the start line and could see a number of runners in their forties and fifties and I wondered what on earth it took to be that fit at that age and if there was any way I would still be competing when I reached that point. Back in 2011 I didn't really understand what it takes to succeed thinking running was the key and everyone gets slower with age. I didn't understand that running was only a small part of what it took to succeed. Pacing, nutrition, hydration, kit choice, navigation, wanting it and training are all of importance so success is balancing everything. Whilst speed may drop with age training may improve.

As I stood in the pack pondering the day ahead the same rising music played with the countdown being in French from 10 to 4 then a 'C', 'C' and 'C' and we were off at 10:15.

This year the route at the start was different as we gained the first big hill through a forested section that is used to this day. Personally, I preferred the 2010 route as the current route is narrow with lots of stop/starts as the pack narrows to one wide at times.

The weather was still good and I was soon up and over the Ferret and down the other side. My legs cramped up again and I tripped but was OK. It wasn't that long before Champex came and E and I had a chat. At this point I thought I could do it and was feeling positive about finishing. Beyond Champex the route changed completely and turned in to a mystery tour in to the unknown. Instead of going up to Bovine we headed to the centre of Martigny. This area is covered in vineyards and many a runner had taken some grapes on to spit them straight back out as they were inedible. The rain was now teeming down as the route crossed the railway line and then there was a chain disappearing up a steep rockface in to the dark. All I knew was the first person was walking up the rockface holding on to the chain with their hands and the chain was swinging all over the place. I wanted to wait to be the only person on it but that would never happen as there were hundreds behind me so I just grabbed the chain and walked on up the 20 or 30 ft until we were back on the level. This was my first experience of via ferrata, or the iron way, the occasional staples or chains that make many an alpine path more passable. I was quite pleased with myself having gone up it with no problems and was confident I'd be fine if another one occurred on the route.

The rain continued to pour down and at one point I was walking along on my own in the pitch black, the headtorch lighting up a little of the way in-front but mostly reflecting off the rain, when a lightning flash came. For a tiny fraction of time the entire mountainscape lit up and it was truly magical. I could also see about a foot to my left was a drop and then the lights went out. Nothing. Just my torch doing the best it could in difficult circumstances. That momentary glimpse has been permanently etched in to my brain as it was such a remarkable thing to see – someone turning the lights on for a fraction of a second in the middle of the night – the snowy mountains all around. There is nothing that beats a flash of lightning in the dead of night in the mountains – the clarity of glaciers under such light is absolutely stunning.

We carried on and came to a CP and I asked how far to the next one and they did not know. I asked if there were any hills and they did not know. It was now about 01:00 so off I headed in to the night following the markers to who knows where. Walking up a hill a man was standing in his garden with a teapot and some cups and offered me a cup of tea which I gladly took. I asked about the route ahead and he told me I was on a very long uphill. There was a road adjacent and some runners could be seen getting in to cars at the bottom. When I eventually got to the top, I could see some different runners coming out of cars. At the very least they had been sheltering in cars, perhaps getting some food in the dry. A more extreme possibility would be that they had taken a lift up the hill and this possibility annoyed me. What does it mean to say you've completed an event if you've had mechanical assistance along the way? I often wonder if such people have regrets as they will never know if they could have done it clean.

The route carried on and now it was amongst ski infrastructure and there was a little snow falling. In a tiny hut at the bottom of a chair lift, the sort often seen at a car park entrance, a man was sitting down staring out in to the darkness. I had no idea who he was or why he was there as he gazed wide eyed as if in a catatonic state. By now it was snowing lightly and things were starting to get really cold.

At around 03:00 I came to a CP and was glad to get out of the atrocious storm that was building outside. Inside there was space for about 40 people to stand and a few heaters. Some runners were hogging the heaters trying to dry all of their clothes out. Other runners were really cold and shivering at the entrance to the tent. I got myself close to the heat for about 5 minutes and got a tiny amount of warmth but my clothes were soaked through. Another runner who was further back was really cold and asked if I could help to get his foil blanket around him and I did. He put it under his coat and said he was still going to continue with the race in to the night.

I gritted my teeth and headed out in to the biting wind. It was the sort of wind you have to really lean in to for any progress to be made and it was ferociously cold. It was hard going and after about 50 metres I thought it was too much so turned around to go back to the tent as I was hours ahead of the cut off, I could wait until daylight at least. I took a few steps back to warmth and safety and had a word with myself and said if Captain Scott had quit, he would never have got to the South Pole so I have to turn around and push on and I did! After the event I remembered things didn't work out well for Captain Scott but, at the time, I thought he was heroic and I was not going to be a coward and take the easy way out.

The next few miles were very wet walking along a forest path. I was pleased to see two very wet poncho clad ladies who were a mobile CP scanning my barcode to track my progress. It would have been tempting to have walked along the parallel road as it would have been quicker but anyone doing that would have missed the CP and been caught out. After seeing the car issue earlier, I really hoped they caught some cheats.

The last few miles in to Chamonix were miserable. It was dark, slippy and my headtorch was not that great. My torch needed to be brighter and I needed to have a way of wearing it with my hood up. My NF Voza shoes were letting me down – everyone seemed to be passing me in Salomon shoes - I needed to investigate these. On one long descent about 100 people passed me and they just all seemed to be able not to slip everywhere – it was noticeable that I was about a foot taller than everyone and having a higher centre of balance was a big factor here, however it was not the only one. I'd spotted many had on very tight looking socks so made a mental note to investigate these further. Eventually I came to Chamonix and knew all I had to do was cross the river then there would be a short, paved, section then a loop back in to the town – less than one km to go now. In my head my plan had been to put my walking poles away and run heroically through the town and to the end bouncing along like a hare who had eaten a rather good carrot. I put my walking poles away, licked my fingers and stroked my ears back and set off at speed. About 100m later my bounce had gone and I was now walking feeling more like a pained tortoise so I got my poles back out. I power walked the last mile and jogged (in my head I probably thought I was running) to the end arriving at 06:17 in the morning. E was there having had a reasonable night's sleep. I'd done it. It felt good. Time for bed!

The trouble is sleep doesn't come easily after such events so after chatting for a bit I decided to catch a bit of rest around 09:00. All that happened was I couldn't really regulate my core temperature so I got hotter and hotter and super-heated the bed waking up on a torso shaped wet patch, like a chalk shape drawn on the ground after a homicide. The only thing to do was to get up and hope it would dry by that evening.

Just like in 2010 I spent the day hobbling around Chamonix like I had 10kg strapped to each leg. It would take years until I could walk normally after a race.

My new Black Diamond poles had been great and would be used on many races to come. I'd drunk a good 9-11 litres on the way round but was dehydrated only peeing at 16:30, 20:30 and 03:30. Bearing in mind I started at 10:15 and finished at 06:17 this was not good. I was also really hungry between CPs. This year I'd started training in April but, with hindsight, thought this should have been March. I also realised I needed to work out a way of getting downhills in to my training for future events.

Fitness-wise I was very good on the up-hills managing each nonstop. I was actually overtaking on the ups. On the downs I was slow due to slippy mud and just being tall so off-balance. The back pain wasn't as bad as expected and was manageable.

My notes finish with 'Lakeland50 fall impacted me as could not train in August and it was painful throughout (and in to Sep). The big question is should I have done two races so close?'. I'd had a good Lakeland50 so it was tricky to know what would be best for next year. I was contemplating entering UTMB as felt that I'd conquered CCC so wanted something a bit more.

As things would turn out the back problem would attack with full vigour and it would be a number of years before I would be able to race properly again.

6 BACK PAIN

There are a lot of cliched phrases in any sport such as 'pain is temporary and glory lasts forever' – the trouble is the opposite is so often the case as I was rapidly finding out.

In late 2011 I knew there was something wrong but it would take a long time to work out what it was. My first port of call was my GP who advised resting and taking some over the counter painkillers; these provided no relief. The pain was an ever-pervasive presence that cut in to all aspects of my life. The basic problem was it was incredibly hard to sit down as the pain in my lower back was just unbearable. At the same time, I discovered standing up would give some relief as would walking, however walking slow (like in a supermarket or museum) was excruciatingly sore. In these cases, I had relief by crouching down and curling my spine forward then sitting down and resting, a bit like a grotesque at Notre Dame.

I went back to my GP who put me on the waiting list for physiotherapy and prescribed Co-Drydamol and Diclofenac. Co-Drydamol is a compound analgesic that contains standard pain relief ingredients as well as caffeine to help counter the analgesic effect. It can be thought of as something stronger than a traditional ibuprofen or aspirin; however, when I was taking it, I thought it brought me little benefit. It was only when I started to stop taking it that I realised the benefits it brought – more of that later. Diclofenac is an analgesic Non-Steroidal Anti-Inflammatory Drug (NSAID) that aims to reduce inflammation and provide pain relief. It can be bought over the counter at a chemist for a week-long course. This approach doesn't sit comfortably with me, and I've never done it, as this in the realms of self-prescribing without medical oversight. Taking it for one-week does make a difference as if something is tight it relaxes it. In my case the lower back was perpetually held in a twisted spasm so the theory was the Diclofenac would reduce the spasm and the Co-Drydamol would reduce the pain. The trouble with taking analgesics on a daily basis is they make you feel sleepy so I also started to drink coffee and energy drinks. In summary I was now taking my societally acceptable medically prescribed downers along with my self-selected and self-prescribed uppers to try and keep myself functioning in the middle.

I missed my exercise so decided to get back in to swimming and for about the next year swum a mile three to four times a week (being lucky enough to live very close to a 50m pool). The ritual at the pool would always be the same. I'd tell myself it was too cold to go but then if I didn't visit the pool, I'd get no pain relief so would go along. I'd get changed then put my items in the locker. My left leg had not been functioning correctly since this injury started and was a bit dead at times so took less of the load than my right leg as I'd walk to the pool. I'd climb down the ladder and the left leg would feel like it was having an electric shock – really unpleasant. I'd quickly start swimming and the left leg would calm itself down. I'd do my distance in one go always none stop often doing 2k peaking at 3.5k on one visit. I'd get out and could walk normally and would feel so much better. A few hours later the pain would be just as bad so I would need to go swimming the next day.

Many things in life seem to move at a glacial pace, often for good reasons, but the time was passing by and we were now quite far in to 2012, over a year had passed without an accurate diagnosis. Keen to get results I decided to pay for private physiotherapy and booked up a series of sessions. At the first one the physio did some gentle movements and whilst lying there I memorised the titles of all of the books on her shelf that talked about backs and, when I got home that evening, I ordered them on-line. The medical opinion was that my problem was being caused by my piriformis, deep inside my buttock, but no matter how many hours I did piriformis exercises it made no difference. As I was getting neurological issues down my left leg and in to the base of the foot, I suspected it was something in my spine that was causing the problem. If correct all I needed to do was to work out what and persuade my GP to get me the treatment for it!

At the next physio session, she did a twisting motion with my upper back staying fixed on the table and my lower back rotating. This was horrendously painful and I had to ask her to stop and we ended the session as I was in a whole world of pain. I got in my car to drive away and stopped after about 1 mile as the pain was too much. I walked to the nearby library and sat down in there for a few hours until the pain became slightly more manageable then walked the mile from there to home. I went back for my car the next day.

A friend, Martin H, suggested I try a chiropractor and I was straight along there and the chiro did various manipulations that gave relief for about 30 mins before everything went back to how it was. These sessions were costing about £25 for 15 minutes and the money was soon building. To me, going along three times a week for a temporary cure, that lasted for about 30 minutes, was nonsensical so I decided to learn to replicate all the moves. On the last session instead of the chiropractor doing the moves as she was bending/folding me I'd give the critical muscular input at the required moment and we achieved the same result – my spine would be straight for about 30 minutes. I've no idea if she was aware that I wasn't relaxed on the last session and providing the input or not but she seemed pleased with the result which was great. To this day I do these exercises several times a week – those close to me call it 'clunking my back' due to the noises that are made.

The NHS physio sessions came along and the outcome here was also a diagnosis of piriformis syndrome which is deep inside the buttock. I'd now read a lot and this didn't seem correct to me – I had my suspicions about a slipped disc in my lower back.

I went back to the GP explaining what I thought and he referred me for an MRI scan and the appointment came through a few months later. It was for a Saturday afternoon at Frimley Park Hospital and E & I went along for the appointment. There was a delay at the hospital so we spent longer than intended in the waiting room as the pain just kept building. I went through for the MRI and was told I had to be very still for it to work so, in a lot of pain, I lay there. A few weeks later I found out I had a slipped disc L5/S1 and, having paid £15 for the images, I could see the problem myself. The specialist asked did I want to go on the waiting list for an epidural and, having read about how these may help, instantly said yes.

I'd been aware that epidurals are used in child birth but, until my back problems, didn't really know much more about them but knowing I might be offered one decided to learn about them. Within the back is an area called the epidural space that has lots of nerves in it. Under general anaesthetic the surgeon inserts a needle between two of the vertebrae in to the caudal hiatus, and injects an anaesthetic, along with a steroid, in to the epidural space close to the nerves. The desired effect is to reduce the inflammation around the nerves so the patient can try and do some strengthening exercises to help things. The effect of the epidural wears off after a few weeks so the window of making a gain is small. I knew I may have to go back for several epidurals. As with anything there are risks – in this case infection, nerve damage etc. but in the position I was in I'd have given any established technique a go as had little to lose.

It was good to have a diagnosis in early 2013 so I could now move on with things – I just had to wait for the epidural appointment to arrive. I think the GP now realised I had a real problem so prescribed Amitriptyline to help at nights. Amitriptyline is often prescribed as an anti-depressant but is also prescribed for neuropathic pain (as in the case here) the idea being it would help with sleep. Up to this point my left leg was so painful when lying on my back that I had to rotate to my side and so the constant turning of the small hours would commence. As any insomniac knows the middle of the night is one of the loneliest places to be as all you can hope for is daylight to come. Daylight brings only a temporary relief as the fatigue from lack of sleep kicks in and the individual rides the roller coaster of sugar highs, sugar lows and caffeine highs until it is time for bed and the whole ghastly night time experience starts again. At times at night the pain was so intense I imagined being on a stretcher and

6 BACK PAIN

the head end being raised so I tipped forward in to the dark abyss and the pain would be no more.

To help manage pain I also had the benzodiazepine Diazepam which is taken in a week-long course. I found this provided relief but it also slowed me down in general and induced apathy. I only went on this twice throughout my problems. On both times I had to have a snooze at lunchtime each day as these tablets really do take it out of you. Diazepam does make a difference with pain relief but it really slows everything down in a way that is unimaginable unless tried. So now I was taking the triumvirate for pain relief – Co-Drydamol, Diclofenac and Amitriptyline and had options on Diazepam; noting I was still countering the analgesic effects with coffee to bring things back up a little. I considered my Diazepam to be in a virtual 'break glass in an emergency' box that should not be touched unless things were really bad verging on unbearable – I had an emergency weeks course always in my medicine box just in case.

It was about this time that I met one of the reviewers of this book, DJ Alf. Whilst we have never taken part in any run together, he has offered constant sage advice on all manner of subjects for which I've been very grateful. I remember vividly during one Diazepam course DJ Alf commenting on how I was slower at everything – in this case it was turning to talk to him as he sat to my right. It started to make me think of the negative aspects of the medication. However, I was cossetted in my analgesic duvet so it wasn't something to overly worry about.

I was busy rescaling my ambitions now moving from competing in ultras to thinking of being pain free at some point. Whilst doing this I also had part of my brain thinking the 'what if' of the future and had settled on completing the Lakeland 100. In many moments of despair, I focused on succeeding at this at some point in the future. This was a major reason for persevering and not going for stronger medication as I didn't want a life of medication but wanted to get fixed. This is not to trivialise those who are on lifelong medication but more to say I wanted, if possible, to get to a pain free point and be off it.

Taking all of these tablets had put me in some sort of permanent analgesic fug. I was well aware of it and was being very careful only driving when I felt safe to do so. Others around me commented that everything was a bit slower in how I would answer things. I also think all these pills start to emotionally flat line an individual e.g. if 'mood' is rated from 1 to 10 everything sits around 4.5 to 5.5 no matter what it is. It's really hard to get excited about anything when all you want to do is to take a large mallet and bash your spine to relieve the pain. I was never going to do such a thing but there was always part of me that thought it just might help.

As well as the frustration with the pain there is also pain with the frustration as both physical and mental well-being are inextricably linked. To not be able to do things everyone thinks of as normal is frustrating – due to the 'pain sitting down' thing I was avoiding many social situations. I didn't have the strength to lift things and this was frustrating. All said those close to me were very accommodating then, and have been in periods since, when things have taken a temporary turn for the worse for which I'm very grateful. My standing joke is I'd like to think I'd do the same in the reverse situation – not many hear the 'like to think' clause when I say this!

Any sort of long-term illness grinds a person down as their body cannot do what their mind wants to do. There are feelings of depression and despair. The meds don't help in giving feelings of passivity and letting what happens happen regardless of whether it is good or bad – a bit like standing in the sea and if the wave knocks you over so be it. Within a forest that is dying there are small plants with green shoots poking up through the soil. As much as possible the focus has to be on the green shoots as without this there is only a life of accepting the pain and despair and the crushed dreams will always be there. For sure some have no choice and then have to cope with this and find acceptance in themselves to continue and this must be very hard. I had a chance as there were green shoots and I had to put every energy into nurturing and growing them. Up to this point I'd been doing about 300 hours exercise a year and now

I ramped things up to around 600hrs per year and have done this every year since.

On October 24th 2012 I had my first epidural. I was quite relaxed in advance about the procedure (who wouldn't be when on all those pills!) and went in to the local hospital late morning. After some forms and a fair bit of waiting I was taken through and anaesthetized. Coming to an hour or so later I cannot say anything felt different but I had an open mind. A good friend, Mike L, collected me and drove me home and I rested for a few days. I bought 'The Big Walks of the South' by David Bathurst in the local book shop and wrote inside the cover '1 day after 1st L5/S1 epidural! It seemed as if I would be able to go long again. One day.' I'm obviously writing a note to myself justifying why I bought it (the 'seemed') where others may question why. It is also interesting I'm thinking there will be more than one epidural.

About 2 weeks later E and I visited the Lake District by train (we had booked the trip months in advance). E went horse riding and I went up the nearby hill of Black Coombe (600m). For the first time in months I felt freedom from the pain (albeit still taking all my meds) and was elated to get up and down in about two hours. It was a real corner turning moment as now it looked like I'd be able to do hill climbing at least in the future, and with any luck something more!

The reduction in pain only lasted a few weeks and then I was back to where I had been however the door had been opened to what was there so I visited my GP and was put on a waitlist for the second epidural. I knew post this I'd have a small window to try hard to get things to work. I had this in March 2013 and again Mike L collected me and drove me home. I worked really hard after this one and it looked like I may be able to run again at some point in the future but not yet.

The next thing was to enrol in 1:1 core strength training sessions with Rich, a very competent gym instructor. Over the next 10 months we worked together for one session every Weds afternoon and whilst the epidurals were the building blocks these 1:1

sessions are what made the difference. Slowly but surely, I'd try a tentative run – 500m at 10kmph on the treadmill and things like this – to see what would happen. Without Rich I don't believe I would be able to do what I do now so I'm very grateful for all he did.

I was now starting to get increasingly positive about things as 2013 progressed and managed to secure a place in the Lakeland 50 and finished in 13:37. This was over an hour slower than in 2011 but it didn't matter – I'd completed it well within the 24hr cut off. It was now time to enter the Lakeland 100, the dream of completing had been my constant companion through many a dark hour. This may seem an odd choice to many i.e. not aim for something simpler but I was still developing in ultras and needed a challenge.

Coming off my medication was a lot harder than I expected – I naively thought I'd just stop one day but my GP explained it needed to be controlled. I came off the Amitriptyline first by reducing the dose then stopping about a week or so later. The Co-Drydamol and Diclofenac took a lot longer – about two months – to slowly reduce things down. Sometimes I'd reduce too quickly and have to go back up. Each time I reduced it was like the pain tap was being turned back on so it was hard to try and stay at a level and not go back. I'd try and hold it for a few days but sometimes it was too much so I'd up my dose again slightly and try and stabilise for a week or so before coming back down. I eventually managed to get off them and it was only several months later I realised how my clarity had been fogged during the period from late 2011 through to 2013. Lots of things I'd done with friends I could not really remember – I needed to look back at photos. I became aware my reasoning was a lot sharper and quicker when off the meds – it's a hard thing to describe unless you are ever there.

Pain wise I could now do about a 600m treadmill incline, say 4k at 15%, in 45 mins before the pain got really bad and I had to stop. This was better than nothing but not that good but at this point in time I started to accept this may be my limit moving forward.

My perspective on many things had changed as a result of my experience – firstly I was now more about completing an event than putting down a good time.

All of this meant the path was now set for an attempt on the Lakeland 100 in 2014.

7 LAKELAND100 RECCE 2014

It was now time to see if my body could perform as my mind wished and the test chosen was to walk the Lakeland100 course. Success would give increased confidence for the main event.

Each July around 1000 runners gather at Coniston in England's Lake District to take part in either the Lakeland50 or Lakeland100 races. Entries open in September the year before and the race typically sells out in hours. There are no ITRA points associated with the events but that makes no difference. The Lakeland100 weekend is to the Lake District what the UTMB weekend is to Chamonix. These events are popular for all the right reasons – excellent organization, friendly checkpoints and an interesting route through stunning scenery.

The 50-mile has a generous 24hr cut off so is an entry event for many aiming at their first 50. The 100 has a less generous 40 hr cut off and is a significant challenge for many who take part. Those taking part in the 100-mile race set off at 18:00 on the Friday heading out on a clockwise course. At 09:00 the next morning the 50 runners set off by bus to the approximate mid-point at Dalemain and then wait for their 12:00 start.

I'd waited at Dalemain three times (my Lakeland50 races in 2009, 2011 and 2013) and seen tired Lakeland100 runners pass through the CP. In my Lakeland50 races I'd overtaken many of them on the 50 miles back to Coniston – many walking like zombies but somehow managing to keep going. Whilst recovering from my back injury I'd decided I wanted to become one of those who succeeded on the long course, knowing that there is typically a 50-60% drop out each year, but I still thought it was worth a go.

I'd met Big Andy in 2013 and we had finished the Lakeland50 together – he had done the Lakeland100 the year before in 36hrs and I had his time plan to base things on. His take was the 50 was more enjoyable compared to the 100 which was a more akin to a 'death march'.

In April 2014 I headed to the Lake District to walk the entire course. With typical enthusiasm I'd loaded my big rucksack and my plan was to set off at 18:00 from Coniston school and see how I got on putting my tent up once or twice on the route. I'd allowed myself four days so had plenty of time so no pressures there.

Arriving in Coniston I could feel the excitement in the air of what I was about to take on. I got to the school and took a few photos of myself with my arm extended to my side to show my massive bag. I'd stuffed some last-minute cake in so it was now about 14kg all in which was quite heavy. Come 18:00 and I set off up the road and up the first hill on the Walna Scar Road which is a very rocky path, thinking it will be a lot easier with a lighter rucksack come July. Down the other side the CP location at Seathwaite was easy to find then it was inwards and upwards to the remote farm of Grassguards. I was sweating buckets but thought this OK as the bag was heavy and it was hot. I was navigating by paper map only and pushed on along the route having no fixed place to pitch the tent but thinking I'd do it around midnight depending on where that was. As so often happens when things start to go wrong, they start to go wrong very quickly. It was about 21:00 and I fell in to a bog – one-minute walking along and the next waist deep in sticky mud. The first thing I did was to undo my chest and waist strap as I didn't want the extra weight of the rucksack on me – I then took my bag off and threw it to dry ground – next I had to work out how to get out. I quickly realised I could not walk out as any step forward got me nowhere. I now realised I was acutely alone on the fell with no-one within sight or shouting distance and it was starting to get dark. What made it worse was my phone was in the bag I had thrown to the side so I really had to get out. The cooling effect of the water wasn't helping either as I was going goose-pimply whilst stuck in the bog. There was only one person who was going to get me out of this mess and that was me – no-one was passing tonight and the earliest walker, if there were one, would be mid to late morning tomorrow. I knew there was one safe exit point which was the point I had come in at so turned around and put my energies in to exiting there. I did the one thing that seemed obvious which was to throw my body weight forward on to the mud and hold on to any plant life I could to drag myself forward. A few large drags later and I was at the side with my front covered in wet mud and my legs drenched. I knew my priority now was shelter and warmth so whilst still in my wet gear I found a bit of flat ground and put the tent up. Next, I stripped off all my wet gear and tied it to the outside of the tent so it would not blow away in the night – I was hopeful it might just dry! One advantage of being completely alone was there was no risk of flashing anyone whilst I flapped around erecting my tiny tent. Finally, I got in to the tent, put on my spare clothes, and got in to my sleeping bag and shivered for a long time until I could get warm. I'd covered less than 20 miles and got very wet which was not a good start. Being remote meant that my sleep was peaceful and I woke up naturally around 05:00 ready for the day ahead. It was important I kept my spare clothes dry so I put these away and got in to my wet clothes that had not dried in the night and set off on the next leg to Wast Water. This leg is beautiful with Scafell on the right as the path traverses the high ground and down in to Wasdale Head. My bag was feeling heavier and heavier at this point and I started to question if I could complete the course in time. I rescaled my ambitions, now planning on doing half of it (walking to Keswick about 40 miles in) and stopping there for the night. As I set off the rucksack straps now decided to progress from making red marks on my collar bone to actually drawing blood through friction so I stopped and put some plasters on but this didn't seem to do much for the pain. I crossed Black Sail Pass and realised this would be tough in the real race as the path was indistinct and it would be easy to twist an ankle. Heading up Scarth Gale Pass I knew I was stopping in Buttermere for the night and my Lakeland100 attempt was off as I was not covering distance quickly enough.

In various countries around the world there are collections of mountains that walkers/runners set off to climb. Some will have a concerted effort to do them quickly. Some will do it over a series of holidays/weekends spanning their lifetime. The Lake District contains 214 Wainwrights that many set out to complete. This list was established by Alfred Wainwright and his ashes were laid to rest on one of the Wainwrights, Haystacks, which is very close to the Lakeland100 route. Steve Birkinshaw holds the record summiting all of the Wainwrights, covering the 515k and 36,000m in 7days, 1hr and 25mins. My progress is far more leisurely completing a few on each visit to the Lakes, at time of writing having completed 115 with a hiatus since 2015 as spare mountaineering time has been spent in the Alps. My reasoning is that the Alps are not going to get any cheaper to visit, and I'm bound to be tackling less arduous hills with age, so may as well visit the harder ones now and keep the Lakes for later.

I decided to visit a Wainwright I had not visited before, Haystacks, which was busy that day with many people eating their lunches and admiring the view. Moving on from this I descended the rocky path to the picturesque Buttermere. There is a small campsite here that had just what I was looking for – it had toilets, it did not have the possibility of falling in to a bog, and I could dry my clothes. Sitting in the pub eating fish and chips was nice – probably more appetising than my original plan of half a malt loaf and a banana – and I sipped a pint of local beer whilst planning what to do the next day.

The next day dawned and off I went on the course heading over the high pass and down to Keswick where I spent two nights in the campsite bagging many Wainwrights during my short stay there. All in it had been a learning experience. I'd learnt I cannot really carry 14kg day in day out (I'd make this mistake again in 2016 when recceing the TDS). I'd learnt that part of the route is hard to navigate due to a bog. I'd also learnt that, on the right day, I could probably do the event as nothing on the course fazed me i.e. no nasty drops or anything like that. I would return!

8 LAKELAND100 RACE 2014

Having had a non-successful Lakeland100 recce it was now time to see if I could pull things together on the day and complete the event.

July came quickly and I headed to Ambleside on the Thursday staying overnight in a B&B before catching the bus to Coniston to register for the race. It was a lot busier than a few months ago when I'd been the only person at the start! Having registered several times previously I knew what was expected so registration all went quickly and I put my tent up in the field and tried to get some rest until the 18:00 start. From about 16:00 onwards I chatted with a few other solo runners who had no support – we were the minority and had our various thoughts to share on what would be a very warm weekend for the Lake District.

One runner, Bob, had done the event before and he advised keeping our eyes shut over these hours.

Next to him was Mike who had found a variety of legal stimulants on-line that he had imported in from abroad. His plan was based around when to take what pill and was limited in terms of other details.

Then there was me. I was recovering from quite a bad back injury and was not fully fit by any stretch. I'd done the Lakeland50 three times but had never gone beyond 50 miles and now I was attempting the double. I knew I was going to push myself in to the unknown in many senses but had decided I was not going to be reckless and if it looked like I may do permanent damage I would stop.

At 16:00 the race organiser, Marc, got us all in to the hall and gave a serious race brief talking about weather, carrying mandatory kit, safety and such things. Everyone sat there very seriously then we all went our ways for our last preparations. For me this was lying down with my eyes shut. Time was now marching very quickly so at 17:30 I got up and went to the start pen. About two hundred of us stood there whilst an opera singer sung 'Nessun dorma' live. Hearing this really rips through you at the start of such an event and a number of runners had bits of grit in their eyes they needed to remove.

Come 18:00 and we were off – the ones racing the course sprinted off up the road whilst everyone else ran at a more leisurely pace until we hit the Walna Scar road when the pace dropped to a very fast walk. Up and over the top we were soon down at CP1. Of all the CPs I've ever been at in a race this was the most hectic one. There were about half a dozen volunteers pouring out drinks in to cups and competitors grabbing them as if their life depended on it – no airs or graces or politeness but just going for it and grabbing – it was a bit like being in some sort of whirlwind. I was glad to get out on to the relative calm of the course. On this next section I did not want to fall in to the bog from April so I kept on the back of runners and successfully got to CP2 at Boot. It was now getting dark so with the headtorch on I set out on the next leg. Everyone around me was now walking so this next section was really about everyone talking about races they had done and their dreams for the future – the miles went by quite quickly on the way to CP3 at Wasdale Head. This was the first calm CP as the pack had thinned out – plenty of food and a disco ball hanging on the ceiling of the hall – all the volunteers dressed as if they were from the 1970s. Now it was time for the two big passes on the way to Buttermere. I was really glad I'd recced these in daylight as I had a feel for how long sections would be – most useful. Buttermere CP4 was outside a small building and we took drinks and food on the grass. The cut-off here is 03:18 and it wasn't even 02:00 so things were looking good as I set off on the long hill up to Sail Pass. On this section I got talking to new people and we exchanged various race stories. Coming over the top of the pass was amazing – seeing lights on some very high pylons miles away. At this point I met one runner, Ross, who had entered, and not finished, on four previous occasions and was planning on not finishing again. As he saw it if he got a little further each time it was a good thing and, one time, he would reach the end. I admired his dedication to the race.

Throughout the night I'd been using my walking poles a lot and my upper arms were really painful. I knew I could not use them for the entire race so put them away and took two Ibuprofen tablets to help with the arm pain. The Braithwaite CP5 gave a welcome relief from the pre-dawn chill and I sat down inside to eat cold rice pudding and goodness knows what else. Everyone looked sleep deprived and half-dead. I just wanted to get going so headed out as the sun rose and things got a bit warmer. For long races the hardest bits are bedtime and an hour before sunrise – get through these and things should be OK. This next section was familiar to me and the miles slowly but surely got eaten up. At each CP I took on food and water and just kept going along. At one CP I was absolutely delighted when the lady manning it asked would I like her to make me a cheese sandwich and I left munching this as I walked along the route.

I worked out I'd go through Dalemain around 12:30 so would get a boost from the Lakeland50 runners – this would be good. As I approached Dalemain the runners started to pass me (they do a 3-mile loop before going through the CP) and I headed in to the 'Lakeland100' tent for some food. At this point I'd been awake for a long time and my memories are a little vague. I remember sitting down and opening my drop bag to have a tin of mackerel (salty fishy protein as I saw it) and a tin of fruit (fluids and fructose in my eyes). I changed in to some spare socks I'd put in my bag and decided to unload some of the extra layers of clothing I'd been carrying as it was a really hot day and I didn't think I'd be needing them.

Next to me a medic was giving some painkillers to a runner and asked if anyone else wanted them. A few to my left put their hand up, a few to my right did, then everyone around me did, not wanting to miss out I did also. The medic then said it was only Ibuprofen and there would be a form to be filled in – all the hands dropped. I think it is interesting that so many people, in the comfort of their armchairs watching sport on TV, get annoyed at 'drugs cheats' in sport saying they would never be susceptible to it. I've always taken a different view that some things are not black and white and there is a scale of grey between. The reason we all put our hand up for the pill was that we were all suffering so would take anything that was offered that would help. If I were a professional cyclist trying to make a team would I be similarly weak in putting up my hand to something offered? I cannot say but I do know I'm human and no-one sets out in life to do a bad job or cheat at something but sometimes things just happen.

It was noticeable that others were thinning out their bags so in the roasting heat, and blue sky, I thinned out my race bag to the bare minimum putting bits in my drop bag and headed off. This was potentially a big mistake and I've never done this since – always carry extra clothes just in case!

This next section was very familiar to me but I was not feeling good. I'd eaten a lot and was feeling bloated. A friendly man started to walk with me and kept telling me how wonderful and strong I must be to have entered such a race and he would like to walk with me for a few miles (he was going to the next village) to understand what it takes. I was feeling rubbish and whilst his questions were good for the ego, I really just wanted to be alone. He took none of my hints so I said I needed to go for a pee and wished him well. I went in to the bracken and came out and he was standing there waiting for me. We carried on. I found his well-intended chat more and more irritating and needed to escape him. I told him I needed to do a poo and it may take some time. He said he didn't mind waiting. I went in to the bracken not really needing one but thought I should try as I had to waste five minutes pretending so may as well see if I can do something with the time. Suddenly, out of nowhere, I had a violent bout of diarrhoea. Whilst not good in many respects I thought this may be a lifeline to solitude. To my new-found friend I shouted very loudly what had happened and said I would be about 30-minutes so can he leave me and he said he would and off he went. After wiping with bracken, and burying my mess, I set off down the course to CP9 at Howtown. I picked up some food and water and went on my way. It was a very hot day and about a mile out of Howtown I got the shivers. It was decision time. I could go on but if I stopped at CP10 (Mardale Head) I knew the rescue bus was at 23:30. If I went back to Howtown the bus would be at 18:00. It was now 15:00. Of course, I could have gone on but I didn't understand the shivering and did not want to have to get the emergency services out if I collapsed. I was clearly dehydrated, and shivering, on a hot day so something was wrong. This has to be taken in the context of someone who had been up since about 08:00 the day before so it was, at times, hard to think totally rationally so being risk adverse seemed a good strategy i.e. to withdraw. Other competitors encouraged me to carry on saying we would do it together. I knew my Lakeland 100 attempt was over having covered about 2/3 of the distance. With a tear in my eye I walked back go CP9. The CP staff asked me what I wanted to do and I said withdraw. They said they had been told not to encourage anyone to continue and respected my decision.

Over the coming hours they kept a good eye on me and got me food/drinks and chatted so I was not alone with my thoughts. Slowly but surely more people stopped here. My shivering stopped very quickly and I've since learnt this is about my ability to thermoregulate and over compensate at times. In the Ut4M in 2017 I had the same problem with being very cold in heat after climbing up a downhill ski slope in blistering heat on day one – in that event I pushed on and things stabilised quickly. With the power of hindsight, I, perhaps, should have spent 1-2 hours resting at Howtown then continued along the course as I was well within the cut-off times. However at least I learnt from it for future events.

Some competitors who arrived at Howtown had foot problems so, to pass the time, I took on the role of 'foot fixer' looking at blisters on the like – at least I was doing something useful. As the minutes and hours passed, I had some regrets about having withdrawn as I was now feeling fine but I had to live with the decision I had made only a few hours earlier. This decision would haunt me for several years and in my head moved from 'making a risk averse decision due to health' to 'taking the easy way out when things got a little tough'. These two perspectives are very different and many ultra-runners will beat themselves up over perceived failures. The nature of the sport attracts self-reflectors, after all there is a lot of training to be done so plenty of time for analysis. From each 'did not finish', or DNF, the runner bounces back and this is made all the easier by believing a self-selected DNF was the wrong decision.

Around 19:00 the minibus came and took us back to Coniston. It was disappointing to withdraw but the right decision. The night brought horrendous rain so I would have been very cold with my minimum kit had I been racing still – a lesson identified for the future – don't remove kit when tired at Dalemain! I struggled to sleep that night as my mind went through the 'what ifs' about what had happened.

Of the other 100 runners I had chatted to at the start Mike (with the pills) had covered less than 10 miles as one of his shoes had fallen apart. He was philosophical about it but said he would never attempt the race again. I saw a very tired Bob on Sunday morning who had now completed his second Lakeland100 and was starting to think about entering a third.

In my case I believed I could succeed in a 100 miler – I just needed the right one. Mentally I could not face an attempt in 2015 so decided I needed to enter the Lakeland50 and thoroughly enjoyed it, completing in a little over 12 hours. I'll return to the Lakeland100 at some point in the future.

9 TREADMILL INCLINES

The treadmill was originally invented as a form of punishment but has subsequently left the penal system and found its home in the gym. It forms the cornerstone of my training. Throughout this book there are various mentions of training on treadmill inclines. There are many benefits of training this way. There is no need for real hills, it is possible to train safely and make things harder/easier and to stop when as necessary. Against this huge safety net is the realisation that there is nowhere to hide on a treadmill. In the real world there are gates to go through, walls to climb over, views to admire and maps to check – all important things but if a little tired it is possible to spend a little longer to get a microbreak and a quick chance to recover. The treadmill has no room for such excuses and is a core piece of equipment for building mental robustness. There will come the point when the legs tell the mind it is time to stop however never ever let your legs control your mind.

A standard gym treadmill will typically go from 1 to 20 kmph in inclines from 0% to 18%. There are some rarer more expensive ones that will go faster, offer negative inclines (i.e. descents) and even positive inclines to 40%. All of my treadmill training has been done on machines that can incline up to 18% which has been more than adequate for my needs.

In many hotel gyms a treadmill can be found but often gyms are in normal height rooms so as soon as an incline is used it can be a real problem with the head room for taller people – this can be highly disappointing when stuck away in a hotel somewhere when spending an hour on an incline would be a very good use of the evening. It's easy to get in to a habit of spending the evenings in hotel bars with others which whilst sociable, won't really help with training. If possible being sensible in both the gym and the bar will probably yield more benefits all round.

Any incline is a shock to the body if the runner is not used to it as everything is just harder. I'd say to anyone who has not used an incline before to start at 2% then if things are OK over a period of sessions move to 4% then 10%. Only progress beyond 10% if no problems then try 12%, 15% and ultimately 18%. This typical top end feels really steep and can be very hard to run on due to angles of various joints in the body – I've found I can maintain about 7.5kmph for a few minutes but I have to drop to 6.8-7kmh to recover and get my heart rate down a bit. In the races described in this book there are sections that are steeper than 15% but these are typically when hands are also needed to get up some rocks etc. Most path inclines are 15% or less so actual hills don't feel nearly so bad after training on treadmill inclines!

Other numbers come in to treadmill incline challenges. Many people think they can walk at 4mph (6.4kmph) but very few could actually walk 4 miles in one hour. 1 mile is 1609m so 4 miles is 6436m. As treadmills typically go up in 0.5kmph increments this makes hitting 6.5kmph a good target. The trouble is when running it is an odd number to do calculations on, 6.6kmph is far easier as this means 1km in 9 minutes. If aiming for this, and to play it safe, best to go with 6.7kmph though to allow a small buffer to build.

Before going for a personal best (PB) attempt I have to really believe I can do it in my head – I need to believe this at least the day before and on the day. As an example of this I'll describe a recent 10k at 15% treadmill incline PB attempt. My previous PB was 1:37:48 in April 2017 which was my final push before the Transylvania 50 - in the intervening time I'd convinced myself I had a sub 1:30 in me. On the one hand sub 1:30 is good psychologically but it doesn't mean that much as it is just a round number in relation to the time system we all use. It's more about shaving 7 mins 49 off my previous time and despite being a year older still being able to maintain, or hopefully beat, what I could do then.

Being a scientist, I was interested in a few other aspects of the attempt so weighed myself at the start (74kg), filled up my water bottle (water with some electrolytes) and walked to the treadmill. In the local gym I like one particular treadmill largely because it gives a view of the TV and is in the middle of the row so I might get someone running on either side. It doesn't matter who is fastest but having others running as well always seems to help me and I like the mutual encouragement people give each other. As things turned out today, I'd have no-one next to me for my attempt.

The simple maths was I had to average 6.7kmph to meet my time target. I'd told myself that I'd only drop below 6.7kmph if it was looking like I'd fail to complete the distance through trying to maintain the target speed. I'd also told myself I'd try and do what I could to stay above 6.7kmph so I could build a buffer to be called on if needs be. I set off at 8.1kmph for the first two minutes which bought me a 40-seconds buffer to use if required. At this point I had a heart rate of around 140bpm so slowed things down to 7.1kmph as I was in this for the long haul to get the heart rate back under 100bpm which it soon did. The first 5k were a mix of 7.1kmph and 7.5kmph looking at the distance and time every minute and making a calculation.

At the half way point I was 2mins 20 up meaning I had a predicted finish time of 1hr27mins40secs if I could keep at 6.7 kmph or above for the next 5k. It was now time to really dig in and tell myself why I was doing this. I was drenched, feeling a bit wobbly and light headed, and getting funny looks off other passing runners. They would do 20 mins on a (non-adjacent) treadmill then head in to the changing rooms, have a shower, and leave giving me a curious look on the way out. In my head I started doing calculations as to what would happen if I dropped to 6kmph and worked out I could still come in under my previous PB but under 1:30 was unlikely. I then considered going for 7k in under one hour as a new target but I knew I was cheating to think of this. I also knew I'd been keeping something back so whilst it was possible, I knew it would not be my best 7k. For all the effort I was going through I was in this for 10k and there would be no quitting. My mind then drifted to races and why I'm doing this; how in a real race if I were struggling on a hill how I'd regret not training hard. After all I was attempting 1500m vertical which is nothing compared to some of the hills I'd face in the TDS in August 2018!

The trouble was it was getting quite hard and 1hr 27 seemed an awful long time away. I was wringing out my T-shirt about every 2 mins and the rubber belt of the treadmill was getting wet from my sweat and this was surprisingly slippy. All this and I was only half way. Getting to the end would be a massive internal battle with one part of me saying 'you've done well, take it easy now and go for a shorter distance' and the other part saying 'training is tough but it reaps rewards, do you think all these elites look for excuses and easy ways out?'.

There was a property programme on the TV with subtitles whilst classic dance tunes played over the radio. A tough treadmill incline is relentless so any distractions are welcome. On the TV a couple wanted to move out of Wokingham as they did not like all the green space development that had been going on around their house. They wanted to move to the country and do a self-build on the edge of a small village so they could get fields around them on three sides again as that is what they thought life was about. I'm not sure they realised the irony of their viewpoint.

At about the 7k point I started doing calculations on 500m intervals to work out a predicted end time and could see I was on for 1:27-1:28 if I kept going. I knew I was on the best hill run of my life and all I had to do was to hang on in there. I'd taken an energy gel to the treadmill but as I was so wobbly when trying to do things I decided not to try and open it. Now the sweat was really building and not evaporating off me quick enough so I was constantly wiping down my arms with the opposite hand and the sweat was pouring off.

A rhino of a man walked in to the gym, spindly legs, tight red shorts and a muscle vest that his overly developed arms popped out of, the tight vest accentuating his beer belly. He looked like he had stood against a wall and someone had some tattoo stickers that they had thrown at him from a distance. He strutted around a bit like a baby constipated rhino and after admiring himself in the mirror for a while settled in the weights area. His approach was to make lots of 'huuuuuh' type noises and clap his hands a few times then pick up a heavy weight and get it over his head whilst his spindly legs flexed like those of a heavily laden emaciated donkey. When above his head he was obviously pleased as he would drop it from height to the floor then do more 'huuuuuh' noises as his angry rhino face strutted around the gym staring at everyone giving himself the odd clap here and there.

8k came and it was getting really tempting to stop. The treadmill was relentless and there was nowhere to hide and part of me really wanted to take a breather but I knew to stop would be to cheat and I'd regret it afterwards. The only thing was to continue. Now I was doing my calculations based on 110m distances trying to do more than this each minute as this would then bring me under 1:27. I was running about 40m in every 200m and fast walking the rest – still never going below 6.7kmph. 9k came and I knew I had a sub 1:30 in the bag and had a fighting chance at a sub 1:27. Now the calf muscles started to play up. Both of them kept wanting to cramp and all I could do was to try and walk so I stretched them – I say walk but 6.7-7.2 kmph at 15% is really more of a shuffle run. About every 50m one of them would go to cramp and I had to fight it to stop it doing it. It was getting really hard as I passed through 9.5k but I knew only 500m, or about 10 cramps, to go. At the 9.8k point I decided to up to a proper run and edged the machine up to 11kmph and went for it – my calf muscles were popping all over the place but I had to keep going to get to the end and finished 10k in 1:26:10 so a new PB by a significant margin burning 1293kcal in the process. As soon as it reached 10k the machine went in to 'cool down' mode and dropped the incline to 0% and the speed to 5.1kmph. I slumped over the front of the machine and walked half bent leaning on it for about 30 seconds before straightening up increasing the incline to 4% to help my legs out and walked for several minutes until the machine stopped. In this time, I tried to open my energy gel but failed. I got off the machine and found in lifting my leg to drop it to the ground my calf cramped again so I hobbled over to the disinfectant and came back and gave the machine a good clean. I got some scissors and finished my gel. I changed my clothes and got back on the scales and was now 72kg so despite drinking a litre had dropped 2kg so sweated 3 litres. This meant I had to drink about 4 litres (two for each kg lost) over the next day to put it back on. Fearful of my calves I went on the exercise bike to cool down and did some gentle pedalling for 10 minutes and some stretching. For hours afterwards, my calf muscles kept spasming.

There were some other interesting physiological changes. Firstly, my fingers were a bit macerated as if they had been sitting in a bath. My eyes looked very red and sunken. As well as this as my blood had been in my vital organs and muscles not a lot was getting to my extremities so even an hour after this the ends of my fingers looked like waxy milky candles and had very little feeling in them. That evening I was surprisingly warm and despite it being cold outside needed no bedding. I woke up repeatedly through the night with either the calf muscles trying to cramp or feelings of dehydration so drunk a lot of water through the night. I'd also picked up a sweat rash from my shorts and had a lot of red spots tracing out the lines of the seams. On my head I had a lot of sweat spots just under my hair line. I'd pushed myself reasonably hard.

The treadmill had given me a good feeling for racing as it was the 8th March which is a long way from TDS. The trouble with treadmill inclines there is always the 'what if' – the decision for next time will be to either go for 11k (so more than a vertical mile as 1650m) or seeing how much under 1hr 7k can be covered in – 7k gets the magical >1k vertical as 1050m. There is also the stretch target of trying the big hill in TDS – about 2000m which would be a significant undertaking on a treadmill.

10 UTMR RECCE 2015

Entering increasingly technical races is like a game of dare. Get it right and it will lead to upping the stakes for the next event. Get it wrong and it could lead to not finishing or worse. Like a squirrel running across a busy road it is all about how risk is assessed.

During 2013 and 2014 I'd successfully completed a number of multi-day events in the UK and was quite enjoying the challenge they presented. The first one I'd entered was the X-NRG 2-day event circumnavigating the Isle of Wight and it opened a whole new aspect of racing for me – the social side. Whilst the first day was a little quiet, in the evening everyone chatted about the race and the course on day 2 was all very sociable as over the kms strangers become friends. Since then I've done many X-NRG events as find them a great way of training as cover 30-40 miles a day for 2-3 days – they also have the benefit of coming with ITRA points which helps keep the balance topped up! One disappointment I had with CCC was that I was paying a lot of money (not in race entry fees but accommodation/flights) to pass through somewhere that is stunning, but none of it could be seen during the night stage. There was now a new need – the need to find a daytime multiday in the Alps!

What next?

Most of the multi-day ultras abroad are what I'd consider to be lifetime events – crossing a desert or jungle and priced accordingly. I needed to find something that was more amenable to my budget.

Simultaneously I was also considering an attempt at TDS in 2015 but was hesitant in entering as I didn't believe I had the skills to complete the technical aspects of it.

I'd read about a new race, the Ultra Trail Monte Rosa (UTMR), which was having a proof of concept 'zero edition' in September

2015, with a view to launching a full first edition in 2016. The race organiser was the legendary UTMB (and so much more) runner Lizzy Hawker who, until late 2018, held the women's world record for the longest distance covered in 24hours, a phenomenal 153.5 miles.

Just like businesses many races don't last due to the relatively low returns for a high amount of effort. I've spoken with some organisers, from other events, who have a business model where they make a loss (noting they are giving their own time for free) for the first four years and aim to break even in year five then a small profit each year beyond. These organisers are not in it for the money but want to give something back to society and the sport they love, and give people experiences and dreams to last a lifetime. I wanted UTMR to be a success but knew that there was no guarantee there would be a multi-day option, or even if the event would take place, in years to come. If it were not a multi-day event, I thought I wouldn't be able to do it as not having the body to cover over 100k and 7000m in one go over such terrain. This meant if I wanted to do it, I really had to try and get a place in 2015!

The UTMR website had an application process and applicants would be sifted based on experience etc. and be informed if successful by some date in Jan 2016. The trouble was this date was beyond the date for applying for the TDS lottery i.e. if I applied for UTMR I may get rejected and at that point it was too late to apply for TDS. I wanted to keep my options open so contacted UTMR explaining my position and Lizzy replied saying she understood and if I applied for UTMR she would give a definite yes/no prior to the final date for the TDS lottery so, if UTMR rejected me I could apply for that. This seemed very fair and reasonable and this flexibility gave me a good impression of how future questions would be dealt should I get an entry in the race. I was never let down.

At this point I submitted my UTMR application and within a few days I received an 'accepted' e-mail which was great. All I had to do now was to ensure I was ready for 104k and 7070m (both distances subject to change as the race was planned) over three days in August.

At this point the reader may be thinking that 104k and 7070m is not that much and many races would do this over one day but these numbers hide the technical nature of the terrain. The trails are far more demanding than that found on, say, the UTMB course. They are narrow, they are high, and there is what is euphemistically referred to in the sport as 'some occasions of significant exposure'. This phrase means trails that are very narrow with significant drops where, at times, hands may well be required as well as feet. It's a bit like being a moth and seeing the candle burning in the distance and for many ultrarunners it is about how close they can fly to the point where their survival instincts kick-in and nothing matters more than getting through something and living. I've flown very close to the flame a few times and at these moments the real value of living becomes apparent. When clinging on to a rockface with four points of contact, and no ropes, and seeing a large drop below knowing I may be ten minutes from safety or seconds from death, is when I find my senses are dialled up to 11!

Of course, fear is a subjective thing that is based on physical ability, experience, perception of danger, actual danger and how the brain deals with all of this. On some courses I am fine where others are frozen in a grip of fear and visa-versa. It differs from person to person for a variety of reasons including the prevailing weather, past experiences, available light, and fatigue.

As things have turned out UTMR is a highly successful event, and now offers a 170k and 11000m option for those who are looking for something that is so much more than UTMB. True to the original edition they do offer a four-day version of the route also. In 2018 they introduced a '3 passes' version for those who want to do about ¾ of the route that I raced in 2015.

What was fixed for the zero edition was the start and finish of the race, the cut-offs and the approximate distances each day. For the zero edition the UTMR would start in Breuil-Cervinia and proceed in an anti-clockwise direction finishing in Grächen three days later; detail in Table 2 below.

Stage	From	To	Distance	Ascent	Descent	Time Limit
I	Cervinia	Gressoney Staffal	27 km	1800m	2250m	12 hrs
II	Gressoney Staffal	Macugnaga	36.5k	2670m	3200m	12 hrs
III	Macugnaga	Grächen	41k	2600m	2250m	12hrs

Table 2: UTMR distances (Ref: https://www.ultratourmonterosa.com/race-information-stage/)

Training

For my early races I'd done virtually all my training on treadmills in the UK as this was cheap and could be fitted around everyday life. I could have trained for UTMR on a treadmill in the UK but wanted to try the approach I'd heard others talk about i.e. heading to the Alps so I could get some downhill practice and have the opportunity to train on representative trails with all their associated hazards. I've since found it to be an effective way of training however it does cost both time and money which should be factored in to any racing budget. I typically do four or five races a year and my budget for entry fees, flights and accommodation is £1,500 per year so I need to choose carefully how I spend this.

Soon after being accepted I decided to book my flights to head out to Zermatt to do some training. I decided to go in April as I thought the snow would be gone and it would be a good chance to see the terrain – if it turned out my fitness was not good enough it gave me a chance to do further work in the UK over the summer months before the race in September. I booked a flight to Geneva then bought a special Swiss rail transfer ticket that allows one return journey to/from where the person enters Switzerland provided each trip is taken in just one day. Geneva Airport straddles the border between Switzerland and France so this was an acceptable entry/exit point. I also purchased a ticket that allowed me to have half-price access on any cable car in Switzerland. It was about February 2015 and I was feeling quite good at this point so decided to ask Lizzy for any advice on training in Zermatt. The helpful and polite reply informed me that there would be snow in April so I should consider this in whatever I was planning to do. Coming from the UK, and never having seen the Alps in April, I didn't think there would be snow but I had to yield to her experience and knowledge and re-think what I would do out there.

April arrived and I headed out to Zermatt with my crampons and ice-axe packed. The flight to Geneva was exciting as I thought about the week ahead – a chance to see the Matterhorn, a chance to use my crampons, a chance for an adventure, what's not to love! I could see the Alps from the aircraft as we approached and could see they had a lot of snow – Lizzy was correct!

Geneva is a great airport to arrive in if your onward journey is by public transport as there is a main railway station in the complex so I was soon on the train for my journey across Switzerland. The carriage I was in had two seats on each side and each seat had a table in front of it so four people sat around one table. It was an eight-coach train and for some reason the coach I was in, at the back, was empty for my three-hour journey. After leaving Geneva the train snaked along the Lake Geneva shore which had a fine mist rising from the water; fortunately, no fire in the sky. After this the train continued along a long valley which has a few aerodromes and a few very large wind turbines in it. There must have been planning issues in siting these turbines here thinking about approach paths for aircraft. It wasn't long before I could see signs for Martigny and this made me think of CCC in 2011.

Now the terrain changed again and I could see a number of railways heading up a mountain on the left. Later in the year, after the actual race, I would be on one of these heading to Interlaken and beyond but, for now, it was time to check I had everything and get off at Visp.

Visp is a small town at a junction to the Zermatt valley. It has a number of shops and feels like somewhere people pass through but never stay. I knew the Zermatt train was a cog one and could spot a cog train on the other side of the station so headed through the underpass to it. I had about 15 minutes to spare so feeling hungry headed out of the station and found a small shop to grab a snack which I took back to the train to eat. I had my first real experience of how expensive Switzerland is spending around 8 swiss francs (about £6) on a bottle of water and a bar of chocolate.

I got on the train and wanted to work out the best side for the views. Helpfully the train had lots of small maps on the walls and I realised both sides would be great, but settled on the right-hand side as I wanted to see a massive landslip at Randa that I had read about. The train set off and we slowly but surely started to gain height. We suddenly got to a steeper bit and I could hear the cog whirling up the rack. We were about 800m above sea level and we had about another 800m to climb to get to Zermatt. The train continued to snake up the valley and before long we were approaching Randa. The train went at about walking pace and I looked way up in the sky and could see a minor rockfall happening about 1000m above the train. This area has a considerable number of large rocks deposited everywhere and is a landslide danger area so I was glad when our train had snaked out and we set off again up the valley. About 5k out of Zermatt is the station of Täsch that, at first, seems incongruously large. Up to this point each station had been small but this one had many platforms and parking for 2,100 cars. The reason for this is that Zermatt is a car free town so for virtually everyone this is as far as they will get by car. As well as the parking spaces at the station there are a further 1,000 in the village. We left Täsch and went below a snow/rock avalanche protection cover and within a few minutes arrived at Zermatt station which, to me, had an odd feeling of being indoors despite it being completely open.

On leaving Zermatt station the first thing to greet the visitor is a square which has a sign in the middle with lots of directions to walking paths – all of these looked incredibly exciting and enticing

– like being incredibly hungry, and not being a fussy eater, and being presented with a large menu.

I'd booked in to the Youth Hostel and to get there I knew I had to stay on the road so headed in to town and along the shopping street. By the Pfarrkirche St. Mauritius I turned left and passed a climber's cemetery and headed over the river and took a right which started to gain some height and ended in a staircase that would take me to my accommodation at the Youth Hostel. I was obviously aware that climbers die in mountains but this was the first time I'd walked past a cemetery and seen a corroding ice-axe attached to a tombstone. This image would play on my mind throughout the week.

To keep things cheap, I'd elected to stay here and to keep things really cheap I'd gone for the eight-person mixed room. The bed came with breakfast and was about 25 Euros a night. On top of this I paid for the meal each night which was very tasty and cost only 20 Euros a night – for the quality of food, and in Zermatt, this was cheap. The meal was either a 'vegetarian' or 'meat' meal and you had to pay in the morning for that night – there was no element of choice as you would get what you would get but that was fine. The meal was available 18:00 – 21:00 but, typically, everyone would sit down at 18:30. If the weather was nice, we would sit out on a terrace. If it were cold, we would sit inside. There was always plenty of space to eat and to exchange stories of adventure and derring-do from the day.

I spent the first few days in my eight-person room and in this no-one spoke at all. Small groups came and went who were doing one day's sightseeing in Zermatt. On the third day I got back to my room with a note 'Mr Byrne. This is important. Please report to the head warden immediately'. My heart was racing as I was trying to think if I'd done anything wrong. I know some people pee in showers but whilst I'd taken a shower each evening, I hadn't partaken in such an activity so, surely, I wasn't being blamed for that? I'd similarly kept the sink for sink related activities so I was innocent on that count. I did have some quite pungent socks but I was keeping them in a locker downstairs away from fellow guests so I could not be blamed for that. I'd eaten rather large breakfasts each day and started to dwell on this. My bowl of fruit followed by a bowl of muesli then some toast, a cheese sandwich and a banana finished with coffee may seem a lot but hopefully I wasn't being pulled up for making them potentially bankrupt? I needed this fuel each day for what I was doing and there was not a sign explaining how much could be eaten – it was a free buffet breakfast after all.

On a more serious note a number of years ago I'd had such a message when someone close to me had passed away – hopefully it wasn't this. My heart raced as I went down and saw the head warden to find out what my summoning was about. It turned out to be very simple; they wanted to paint my room. As I was the only person due there that night, they wanted to move me to somewhere else. Waves of calm passed through me – I could have used that shower after all. The head warden said they would put me in a four-person room and asked if I was OK with that. I said I was, provided I didn't have a top bunk as being tall, and having fallen out of a bed previously, I didn't want to do that again. She offered no guarantees and gave me a room number to go to. I was certainly not going to take a top bunk so went along to see if there was going to be a problem and was pleased to find there was only one bottom bunk taken. I spread my bits all around the other lower bunk and wondered who I'd be sharing with now – with a bit of luck they would be conversational.

It wasn't long before the other person came back, a New Zealander called Andrew. He'd retired at 28 and had no need to ever work again – he didn't share this in a big-headed way but in a normal conversational way. He was spending some time skiing the world – he had just come from Japan and was booking his flight for the following week to South America. He was very pleasant to talk to and explained his family was a bit split and he didn't see as many of them as he would like to despite having the time and money to do it. What really struck me was that despite having means he was quite lonely and didn't have anyone to share his experiences with. I suspect this was why he was sharing a room in a youth hostel as opposed to staying in a hotel. The loneliness of solitary trips is interesting as I've done many by myself, contrasted by many with others.

When I'm by myself there are times when I think it is great as I get the casting vote at every junction and every decision point. The downside of this is that it is harder to objectively look at a dangerous situation when there is only one viewpoint so I do err on the side of caution at times. Sharing with others is great as you can connect in the months and years to come and re-live your adventure, however it only needs one in the group who is not up for it on the day to mean we all turn back so no-one reaches the summit. I think there is a balance to be struck and both have advantages, ultra-racing is somewhere in the middle as it is possible to do some quite extreme things in the company of others with some sort of safety net should it be needed.

The next person to arrive was a Canadian called Dave who was in his 60s. His wife had recently passed away so he was revisiting everywhere from their honeymoon 30 years ago. He thought it would be the last time he would visit any of these places so there was an element of melancholy about him and he was clearly still grieving his loss. After the meal each evening, I'd taken to going out on a night walk for about an hour in the snow, alone, with my headtorch exploring the starts of the trails to work out what to do the next day. One evening Dave, intrigued as to what I was doing, asked if he could come and I welcomed the company. We set off to a steep gully with an aerial assault course just at the end of the ski run in to Zermatt. For anyone who has ever skied to Zermatt from the Matterhorn direction they will know the piste ends in a road section and it was this road we were heading up. We got to the gully and peered in and then headed back down to Zermatt. Dave was a little scared at times on our night adventure and wanted reassurance that we would be OK. Each time we stopped and I explained the route I was suggesting – if he had not have been OK with each stage, I'd definitely have headed back with him as I wanted him to have an adventure and a good time wandering around snow slopes with no paths in the dark! As we walked back, he said he was pleased we had met up as there was no way he would have headed out by himself in the dark. I enjoyed the company as every other walk, both night and day, was a solitary affair so it was nice to find someone to share the experience with. When we got back to the room Dave was telling me how he thought his friends would like me and he thought I'd love to come to Canada and I could stay at his house but I politely declined. I think Dave was very much in the moment, and I know thus far his holiday had been by himself, so was being very genuine honest and friendly. Some would say he was verging on desperate inviting a stranger to his house but I see him more as vulnerable and lonely. I really hope no-one takes advantages of Dave's good nature as he really is a true gentleman.

The final bed was taken by South African Bob who was travelling around with his girlfriend Lucile who was staying down the corridor in a different room. Bob liked to lie in his top bunk and do very little but scroll up and down his mobile phone. At the end of each day we'd talk about what we had done but Bob never really shared anything, comfortable in the company of his smart phone scrolling up and down things. He'd go downstairs to sit in the lobby for some quality mobile phone scrolling with Lucile – that was really the only time I saw them together each on their own phones with their thumbs going up and down rarely talking to each other.

I had five days of training out here and the snow was deep. As well as this a number of the ski runs were closed for one week's maintenance which would have advantages, and disadvantages, as I was to find out.

For those who want to appreciate the area from the comfort of an armchair Michael Portillo did a really good episode of his railway programme that showed many locations. The BBC also chose a location in the area, Gornergrat, to be where Jonathan Pine worked at the fictional Hotel Meisters in the hit series 'The Night Manager'.

The first day I decided to head up to Gornergrat (3089m) which would be a snowy walk of about 10k and 1700m ascent. As I was by myself my plan was to stay on paths. The start of the trail, to the Furi (1862m) ski station, was a 3k walk going up about 300m and was quite easy going. I did this every day as it saved about 8 Swiss Francs each time and I was here to hill train after all! Beyond this I could see a few paths on my map but, unfortunately, the snow was covering everything. I set off anyway as having crampons, and an ice-axe, I thought I'd be fine. After about an hour I met a Swiss man coming the other way who had descended from the Monte Rosa hut on the other side of the Findelgletscher. He said crossing the glacier was not nice as, at places, he could see through the ice and see water rushing below. He had put on skis to cross it to reduce the likelihood of falling through and said it was scary and should not be attempted. I explained I was going up the left shoulder of the mountain and we said our goodbyes and went on our way.

I carried on up not finding the track at all, except the odd sign or bench covered in snow, and got to a corner where a handrail of rope disappeared in to the snow. At this point I knew I was getting in to increasing danger as I was several kms from the nearest person and I was tackling, at that time, the biggest snow climb of my life. I continued cautiously up and got to a flat area with huge rocks with a cliff face behind. All I needed to do now was to cross the rocks, pick a path up the cliff, then walk out at the top to the railway at Gornergrat - easy. It took about 30 minutes to cross the rocks, the problem being it was easy to fall through the gaps when walking over them as many were over 2m tall – a twisted ankle would be very serious here so I was very careful in what I was doing. I then got to the cliff and started to climb up the rocks and now it was starting to get really dangerous to the point where I was unsure whether to continue on up or to turn back. In many cases it is safest to go up than down so I decided to continue as surely it was not going to be long now. One part of my mind strayed in to 'you idiot – what are you doing here so far out of your depth – you could die here' but the dominant part quickly took over and said 'you are in the now and this is what living is about – take things carefully and logically and you will be OK'. I carried on up. On an exposed part of the rockface there was no snow – just slippy rock. I took my crampons off and was alarmed that my boots didn't want to grip the rock. I took my ice axe (at this point I had only been carrying it) and plunged it in to the moss. It held my weight. Brilliant. I moved up step by step not looking behind me at the large drop but at the snow on the shoulder up ahead. I knew if I reached that then the gradient would decrease and I could get my crampons back on and hopefully have a simple walk out. The next ten minutes were very frightening as I edged my way up the slippy slope - the ice axe being the one item that held me each time. I eventually reached the edge of the snow and felt more positive as the fact it was holding meant the gradient had decreased. The snow was probably 1m-2m thick and when I walked on it, I typically sank about 30cm. I could see a finger sign post about 100m vertically above me so put my crampons on and headed on up. I knew reaching this would mean the worst danger had passed. I carried on up towards the sign and the fear started to kick in again as whenever I looked back the drop was enormous in to the valley below. I carried on and the mountain eventually levelled out and I could see the train tracks in the distance. I knew I was safe now and carried on up to Gornergrat station where the view was fabulous. The café was open so I had a coffee and a cake then caught the train back down to Zermatt. I'd taken some big risks today so decided tomorrow would be a little more benign.

Back down in Zermatt I decided to visit the Pfarrkirche St. Mauritius climber's cemetery. On the face of it this may seem an odd thing to do but I wanted to learn where people perished on these mountains. I suspected many came, like me, seeking adventure and got quite excited with what was around them. In some way they all got unlucky and things ended very badly for both them, and those they left behind. One mountain kept coming up as I read the gravestones, the Breithorn, which sits proudly in the sky and most guide books will say is one of the easiest 4000m peaks in the Alps. Having had this reality check I headed back to the accommodation and the evening meal which was, as ever, exceedingly pleasant and filling.

The next day I wanted something more benign so decided on the Rothorn (3103m) which is a high whaleback of a mountain with no big drops – just what I needed. I set off up a well-used path that leads to a high metal railway bridge that gives a really good elevated view over Zermatt and quickly found the trail that would lead me up through the forest – the trail leaves the railway just before the bridge. After about an hour I came to the deserted ski village of Sunnegga (2288m) just as a van full of ski workers were arriving. They got out of their van and sat down in the sun as I slowly walked up the hill past them. I would now walk up the blue 7 to Blauherd (2571m) and when I got there a helicopter was dropping off some repairmen with big power tools. As I walked out of Blauherd I had the real feeling of walking in to the wild, my only distraction being the piste basher I could hear up-ahead. After about 30 minutes I met the piste basher which was working its way up the mountain shovelling large amounts of snow in to the valley below. I always approach mountain vehicles tentatively to ensure they can see me and the driver stopped the engine and I passed him on the outside i.e. above the big drop in to the valley below. I kept on walking up now on virgin snow where no skier or vehicle had been in a while and the path got steeper – I was on red 11 now. The approach now was to continue on up and at some point, I knew the path would double back to the summit. It was really hard going as despite the snow there was not a cloud in the sky so I was very hot trudging up the hill. I turned the bend at around 2900m and started the final climb to the summit. My nose felt a bit funny and I looked down and spotted blood. I've never had a nose bleed yet now, of all things, it decided to start. I knew this was not a good thing, to be high on a snow slope by myself in a remote spot with a nosebleed, so I had to make a decision. If I headed back down it would take me at least an hour to get to the workers, that's if they were still there. The top looked about 20 minutes away and had a building (albeit closed) but I could get some shelter against it to sort myself out and, if things got worse, it would be easier to get help there. I pressed on up dripping my way up the slope but, after a few minutes, it stopped. I reached the top and savoured the view being so far from everyone – I looked back down the slope and only my single footsteps broke the whiteness of nothing. I sat down to have some food and enjoyed the views – the Matterhorn straight ahead and the Breithorn off to my left. I was feeling quite good with my nose bleed having stopped and thought I'd taken manageable risks today and the ski runs worked for me. I headed back down red 11 and things were fine. I next decided on blue 8 and this was a bit of an error of judgement. Red 11 is a road run so has something hard underneath it. Blue 8 is down a slope so had plenty of opportunity to fall through – several times I was walking on the top then dropped in waist deep. After some time, I got to Patrullarve (2000m) and was again feeling quite good. I thought I should try and find the Europaweg thinking that if I ever did come back for another UTMR, and if they did the full route, I'd need to take this trail so it was a good opportunity to have a recce. This quickly turned out to be a big mistake as the terrain was either very icy or I'd fall through the snow. At one point I dropped through to my waist and an ibex came along and stood about 10ft away and just looked at me in my hole then walked off. As things were getting bad, I had to climb back up as I could not afford to slip down and off the mountain. After about an hour I managed to circle back to where I'd started the Europaweg escapade and decided to head down the mountain on blue 2, passing the closed piste-side champagne bar, and heading back in to Zermatt. The final half hour was interesting watching the helicopter deliver supermarket shopping to the houses high above the valley – it cannot be a cheap delivery service. I'd had some good training on hills, learnt a bit more about how things can get bad quickly, and had built an enormous appetite for the meal at 18:00.

Any walker/trekker/mountaineer who comes to Zermatt will have a watching eye on the Breithorn, to many the easiest of the alpine 4000m peaks at 4164m, but not without hazard and many have died trying. I'd seen it sitting up there every day and knew it was a relatively easy approach from the Matterhorn Glacier Paradise (3883m) – the standard approach being to catch the cable car to this point and walk across. A few days ago, I'd visited the Zermatt cemetery and seen the tombstones of those who came to Zermatt and died on the mountain - one that sticks with me is a tombstone with a rusty red ice axe attached to it, a safety device that, on the day, didn't save the person from tragedy. Clearly it was going to have to be a sensible attempt and having seen how quickly things can go wrong I was not going to take huge risks to summit today. Being there for hill training meant there was no way I was going to cable-car to 3883m which is the standard approach to tackle the mountain. I walked to Furi (1867m) then caught the cable car to Schwarzsee (2583m) and this would be my start point. From here I'd walk red 63, 65 and 66 to Trockener Steg (2939m) then blue 73 and red 80 to the high pass of Testa Grigia (3480m) then red 85 to the glacier paradise (3883m). As I set off up this route several things struck me. Firstly, there were only a few people walking up and, in each case, they were in small groups all roped together. Secondly the slopes had very few skiers on them and everyone gave me a good stare. Thirdly until you've walked up a ski slope it is hard to describe how hard it is. By the very nature of what you are doing you have to keep a tight line on one edge so have to tackle each bit in a straight line and the work on the legs is relentless. The only saving grace is the view that keeps on opening up and getting better and better. After several hours I got to the Glacier paradise and things were looking good for a Breithorn summit attempt. I could see the top; the sky was clear and I could see people. There are two main dangers on the Breithorn – one being the crevasse field that needs to be crossed at the start, the second falling off. I looked at the crevasse field and could see these large clefts down in to the icy cold below. To cross a crevasse field without a harness, particularly when solo and not roped to anyone, is risky. The reason being is that if you fall in you need to have a harness on to get winched out, assuming you can get help. It is reckoned to be virtually impossible to put on a harness when jammed in the bottom of a hole in a crevasse field so a fall down a hole could end in a painful cold death. I spent a few minutes looking at the crevasse field and I could see footsteps across everyone seemed to have taken. The temperature was about -10 degrees, and there was about a 20-knot wind so I didn't fear any real melting so set off over the crevasses being careful as I went. After about 10 minutes I was on the other side so now just had the summit slope to contend with. I set off and as I got higher it started to get really cold. I hunkered down in the snow and put every layer I had in my bag on and set off again. To do this meant I had to take my gloves off and within a minute my fingers were useless and numb. Quickly getting my gloves back on I put my hands in my armpits to get some warmth in them, all the time sheltering in my tiny snowhole. Feeling returned so now it was time to get up and start moving up the mountain again. The wind was now bitingly cold – the coldest place I've ever been. I looked behind me and no-one was coming up. I looked above me and could see four people coming down. The groups I'd overtaken on the way up had already turned back not getting as far as I had come. I could see a scenario where I got to the top in about an hour but where coming down was not a certainty. I was only about 200m vertically from the top but with every step I went up the danger was increasing and increasing. It's one of these moments where you have to think rationally about what you are doing and how the risk is exponentially increasing and you may die. I thought about the cemetery in Zermatt and the decisions that faced those climbers and what they might have done on the day. The only thing I could do was to turn around and head back down, each step being one step closer to safety. Feeling a bit disappointed I decided to make the best of a bad situation and head for the easy summit of Gobba di Rollin (3899m) – when I got there the ski infrastructure was mostly buried so the hazard now was not getting tangled in it. After admiring the view from the summit, I followed my tracks back only this time avoiding the crevasse field completely to get back to the glacier paradise. I headed up to the viewing platform, ice axe and all, and some tourists wanted to borrow it for a photo. Others were interested in how I'd walked up and turned around on the Breithorn. After a warm drink I bought my ticket for the way down and headed to the gondola. Standing on the platform awaiting the cable-car I had an odd vertigo like feeling and had real doubts in myself if I could actually get on it as was scared of the height. This may seem very odd after what I'd been through but the fear was apparent. After some inner soul searching, and rationalisation, I managed to stay on the platform and caught the ride down and walked out. I think I had learned something about risks and had got some good hills in. Perhaps I could have a go at the Breithorn later in the week!

On the fourth day of hill training I was interested in exploring the North side of the Matterhorn to see how far it was possible to get. In the traditional Matterhorn photo this is the bit on the right-hand face that you don't normally see. I set off on a pleasant valley route that was easy to follow. It soon gained height and got more and more snowy and, more worryingly, icy. To my right the mountain went up and up and to my left and I could see a river that, in places, looked like I could cross it. As I carried along the path looking for a way down marmots would come out and squeak at me, possibly in indignation about being on their private path. After my experiences earlier in the week I knew this path was not a good idea so when the path came within 100m of the river I decided to descend towards it. This quickly turned in to a big adventure clambering over rocks, over fallen trees, in to icy tributaries as I cut through the snow to the main river. As I approached, I now realised that I'd not judged the river correctly and to cross could be very dangerous as it was a lot larger than it looked – such is the problem of viewing something with nothing to gauge its true size by. I carried on knowing that there was a bridge about 500m up stream and after about an hour got there mightily relieved. I was now definitely going to keep to main piste basher routes for the rest of the day! Heading via Zmutt (1936m) I headed up red 51 that opened out at the bottom of a chairlift. This is an excellent spot to rest and take in the views and the sun. I now had the choice of going up a black or a red run. As I was here to train on hills black 54 it was. This run is really steep in places but I persisted up it and got to the end of the ridge for the Hörnlihütte. I started on the metal walkway along the ridge but realised it wasn't a good idea due to the ice so headed back to the mountain and circled below the main face of the Matterhorn on undulating terrain - the main fear being falling through in to a lake I could not see – however I kept on the piste basher track and had no problems working my way to Schwarzsee where I took the cable car down.

So far this week I'd had some amazing views, and some great adventures, but had been scared several times and was aware how quickly things could have turned out far worse. Based on this I wanted something more benign on the last day as wanted to get home in one piece! I decided on a nice safe run going down the valley to Visp travelling lighter than usual. I set off as normal and headed out from Zermatt past the station and here the path does something a little different. The railway is covered by a concrete shuttering to protect from landslides and the footpath goes right on top of it giving a great view down the valley. I looked to my right and spotted an ibex struggling on a scree slope beside a fast river and thought it was either going to just make it or I was going to see something horrible. There was little I could do as I watched as its legs claw at the scree about a foot from the water's edge. It slowly managed to get away from the water and after about 10 minutes got away to live another day. My situation was nothing like that but was not without peril. The path diverged from the railway and came to a point that had been engulfed by a rockfall with snow on the top of it and this took about 10 minutes to cross. The path then opened up and is very runnable – a good surface with lots of twists and turns all the time heading along the valley critically below the snow line. Approaching Visp, I spotted the primary school that Sepp Blatter had attended – it says this in massive letters on one wall – then approached the station and caught the train back. Zermatt to Visp is marathon distance and it had taken six hours but with the terrain the way it was I was quite pleased!

All in my training had gone well. I'd got in some big hills, I'd gained a feel for the landscape, and I'd seen some exciting places. All I had to do now was to come back and complete the race!

Having walked a lot of the ski slopes I also had an inner desire to come back skiing at some point and was lucky, in 2017, to be able to do this with E, Hannah (from the Yorkshire 3-Peaks) and Darren.

For me it was the best ski area I've ever been to – beautiful views and long quiet pistes. In a week we probably only went to a third of it so there is so much more to explore. I'd say the most pleasurable skiing I've ever had was to ski on our last day on Gornergrat where we repeatedly did runs together on the uncrowded slopes looking across at a view my eyes never got tired of the Tobleronic Matterhorn.

11 UTMR RACE 2015

Despite a few close calls I'd survived the UTMR recce. It was now time to put my new mountain experience in to practice and hope the weather would be kind.

The only sensible way to get to the start of the race in Breuil-Cervinia was to fly to Milan and take the UTMR organised transport from there. I took a budget flight to Milan and was surprised how cheap it was to get a city centre hotel for the night two days before the race started. After one day sightseeing, I relaxed knowing tomorrow was a travel day with the race the day after. The arrangement was to catch the UTMR bus at the exit of Milan airport. I went to the airport in plenty of time and now realised there were many exits so had a bit of a problem. I decided to do laps between them so the driver, and other runners, would spot me. After a bit I spotted another lost runner so introduced myself and learnt Ari was also running the UTMR – result! Ari (who I would see again in Romania in 2017) had phoned the organisers and knew the name of the driver. We decided I'd wait outside with both of our bags and Ari would try and find some more runners or the driver. Ari found another runner and brought her out and then the driver turned up. We were now just one runner down, Antony. After a few minutes Antony arrived and we were off. On the way to the start we all chatted about races and our thoughts of the race ahead. The conversation centred on how difficult it would be, how challenging the terrain was and what fears we all had. Fears of getting lost, fears of falling off a path and fear of failure. About 10km from our destination as we were going up a steep hill the minibus rear door opened and some of our bags tumbled their way down the road. Fortunately, they didn't hit any vehicle, person or animal and our driver did a few embarrassed shuttle runs to pick them up and we were off again to our destination! We were dropped at the hotel and learnt we all were paying different amounts for the same type of room – I was lucky having the cheapest one – and we went our ways to prepare for kit check. This side of the Matterhorn is very different to the Zermatt side – on the Italian side it is a bit of a bowl of a mountain with ski infrastructure on it. I tried to spot the route for tomorrow and could see the start of it heading away from the village.

As with any race there is the ritual of the kit check and UTMR was no different. I headed down to the golf club at the allotted time and could see a few people with tables and lots of runners bent on the floor or in the corridor with bundles of kit. As space was limited what a runner did was to lay all their kit out on the floor and the organiser would come and check it then issue the race pack with the running number etc. In the race pack was a list of restaurants that would offer a discounted evening meal to runners so I went to the first one of those and asked about the meal. They said they had never heard of UTMR and there were no discounts. At that moment Ari walked in and said the same thing and was also told there were no discounts. Ari was far better than I could be in the way he handled this. I'd have just paid for something on the menu at whatever price it was but Ari took a different approach. He simply explained there would be about 100 runners who would be told about the restaurants and as this was the closest one to the kit check most would come in here. Based on this they should expect to have a lot of people coming soon so should provide a menu with a few options at a discount price to feed everyone. The restaurant staff had a little private chat and came back with some options so we ordered. As we sat there more runners came in and they probably served about 10 runners in the time we ate. The pasta dish came out and Ari wanted to put some olive oil on the bread that came with it. On the table was some olive oil. Ari looked at this and decided it was not good quality so asked the staff could he have some good oil and not the stuff on the tables and, lo and behold, they produced an expensive looking bottle. I quite liked Ari's polite and direct approach to doing things in an unflustered way as it did achieve results.

Finishing our meal together we headed back to the hotel then went our separate ways so we could prepare for the race the next day.

Day 1 Views of 4000m peaks

The start of the race nearly didn't happen for me. After all the training, money and preparation I'd done everything correct and headed to bed around 21:00 knowing breakfast was at 04:15 the next morning. I set my alarm for 04:00, laid all my kit out on the spare bed in the room, and went to bed. The next thing I know I woke up around 04:35 and realised I'd missed my alarm. I frantically got down to breakfast, quickly ate some food, then headed back to my room for final foot prep etc. then left the hotel at 05:00. All of us runners had been told where to leave our overnight bag so it would be collected and taken to the end of each day so I went to this spot on one of the main streets and dumped my bag with the others that were sitting there. It was a dark spot beside a hotel but there was a bundle of bags so mine would be in safe company. I then went to the start and shuffled in the cold air with everyone else – after all Breuil-Cervinia is at an altitude of 2050m and it was early in the morning. In total there were around 100 runners at the start line and after some start speeches by the organisers we were off as planned at 06:00. About 100m in to the course is a staircase and the lead runners were bounding up this two at a time. I took it more sedately as there was a long way to go. In the space of 7.26km the course goes up a ski road – as there was no snow it was like a rocky farm track – to a plateau at Cle supre delle Cime Blanche at 2982m. My target was to get here by 09:00 and I was inside this getting here at 08:15. On the way up I'd started to get in to conversation with other runners as we walked up this long hill. From this point the path heads south for about 1km to the Cle infre delle Cime Blanche and the landscape was stunning. Behind was the Matterhorn, to the left was the Breithorn, Pollux and Castor and ahead mountains as far as the eye could see. There were little bits of ice/snow on the ground so many took some photos before heading on past the Gran Lago which is the body of water used in the adverts for the race.

The trail now wound down the mountain to Rif Ferraro (2066m) which was 17.4k in to the course with a cut-off of 12:00. This was our first check point and the food options were limited – bits of cheese, fruit, biscuits and water. I grabbed some food, filled up my bladder then was on my way. There was now only about 10k to the end and I had more than six hours to do it in so things were going well. The trail started on a path which wound its way along a valley with beautiful views on every turn. After a few kms this gave way to a rocky and blocky ascent and up ahead I could see the dots of runners weaving this way and that, around and over the rocks. The course marking throughout UTMR was excellent – Lizzy had been along the course and put temporary markings down (chalk or quickly degradable paint I think) that led the best way through the mountains and it really came down to looking for the next pink dot and heading for it. We kept going up and I met some Swiss runners who were interested in how I could have trained for the course in the UK. They took the view that to compete in this sort of race you have to walk on the actual course in advance but I'm not so sure and explained what I had done. We got to the Pso del Rothin (2685m) and part of me wanted to linger for the view as I was hours inside the cut-off. Another part of me wanted to explore the terrain off the course but to do so would be unfair to the organisers should I come in to problems so I did not. I left this area, the view etched in to my brain forever, and headed on down the trail to the end. The final few kms were on ski slopes and there were some recreational walkers out to cheer everyone on. I finished early afternoon so was well within the time so picked my bag up from the bundle and asked where the accommodation was. The arrangement for each day was that you would be told at the end where your accommodation was which added to the general pioneering nature of what we were doing. I was told it was the 'pink building' which I said I could not see but was directed up a road and told I couldn't miss it so off I set. I got to the Villa Della Regina and checked in and was given a room number. I was told it may be locked as I'm sharing and there is already someone there and they may have gone out so if this is the case come back to reception and they will let me in. I went to the room, it was locked, so went to reception who let me in. Inside the room was actually a self-catering ski flat with a lounge/kitchen, bathroom, one room with four beds and one with two. In the four-bed room one of the beds had been taken and in the smaller room one bed had been taken also. As someone who feels the cold a lot, I wanted the warmest room. I also wanted to minimise the chance of a snorer. The smallest room seemed the best option so I took that. As things turned out although the larger room had four beds the intention was for only three persons to be in there. Part of the race package includes an evening meal and that was going to be a 15-minute walk away at 19:00. I'd eaten little today and was really hungry. I went to the one shop in the village and bought snack food and ate some of this down by the river and brought the rest back. By about 15:00 I'd eaten it all. At this point I thought if the meal is 19:00 I may not get back until 20:00 – 21:00 so will try and get more snack food to eat instead. I went back to the shop and bought some more bits that would form my evening meal.

Back at the room I met a fellow runner, Antony, who I'd first met on the minibus on the way out. We got chatting and it turned out he had his own travel kettle and plastic tub to eat out of as he'd been caught out at races before. This approach I was to copy in Ut4M in 2017. The two others came back to the room and we chatted some more before they disappeared to the meal. My roommate was nowhere to be seen as he had taken a taxi down the valley for a massage but he did come back early evening before heading straight out for food. They returned from food around 21:00 and we were lights off at 22:00 for the 04:00 breakfast the next day.

My roommate dropped off instantly and even with my earplugs in his snoring was enormous – not his fault but just the way it was. He sounded like a food-mixer full of walnuts on a slow speed so I had to do something. I took my sleeping bag to the lounge and slept there. The next morning, we talked about it and he said he was surprised I said he snores as his wife has never pointed it out.

Day 2 Two big hills

We had breakfast, dropped our bags off for onward transportation, had the race brief and we were off at 06:00. Day 2 was going to be two big hills.

Within the field there was a general feeling that Day 2 was important to get through with some spare capacity for Day 3 which would contain, for many, the biggest hill of our lives.

We left Staffal (1825m) and the path suddenly got narrow. For me this was annoying as several people had cut in-front of me just before it narrowed and now they didn't have the legs to climb at the pace I wanted. I waited for my moment and after about 20 minutes got past then sped up to make a bit of a gap. The path now opened up as we went up the red 7a ski run to the first ski hut. This hill can be thought of as a hill of two halves – the entire hill would be adjacent to a gondola with an interchange at Lys (2342m) and the top being at Pso del Salati (2936m). It was a misty day which meant that visibility was not that great but it was cool. 2342m was soon passed and now it was red 6 to the top – the path here was naturally wider being a piste so it was pleasant to have a chat with others all speculating on what was ahead. We reached the top and topped up our water and now had an amazing descent to make. At the top it was very narrow and rocky as the path twisted down the other side of the mountain. This quickly gave way to a narrow sheep track of a trail cut on to the hillside with a significant drop to the left. Antony, who I'd shared accommodation with last night, was running first then it was an American lady then I was in the rear as we sped along the trail. Suddenly Antony took a tumble and ended up resting with his feet on the trail with the rest of his body hanging off with his head facing the sky. We had to stop very quickly not to trip on him but he got up like a scalded cat and bolted down the trail really fast for a few minutes. Afterwards I asked about this and Antony told me he had a massive adrenaline burst from the fall so just went for it. The trail slowly turned to grass and we kept going.

In this area the Walser people settled in quaint looking wooden houses– very sturdy and look very dark inside. The Walser people are named after the Wallis area in the upper Rhône valley where they originally came from. For reasons that are unclear in the 12th and 13th centuries there was a *Walserwanderungen*, or Walser migration, where many of the Walsers moved south and originally settled in the Swiss canton of Valais where the race was running through today. After what seemed like an age, I passed one of the Walser houses with '1826' written in a sign above the door. I thought this was good as it must mean we are 1826m ASL and we only had to drop about another 600m to the CP at the village. After about 30 minutes I realised I was very wrong and it must have been the year of the build. I carried on with the voice in my knees asking how far is it possible to descend in one go as it seemed to be relentless, it was as if we were going down and down in to an unknown crater in the earth. At this point three runners shot past and after about 100m took a wrong turning. I shouted after them and they did not hear but a few minutes later they passed me again. This happened a few times. They were clearly stronger runners but lacked the navigation skills for a fast race. Alagna, at 15.6k (1254m), eventually came and this was a comprehensive CP with a variety of food. A number of runners were hanging round with no desperate push to take on hill number 2 but I wanted to finish as soon as I could to rest for day 3 so headed off. The humidity was high and the temperature was building as I set off down the road that would eventually stop and become a trail to cross the Colle Turlo (2738m) pass. The road was steep and I spotted two cyclists I was gaining on so decided (foolishly) to overtake them and see if I could hold position. I managed to overtake and said hello and got about 10m in front then puffed like a grampus until the path turned off and I could ease up a bit. The trail now climbed to a mountain hut that had lots of tourists sitting outside of it eating– for many this would be as high as they would get. This looked a nice place but our hill had not really started. Beyond this the track went up and up on a man-made rocky path/road and I met a few runners sitting down saying they could not go on.

The path was relentless and kept climbing in to the mist. It was built in the 1920s and looked like at one point it could have taken a horse and cart but had now fallen a bit in to ruin. Eventually it levelled out at a cut in the rock at the Colle Turlo (2738m) and here was a marshal checking up on everyone. After a brief chat I started off down the other side on my way to the next CP at Quarazza. This would only be 16.4k from the last one but these kms were tough. I passed two mountain bikers carrying their bikes up and over the top as they needed to get to Alagna – they were not having a good time as so much was un-rideable including most of the descent they would come to. Being risk averse I was carrying a reasonable amount of kit and at the CP one of the volunteers joked about what I was carrying – my bag was 35 litres which was double the size of everyone else's. She gave it a good shake and asked about the kitchen sink! The final 5k to Macugnaga I took quite slowly as wanted to save myself for tomorrow. Mountain races are interesting as if you know there is a big up coming soon you naturally scan the sky for it. I could see tomorrow would be an absolute whopper as I could not see the top. I got to the end of today's race in a reasonable time and had an ice cream whilst chatting with others. It turned out my accommodation would be in the Casa Alpina de Fillippi that was at the far end of the village (up-hill) and was sold as a 'nice 15-minute walk'. The organisers offered a minibus and I took that option to get there to find my room-mate to be none other than good old Antony! We had a good chat about the day's adventure, and races in general, then headed downstairs for food at 18:00 then bed.

Day 2 had not gone so well for some others. At the start of each day we left our main bag at a stated location which was typically outside a named hotel. This was never really a problem as there was a big bundle of bags and these villages are such trusting places that theft was never an issue. Unfortunately a few runners had put their bags in one place that was not correct so they had been left behind. This only became apparent when they reached the end of the race. From reading Facebook posts, they were quite aggrieved and questioned the organisation. The organisation responded saying they were sorry and had dispatched someone to pick up the bags but due to the road being the long way around the mountains it would take a few hours. To me this was a reasonable approach. The runners were still very unhappy with things. Lizzy came back with a reply saying just because something has not gone to plan one day it is up to the individual as to how they let that impact them the next day – they can have a good race or they can always be thinking of things to blame and have a bad event. My language here is not as eloquent but this was the point being made. In the years since I've come back to this story in my mind as to how to handle things that don't always go to plan.

Day 3 The narrow path

The final day started early. The joke in the hotel was others wearing 'ultra-stilettos' with the noise of people walking around from about 03:00 prior to our 04:00 breakfast. Breakfast today was strangely quiet – in part due to the early start and in part due to what lay ahead. The course today was a massive uphill, a traverse run to Saas-Fee then a very airy and exposed path to the end. We left the accommodation about 05:00 and walked down to the start line. Here we had the usual brief and we were off. Macugnaga (1307m) is nestled in a deep valley and our first job was to climb very steeply to the Moropass (2853m). The path largely zig-zagged up below a ski gondola and was far from easy as it was not a route that saw a lot of traffic. As we got higher and higher amazing views of Monte Rosa came in to view and many stopped to take photos. Having done a lot of hill training I knew this uphill was where I could make ground so I kept going and topped in a reasonable position. The final pass is on massive blocks of stone, with some iron chains and staples, and over the north side was another world with the Mattmark reservoir nestling below. The trail down to the reservoir (2224m) was highly runnable as was the trail along it but my legs were tired so it turned in to a fast walk for me as other runners overtook. The Mattmark dam is the biggest earth fill dam in Europe and compared to a concrete dam looks very wide at its base. We ran past this almost 50 years to the day of a great tragedy that occurred here when eighty-eight people lost their lives. On the 30th August 1965 two million cubic metres of ice and debris broke off the Allain glacier and engulfed the construction site killing many workers below.

From the Mattmark dam to Saas-Fee takes longer than it looks on the map. Firstly, the trail led to the village of Saas-Almagell (1672m). Seeing the buildings, I assumed we were on the outskirts of Saas-Fee so was feeling quite good only to rapidly realise this was not the case as the trail left the village behind. Along the trail were many holiday makers out for a pleasant walk looking up at the mountains around. Slowly but surely the trail rounded a corner and Saas-Fee could be seen on the far side of a river. To the left the mountains seemed to tower with a ski zone hanging high above. From down below the ski area looked quite small but scale is a hard thing to judge when in the mountains. The ski area itself sits between 1800 and 3500m and has 100k of runs the longest being 15k – from down below it looked nowhere near this size! I crossed the bridge and now there were lots of shops selling souvenirs and one of those road trains slowly came past – about 50 faces staring at the oddly dressed man with the walking poles. Up ahead I could see the CP. It was around 11:30 so I was an hour a head of the cut off so was fine but it had been a tough 5.5hrs to cover the 21.3km to get here. After some food and water, I headed on my way. I'd read a lot about this final trail, the Höhenweg, that traces a contour high on the mountain. I knew it would be the scariest path I've ever been on with big exposure in places but I felt ready for it. The initial climb through the forest was OK – just gaining height in the trees. This hour was a constant battle for the voices in my head saying 'things are going OK and you can manage this' and 'every km you do is one less km that has the potential to be really scary'. Slowly but surely, we got on to the ledge path and it was here that the fun really started. It can best be described as focusing on a point 500m or so ahead and getting there then recomposing. At times the path was barely wide enough for my feet. At times it was absolutely terrifying even though I was on it in good weather, daylight, dry and little wind. At other times it had collapsed and fallen away so a jump was necessary to make progress. Occasionally there would be a sign that read 'UTMR extreme caution' which meant something to be really aware of – typically it was a very big drop where care needed to be taken. Despite all of this danger my confidence grew as I went along it and I found I could travel quicker than others – in part this was probably due to wanting to minimise my time but it was also down to having the ability to be up there. As Lizzy said afterwards – just because a trail or race is there it does not mean you have the experience to do it. I'm paraphrasing but the intent was pretty much that. The ITRA gives a 'mountainous' rating on a scale of 1 to 13 for all races. The Ridgeway in the UK gets a rating of 1, UTMR gets a 10, some of the more extreme races of the world get a 13. I doubt I'll ever enter a 13.

There was one point where the path went along a tiny ledge on a cliff then dropped off down a 10m rockfall that was very steep. It felt good to conquer it. Near the end I came to a bench and a marshal who advised me that a man was just up ahead beyond where the path cut through a hole in the rock. He told me on an exposed section there was a handrail and when I reached this not to hold on to it as it would not take the weight of two persons. He also told me the man was very scared so suggested I give some space if passing. I caught the man and passed him at a wide point. The trail finally ended and now it was a gentle 5k downhill on a road to the end. I felt really good running this section and finished around 16:00 being greeted by Lizzy handing me a small race gift. As well as a race memento, North Face gave everyone a quality holdall. After picking up my bag I dropped it at my room and came back. Antony had arrived just before me and had bought me a beer so we sat down and chatted. As it turned out our total time over the 3 days was exceptionally close to each other – it didn't matter who had beaten who as it was about the shared experience. More runners arrived and we sat down to the race meal, and prize giving, at 18:00. At about 20:00 everyone said their farewells and headed to their accommodation and bed.

Day 4 Heading home

The next morning a bus was taking many back from Grächen to Geneva or to drop them at the railway station in the valley. I'd already walked/ran Visp to Zermatt in April and over the past few days completed most of the lap of Monte Rosa but I had one last bit to do so set off with my bag, waving to everyone, as I headed down into the valley to catch the train back. I'd describe these final 8kms as functional to complete the circuit but not that enjoyable as it was walking down a moderately busy road with no pavement.

All in the UTMR was an amazing experience I'd like to run again – the race organisation was great, competitors were friendly, the views were amazing and the challenge was immense. It's up there with some of the great points of my life – CCC, UTMR, Arctic Ultra, Transylvania Ultra and Ut4M. It's perhaps no coincidence a large part of this book is about these events!

12 ECOTRAIL OSLO 2016

Having secured a place in the 2016 Tierra Arctic Ultra I knew I had to do some 'warm up' races. I'd never been to Scandinavia before, and had some apprehensions about how easy it would be to navigate, what the food would be like, and would there be lots of biting flies etc. so thought I needed to have a warm-up race out there. I'd also read about lemmings and watched some online video clips of them being quite aggressive so quite wanted to try and meet them before the Arctic Ultra (more of that later).

Scandinavia has a reputation, reasonably so, for being an expensive place so whatever race I entered had to be at the cheap end of things for both entry, flights and accommodation. After spending some time online, I came across an organisation called Ecotrail who seemed to run a series of events that were based in cities and the race start/finish would be accessible by public transport. They had a race in Oslo so before signing up my next thing to do was to see how much it would cost to get/stay there. Looking around I found a BA weekend break deal that was flights and 3 nights hotel for 2 for around £400. It all seemed possible so I paid my 90 Euros race fee, booked the weekend break and started to read about Oslo. Our plan was to fly on the Friday, I'd race on Saturday whilst E visited galleries, some sightseeing together on the Sunday, then back on the Monday.

Several months before the race the organisers stated that there would be a free pair of trail shoes provided to everyone by one of the leading shoe brands (up to European size 50) which is possibly the best free gift a race could give. I've come away from races before with free gifts that don't fit so kept my enthusiasm in check to see what would materialise when in Oslo. A few weeks before the race BA phoned up to say that due to a hotel strike across parts of the city on race weekend the original hotel was not available however they gave a few options so we took a conveniently located alternative. This was an advantage of booking a package deal as BA will have spent the time phoning round. As race day drew near there was all the usual packing to be done – second guessing the weather – procrastinating over which pair of gloves and the like. Finally packed we headed to the airport to start our first visit to Scandinavia.

Oslo Airport is in a district 50km north of the city and handles about 25 million passengers per year (compared to Heathrow's 73 million). It is connected to the city centre via a high-speed railway line that takes 20 minutes to take passengers right in to the heart of the city. The line, known as flytoget, is Norway's only high-speed railway and carries 70% of the passengers who use the airport. Having recently purchased my Suunto watch I found it interesting to monitor the speed, acceleration etc. of the train as we were whisked in to the city.

Our hotel was going to be about 20 minutes' walk to the west of the station so the first thing we did was to drop our bags off before heading back in town to pick up the (hopefully!) free shoes and race number. Unlike other events there is no kit check or anything like that, all a runner has to do is turn up with some ID. The race numbers (and shoes in a size 50!) were distributed from the Sport 1 Superstore Sentrum that is about 200m north of the railway station and easy to find. This has to be one of the best stocked sports shops I've ever been in with lots of obscure items and obscure maps – we found a map for Senja that we intended to visit post-Arctic ultra. All we had to do now was to have some food, sleep, then tomorrow head to the start!

Near the sports store was a beggar who we passed at the same spot every time. Begging and poverty is a complicated subject with all sorts of factors but it did feel odd to be in a visibly rich area, spending money on a non-essential activity, whilst someone was struggling to find the money to eat. These sorts of encounters do play on my mind a lot as it is very easy to see how someone can end up in that situation. A few Christmas's ago E and I volunteered in a homeless shelter, Crisis at Christmas, a charity I had been donating to for a number of years. Part of the role was listening whilst doing everyday tasks such as distributing clothing, cleaning, serving food etc. I continue to support Crisis at Christmas as believe they are making a difference and helping others less fortunate.

I think when you have someone along with you in a race, as 'support', there has to be some give and take with what you do with the rest of the trip leaning towards your supporter having the majority vote in things. Whilst I wanted to eat a lightish evening meal early E wanted a proper meal so we went to an Italian restaurant at around 20:00 near where we were staying. The restaurant was highly polished inside with large mirrors with gold coloured detailed frames. There were plenty of people in there. The waiter gave E undivided attention throughout the service. In taking the order he made full eye contact with E but would not look at me when I ordered mine. When he brought the drinks, he only looked at one of us. He came and gave an update that one of the meals was taking slightly longer and he was sorry for that but it was all in control (even though we both didn't have a meal at this point). He brought the pasta and was full of charm for one of us. The pasta was nice if not a little over-salted. When it was time to go E asked for the bill and he brought it straight back and put it beside me and said 'for you sir' which was the only time he spoke to me, although he still didn't make eye-contact. Throughout we both found his mannerisms amusing and E did think the service had been excellent. The trouble with eating a big meal 8ish is that it sits in your stomach and feels heavy. I didn't get the best night's sleep, due to pasta sweats, and decided never again to eat a big pre-race evening meal. E suffered pasta guilts and agreed with this plan for the future.

The next morning was slightly overcast and we headed to the start at Vaterlandsparken park. There were about 300 runners shuffling around trying to keep warm. As well as the 80k ultra there were 18,

30 and 45k races with these competitors starting later in the day further up the course. The organisers had been really clever when it came to planning the course with all of these start points accessible by public transport. I really liked the inclusivity of what they were doing offering shorter options for those who wanted them. This inclusivity is a theme across their events.

The race tune was 'Faded' by Alan Walker which features the Swedish singer Zara Larsson; with race tunes they often stay in your head as you go along the course. When the race markings were missing later on, I could definitely hear 'where are you now, were you only imaginary, where are you now' ringing in my head. The small park had some slack lines which is the first time I'd seen such thing and had always wanted a go on one so, along with others, I tentatively walked along these long rubber bands. A toy to get in the future. All things come to an end and the shuffling around in the cold morning air stopped at 09:00 as we were off on our 80km loop north of Oslo!

The course set off along an asphalt path that was adjacent to a river on our left and over the next few kms we left the city slowly gaining height. There were some interesting looking buildings such as an artist quarter where it looked like creatives lived and decorated their buildings accordingly. There were old wooden buildings with skidoos parked up outside which said something for the weather for parts of the year. At the 8km point we came to the southern edge of the vast Maridalsvannet Lake. The view here is similar to Loch Morlich near Aviemore for anyone who has ever travelled in the Cairngorms. The path now was very twisty, narrow and covered in tree roots and I really enjoyed running this technical section. This section passed too quickly though and we were soon at the CP at around 12k. Up until this point there had been lots of markers to follow (as the organisers advised on their website prior to the race) so even though I wasn't carrying a map the markers, along with my GPS watch which I'd loaded with the route, gave me confidence for the day ahead.

At this point I was probably about ¾ of the way down the field, i.e. most were in-front, and the pack was thinning out with about 5 of us spread over 200-300m. Suddenly the markers were missing which was unnerving but we pushed on relying on a variety of GPS watches – I was really glad I had mine. The route now headed up in to the forested mountains and we stayed in this until about the 20k point when we popped out at the bottom of another lake and here there were a few Saturday day trippers out from Oslo enjoying the countryside and waving as we went on.

The path then continued on through the forests north of Oslo until it eventually reached the CP at Holmenkollen (33k). So far, the run had been what I'd call an average mountain run; that is good (but not great) views, inclined (but not steep) trails and limited (but occasional) hazards. Not necessarily one to repeat for the experience of the course alone. On top of this the wildlife had been non-existent – not even an aggressive lemming blocking the path.

Holmenkollen can be seen from about 10 minutes out as it is a ginormous ski jump protruding high in to the sky. Coming in to it I was trying to work out the route and it seemed we would run down a road to the base of it where the CP was at. There were skin-suited speed demons powering along the road on something that looked like a combination between roller-blades and skis. As it was a downhill section they were comfortably going along with the traffic. These lycra-clad warriors moved very silently and very quickly so I had to be careful crossing the road so as not to get knocked over by one of them. It was now a gentle five-minute run to get to the actual CP. At this CP I ate one slice of bread with cheese, 10 tortilla chips, a cup of coke, 2 pieces of chocolate and ½ a banana. I also took on 1.5 litres of water. I didn't hang around as I wanted a sub-12hr 50 miler if I could so needed to be on my way – so far things were going to plan. Upon leaving the CP the path climbed quickly out to about ½ the height of the ski jump and a junction without a sign. I went the wrong way but quickly realised I was walking in to a holiday compound so doubled back on myself.

The route now started to gain some height and we went through a massive aerial wire course at the Oslo Vinterpark at 37k that had lots of people on it looking down at us. From here it was a tour of the ski slopes dropping down to a small lake at 40k. 40k came at 5hrs50 so, disappointingly, I had to accepted that a sub 12hr 80k was going to be very unlikely. It was very disappointing but I then moved to a mindset of enjoying the race for what it is whilst still trying to cover the ground as best and quickest as I could. I was now completely alone, and had been for some time, so navigation was going to be really important.

The race now entered a closed ski range and headed up and down several pistes. As someone who skis I always quite like seeing new ski areas in races and to think of the skiing line I'd take on the hills – it passes the time.

The next CP was at Sørkedalen (51k) and this is basically a village shop isolated on a road in the middle of nowhere with a large piece of waste-ground beside it. Clearly there had been a lot of people here earlier in the day but by the time I arrived it was a ghost car park with a skeletal staff who were friendly but had limited supplies. There was the shop but that would just take more time and it didn't seem right to go food hunting in there when all food, according to the organisers, was provided. I ate a handful of peanuts, 10 tortillas and a cup of coke and I was off. The weather was now closing in and a heavy thunderstorm looked imminent. I knew the next section had a high exposed area and I didn't want to get struck by lightning on it so I ran off wanting to get up and over as quickly as I could. At the 54k mark was a small lake and there were a few recreational mountain runners out there and we had a little chat. This was the first chat I'd really had in the race so it was nice to talk for a minute or two about the area. The downside of the pack being thinned out is that you really are on your own, lost in your thoughts, and having to make every decision by yourself. The upside is the solitude and being at one with nature, taking on the navigational challenge knowing that failure will not be that great but you only have yourself to blame! After leaving the recreational runners the path had a tiny technical section on rock and I was starting to feel light headed from lack of food so had to be really careful. My priority now was to get to the next CP. Throughout the race I was eating an energy bar / gel every hour from my pack but this, with the supplies I was getting at the CPs, was just not enough. This light-headedness continued to the next CP at Fossum (62k). On the way there, I started to visualise a CP staffed by possums from Finland and pondered how good they would be at serving things.

As I approached Fossum I could see it was a wooden sports hall on the edge of playing fields. The CP seemed to be outside and it was now raining heavily so I needed a quick stop (to keep warm) but needed food. The staff here (humans not possums) were friendly and had more food so I took on 2 slices of bread/cheese, 2 cups of tomato/pasta soup and 1 ½ litres of water. I was now one minute up on the 12hr 50-mile pace so it just might be possible if I got a move on. Earlier on I'd been 10 mins up at 40k and now only 1 min at 62k so on the face of it, things may not have looked good however my ultra-strategy is to always keep something in reserve for the end so I thought I could work with this one minute and do a time check every mile and maintain it. To many the idea of being one minute up and holding it may seem difficult as there are so many variables. I find I can be quite stubborn in my head and push myself checking the watch every few minutes to maintain a pace. If I was 70 seconds up, I'd feel good – if it dropped to 50 seconds, I'd feel bad and drive myself harder. I know if I walk flat out, I can do 6.5 – 7 kmph so all I had to do was to maintain this and accept no excuses from any part of my body and things would be fine.

I ran off in the heavy rain crossing the playing fields and caught some runners up for the first time in hours. This next section is nice and twisty alongside a river with a very slippy and undulating path. Running fast down on to the edge of the river then using the momentum to run back up was the way to tackle this slippy trail– the river always on the left. I quickly managed to get ahead of the others and I was on my own now. I knew provided I made zero navigational errors I could get my second ever sub-12 50-miler, my first one being in the Caesar's Camp Endurance Runs in 2009 when I finished in 11:29.

I was going along the path and passed a man with 3 dogs having a very wet walk coming the other way then came to a junction and the markers went both ways – left and right. The right ones were more dominant so I went with them. I went a few hundred metres and it didn't feel correct so went back to the junction and checked the markers. Definitely right so I retraced my steps now with the water on my right and we seemed to be going uphill at times and now there were no markers. As there was only one path I kept going now alarmed about the lack of markers and also lack of runners. I spotted a man with 3 dogs on the other side of the river heading downstream. My initial thought was that it odd to see another man with 3 dogs in the pouring rain. After about a minute I realised it was the same man and my first thought was how had he got there before quickly realising that I was now going up the river on the other side i.e. heading back up the course. This was most annoying. I recognised where he was so knew a bridge was coming up soon so headed to that then repeated myself on the other side now overtaking people I'd overtaken just after we left the last CP. I'd done 3.43k extra on this loop – I hate it when locals move markers as it is dangerous and frustrating – it was not the last time this would happen to me. I was now focused on averaging at least 7kmph over the race as my sub-12hr 50 mile was not going to be possible unless I did this. I powerwalked/ran my way down the course to the paved path which now circles the bay to get back. I think at this part of an event I often turn in to some sort of machine- a switch flicks in my head and the robot part of me runs some simple code:

1: If a runner ahead comes in sight this means you are catching them;
2: If you are catching them you are going quicker than them;
3: If going quicker you must close in on them and overtake them;
4: If they speed up you speed up more as you must overtake them;
5: You must now maintain your speed;
6: Go to step 1.

It was now very wet and I was traversing the shoreline on a pavement- slowly but surely, I was winding people in like a machine. I approached the opera house at the end and ran in fast to the finish to be met by a few of the organisers and E who had been waiting in the rain. We always knew a sub-12 50-mile pace was going to be marginal but I'd managed 81.87km (50.87 miles) in 12hrs 11 which meant I'd made it which was great. The D+ had been 1863m and the D- 1854m. The goody bag was great – a Helly Hansen long sleeved top, a Helly Hansen t-shirt, another technical t-shirt, a medal and all the usual food samples. I've no memory whatsoever what we did for food my only memory being we walked back in the pouring rain and went in to a shop (possibly for food) and someone asked me what I had my medal for and I explained the race.

The race website was very detailed and the idea of being able to do an ultra by public transport is great. The race was let down by the CPs having limited food and someone moving the markers (although this is not the organisers fault). The goody bag is the best I've had in any race but, taking everything in to account, I don't think I'll ever go back to run it again.

13 TIERRA ARCTIC ULTRA 2016

There comes the point in an ultra-runner's career when there is an inner need to try something different. So far all of my races had been either in the UK or in the Alps and there was so much more out there. At first, I looked at 'jungle' and quickly realised it would be too expensive. Next, I looked at 'desert' and formed a similar opinion. Finally, I looked at 'arctic' and was pleasantly surprised to find a race that was cheap to enter in northern Sweden – the Tierra Arctic Ultra on the 7th August 2015. The race start was in Kiruna which was high on my list of places to visit, and due to the large changes going on there I knew I had to visit sooner rather than later.

Kiruna sits on top of a massive mine, the world's biggest iron ore mine, that opened in 1898. It's impossible to escape the mine which is omnipresent wherever you are in Kiruna. There are the obvious things such as the mine itself, the trains and the slight shake at 02:00 each day when the explosions occur. The town itself is slowly but surely being removed. The ground is sinking and the authorities feel in the coming years it will be unsafe to live in so a new town is being built several kilometres away. The buildings are all getting demolished and in a few decades time it will be a large 'natural deformation park'. A very small number of buildings are to be dismantled and moved to the new town and I was very keen to see as much of Kiruna as I could before it would be gone. Kiruna itself has a population of around 17,000 people, of which 1,800 are employed by the mining company and 400 work underground in the mine. Kiruna is close by the original ice hotel that opened in 1989 and featured on many TV programmes since.

I entered the race early in 2015 then didn't sort out the flights/accommodation as I knew it started in a remote spot so thought it would be easy to get a flight there – how wrong I was. It was about

April when I went to book a flight and could not get one on the day I wanted so I had to take a flight for the day before. I booked my accommodation in a hotel for about 100 Euros a night then started to plan my race strategy.

The rules were really simple. You catch a bus to a remote spot and start on the 125k 2500m course, there are no access roads if things go wrong only a small number of mountain huts, and you have to get to the finish within 24hrs. The organisers offer no commitment to come looking for you or rescue you if things go wrong. If things go wrong the idea was to get to a hut and phone for help. A heli rescue was about 100 Euros but may take days due to the weather. I quite liked the whole self-sufficiency idea as it would be something new for me, so I worked out how much food to take – basically aiming at a snack every 1.5 hrs. Fluid wise my plan was to carry little but drink from the rivers.

In the summer months my hotel was cancelled for no stated reason so I had to find somewhere else and booked a cabin at Camp Ripan which was very close to race registration. It was only when I arrived in Kiruna, I learned why the hotel was no longer functioning. The hotel had been abandoned as it was located in part of the town that was due to move.

The months ticked by, and on the 5th Aug, I was on my way to Kiruna via Oslo. At Oslo airport there was a need to change to another flight and it is about a 20 minute powerwalk from where we arrived to where the next flight went from. A business class person would have a quicker walk as at one point the direct route says 'business class only' and everyone else has to go a long way around. To all intents and purposes, it looks like this 10-metre shortcut was built for this sole purpose! Prior to the next flight we went through security again and one man asked where his bag was and he was asked if he had picked it up off the previous conveyor and he said no. They said he had to come without his bag as it was too late to go and find it. I've no idea when he re-joined his luggage.

As we flew up Sweden the scenery got more and more remote and started to resemble flow country from northern Scotland before becoming truly arctic tundra. My head was pressed to the glass looking at the terrain below wondering what it would be like to cross it completely alone. A solitary event was very likely as less than one hundred people had entered the race so the chances of being split and isolated were high.

We landed at Kiruna and the airport had a real outback feel. We walked down the steps from the plane and across to a small door in the terminal building. Some locals had come out of the door to greet their loved ones. Inside this door the luggage would come out on a conveyor belt and passengers, and those waiting to collect them, all hung around. There were burly looking miners waiting to collect fellow miners. There were ladies with minors meeting their partners who had been away for some time. Finally, there were a small number of runners in their dayglo attire and massive rucksacks. Whilst waiting for my bag I spotted a bus timetable on the wall and realised if I were lucky, I may be able to catch the 16:30 bus, the next one being 18:00. I got my bag at 16:45 and swiftly went out to find a bus there with a big queue. Slowly but surely, we got on. The bus had a side door and all around that was built up with big bags. More people and bags got on until we were all a bit buried in the luggage.

We set off and here was where I had a moment of realisation with myself. I'd assumed the bus would go to the centre of Kiruna and I had a map from there to the campsite. As we set off it soon became apparent, we were driving all over the place and turning this way and that and now I doubted we would stop at the centre of town. After about 25 minutes the driver stopped in a cutting on a busy main road with a pavement to the side and shouted 'campsite'. Suddenly many untwined themselves from the luggage mountain and got out. The bus driver helpfully opened the side door and a pile of bags dropped out and I found mine and set off. I had no idea where we were but we all had to walk in one direction to start with so I kept in the group. We took a right and I could see a 'Camp Ripan' sign at the end so I sped up to get to the front and walked in to the camp site first and checked in. My hut had a small lobby, a bathroom and one lounge/bedroom. I now had to decide what to do with the time, conscious of the need to rest. It was now about 18:00 and about 10 degrees and raining so I headed out to get some food. Kiruna is small so it was easy to find the centre and I bought some bits in a supermarket. There was a beggar outside who looked very cold – every time I went to the supermarket he was in the same place. Walking around Kiruna there were several examples of offensive graffiti on the walls. A lot of buildings had a look of not being maintained, in keeping with their plans of future abandonment.

My original hotel was one such building now sitting there empty – visible signs all-around of the ground sinking. It sat close to a beautiful railway station building that was locked and empty. The train can no longer get this close in to town and there was a temporary station a mile or so out of town. Some buildings had gone completely – just a line of bricks outlining where they had been – like a body in chalk on the ground after a drive-by. There was an exhibition of the future showing how people would move to a new town built several kilometres away. The current Kiruna was being cleared in phases and it may take 10 years for some to move but move they will. There are many reasons why people sell houses some good, some bad and some sad. For good reasons people tend to accept they will lose the garden they built up over the years as there is something good at the next place. At the other end those who move on for divorce/destitution/hardship type reasons will be very sad to see the garden go but due to what is going on in their lives it is possibly not the biggest concern. Knowing you would lose your house and garden in 10 years must put a different perspective on things for some as when do you stop caring for it? It doesn't matter how you maintain it as the compensation has already been negotiated. When does stubborn pride and self-worth give way to the realities of capitalism? There was definitely a jaded feeling in many of the streets as if it already were a ghost town. What would it mean to be brought up in such an environment and how would this mould a child's character for adult life?

Heading out in the rain all these thoughts flooded in to my head and I wanted to explore more but knew it was a good idea to rest so headed back to Camp Ripan for the evening and watched some TV.

The length of the daytime was really striking as it never really seemed to get dark, sleeping made harder by the lack of curtains, but sleep I did and woke up to a new day. Race registration was in the afternoon, and I still had to work out where it was, but before then it was time to explore. I left my cabin and headed up a random path in to the wilderness to be greeted by a massive mountain hare, so much bigger than a typical rabbit in the UK. I'd seen many photos of Kiruna from a nearby hill so decided to climb it. I didn't have a map so used a combination of common sense and luck to navigate. Walking along a quiet road I suddenly came across a second-hand dealership of 1950s/1960s American cars. I cut up to the hill and walked up a short ski slope to get to the top and the amazing view.

I looked down the grassy slope and could see a large bit of waste ground, the classic American car garage being just on the edge of this on the left. Beyond this waste ground lay Kiruna itself, rows of houses in tree lined streets. To the left I could see the new Kiruna – apartment blocks in grey, cream and flesh tones. Looking directly ahead, and over the houses, I could see the massive mine. I could see the hillside sectioned in to layers as if it were built in a mould. I could see the large cleft in the landscape that had the current mine hundreds of meters below. I could see the vast sidings containing lengthy trains of iron-ore. I knew if I came in 10 years the view would be very different with the houses replaced by parkland, the mine taking priority over everything around it.

I carried on down to head to Kiruna and got a bit lost and came to a remote house in the woods that had lots of very loud husky dogs who, fortunately, were in a compound. I cut out of the forest, crossed the main road, and came to the loco depot which had big 'no photography' signs on it. Nearby was a marshalling yard and I was fascinated to see a man with a radio control unit standing trackside driving his engine that was shunting wagons – surely the ultimate train set. Next to this was the temporary station which consisted of a small portacabin sized room up some stairs on a single platform. It all had the look of being temporary and one passenger told me it had already moved once – it just kept moving away from the natural deformation that was occurring. From the station it is about a 15-minute walk to town and still there are signs of the mine albeit on a small scale. Some children's playparks will have animals on springs for children to bounce on – here the animals were construction vehicles. Many young schoolboys will play with toy cars but here they played with construction vehicles. It was almost as if some careers had been determined at an early stage. Arriving in town I ate some lunch in a café and was conscious it was best not to walk miles more today (I'd done 10 already) so headed to the library and bought three Swedish second-hand travel guides very cheaply to 'read' that afternoon.

The race instructions helpfully gave a lat/long for registration and said there would be a tent there. I took the view there must be a sign so was not overly worried about this description. Near Camp Ripan there was a large sports hall that seemed to be getting busy for something called the 'Fjallraven Classic' so, having time to kill, I decided to go in. This was race registration on a grand scale only not for my event. To call the Fjallraven Classic a race is a little unfair as it is really more of an experience. Every year 2000 people start on (more or less) the same course as the Tierra Arctic Ultra only start one day later and most aim to do the route over five days. Although the terrain is the same for both races the experience for the individuals will be very different. In both events I suspect there is an opportunity to find oneself only in different ways. There were highly detailed maps on the wall, camp food for sale, clothing for sale and, most alarmingly, a selection of large knives for sale. I did wonder what use a large knife would be up in the wilderness and what were the hazards and carried on around the hall. In the corner was a small desk with the sign 'Tierra Arctic Ultra' – I'd arrived! The helpful man behind it provided me with a small map (1:75,000 scale), pointed out an error on the map and told me the pick-up was 03:00 tomorrow morning from the car park outside. The race itself has a short and a long distance, the difference being the long one goes on 'the glacier'. He ensured me I'd done the right thing opting for 'the glacier' and wished me good luck as I departed.

I headed back to the cabin and ate/read/watched TV until about 21:00 when I went to bed. Due to the lack of curtains, and it not really getting dark, coupled with the fear of missing my bus, I was up about every 45 minutes going for nervous pees and eventually got up around 02:15 and, after getting in to my race kit, and packing my big bag, left for the car park getting there around 02:45. At about 02:50 another man arrived and we nodded at each other. The light was surprisingly bright. At about 02:55 20 or so people started to appear from the campsite and the bus arrived on time at 03:00. We all got on excited for the day ahead. I was the only non-Scandinavian on board and when a Coldplay tune came on the radio my seat buddy, Horst, told me it was a good omen for me as a British tune for a British person. Abba was never played for me to return the compliment.

We drove for about 45 minutes in the wilderness to Nikkaluokta and all got off the bus. Nikkaluokta is a very small village, with a campsite, on the edge of the tundra. The race started at 06:00 so there was a little time here to sort things out and do some last-minute things. I spotted a queue of people going up to a container with their big bags so thought this must be where we left them. My turn came and I handed it over. One thing less to worry about I thought. Slowly but surely more runners came out of the tents at Nikkaluokta and handed their bags in to the container.

There were a few toilets at the campsite but you needed a particular Swedish coin to operate them and many of us did not have it. A useful lesson for future races – always carry a few coins.

We had a timing chip fitted to our ankle and had to check this worked at a scanner. It seemed to work for some and not for others. I was ambivalent to it as was not sure what value it had as we had no choice but to cross the wilderness and whilst it would give a start and finish time, I could get that from a watch. We also had to have our emergency tag visible – this was a bright orange piece of material which we safety pinned to our rucksacks. This final hour was cold with many in down coats, full waterproofs and hats/gloves.

The time came and we were off. As in many races the pack starts quickly as the 'short' racers sped off. I was happy going at my pace towards the middle as the path wended its way through birch forests, often along wooden boards. The boards kept you out of the rough ground but were slippy, broken and bounced in places so took some skill to run on. We soon came to a tranquil deep blue lake that had a jetty and a small row boat tied up. Deep blue lakes occur where there are low concentrations of algae and other substances and low human impact both in the water and the surrounding area. It looked such a beautiful spot to spend a day – the sunlight bringing out the most vibrant green on the beech tree leaves – unfortunately I had a race to run but I made a mental note to ask E if she would be interested in walking this route at some point in the future. Up ahead I could see what looked like a headwall of mountains and was now starting to think how the path would get through them. The heat was now starting to build and I was regretting starting in as many layers as I had; I could now feel my fleece getting damp from sweat. I knew a sweaty fleece would be of no use later on so stopped to remove it but carried on with my Gore-Tex coat as an outer shell.

For these first few hours I was surprised how slow I was- I was averaging about 5-6 kmph on a path and this was early on in the race – if things carried on like this, I may not reach the end within 24hrs. The lake eventually finished and now the path became very rocky and narrow as we slowly climbed along the base of the mountain making our way to where the course would split. I could see the split up ahead at the narrow pedestrian Tarfalabron Bridge and had to work out what to do. The glacier is an 'out and back' to the right, the main trail heads on. A little part of me thought to head on as was not sure if I would complete in time. A larger part told me time is immaterial as if I'm late to finish so what? No-one is going to come looking for me or withdraw me and I'm only here once so I'm going to see as much as I can even if I go over the 24hr limit. At the split a marshal asked me if I'm going 'up' or 'on'. I said definitely up as I'd seen pictures and it looked stunning. Another runner named David was standing there and he said 'will you go up on the glacier with me as I don't want to be alone?' – I said yes but did tell him I had very limited glacier experience but would try my best. We both agreed to keep together noting neither of us, or any other runner for that matter, had a rope. This would mean a crevasse field could be dangerous so we would trust to common sense and luck – all part of the adventure! The path climbed up a valley and crossed the river many times on a selection of narrow bridges until it reached a plateau of rocks. We reached the Tarfala arctic research station which consisted of some isolated single-story buildings hiding in the wilderness. With every step forward, the views got better as we approached a mountain lake surrounded by mountains on three sides. In the distance I could see a 'Tierra' flag fluttering in the breeze at the far end of the Tarfalajaure lake (1160m ASL). As we got closer, we crossed a small bit of snow to reach the check point that was manned by two women reading books and one man whittling wood with a large knife. The glacier had been kind to us this year and had presented no problems to get this far. There was no food, water or anything like that. All that happened was one of them wrote our numbers on a piece of paper and that was it. I took some photos then we headed back. As it was an 'out and back' I knew there were 36 people in front of me and on the return leg I counted those behind me and knew the field went back to person 70. This gave me some reassurance as if I had a fall there were always those behind me. As we headed back to the Tarfalabron bridge David, and two others, left me with no notice and sped off leaving me all alone. Racing is racing so this was OK from my perspective. After a few minutes I could see they were getting a bit stuck on the boulder field and I caught them up and overtook them taking a different path. I realised I was better at reading terrain so now I wanted to make a gap so they could not spot my precise moves so I'd beat them by some margin. I was thinking if I could get sufficiently far ahead that they could not follow me I'd beat them and make up some spaces in the overall finish. I got to the bridge then headed along the course in to the wilderness.

The area we were now in is similar to being around the Eiger, only no people or structures around – these are the mountains around Kebnekaise. At the time Kebnekaise was the highest mountain in Sweden (2111m) and sits above the route – a snow filled hanging corrie high up in the air. From a technical viewpoint it looked like it would present few difficulties, the major challenge being how remote it would be to get to!

I carried on pushing for about 2 hours and my three competitors continually watched me before committing to things like river crossings. I realised I was fighting a losing battle and four heads would be better than one so stopped and waited for them. Together as four we made faster progress and it wasn't long before another realisation kicked in that I shared with the others. We were completely alone. Everyone behind us had turned back. Looking ahead we could see no-one. We were not on paths, we were out of mobile reception, we could see no mountain huts, we were completely alone. We moved forward together having an understanding if one stopped for anything the other three would move on no-matter what the issue was. The stopper just had to catch-up. This may seem an odd decision to make but the weather was closing in and it would be easy to spend hours extra out there as we were all out of phase with eating/toileting/finding water etc. It was a wilderness race and self-sufficiency was the nature of the game, so as long as no-one was injured this was a reasonable approach to take.

Around this time, I started to have some doubts about my main luggage bag. I had handed it in at the start like everyone else but now I realised I had not asked where it was going to, if it were going anywhere at all. Some runners were staying in that campsite so it might be secure luggage for all I knew. I thought back to Lizzy Hawker's comments on luggage from UTMR and knew there was nothing I could do about my current situation so decided to not let it bother me. This approach really worked and it almost became a game to me trying to work out all the possible places it could have gone!

At about 16:00 we spotted a lady sitting on a rock in the middle of nowhere. She had a small stove boiling coffee and was hunched over a flat rock playing solitaire with a pack of cards. David, who spoke Swedish, approached her and she explained she was a CP so took our numbers. They then had a long conversation about the route ahead pointing at a mountain. At the end I asked David what was said and he pointed out a path we had to take. I said this was different to the gpx track I had but he was sure. To put some context here before coming out I'd watched YouTube videos of people who had got lost for days up here so we really needed to be on the correct side of any big river, lake etc. This particular CP staff member had been dropped off by heli, and would be picked up by heli, later in the day – a truly lonely spot to wait. It quickly became apparent that the gpx track was correct and we got to a most beautiful plateau. We were above the treeline and there was no sign of man, or anything manmade, in all directions. There were no vapour trails in the sky. There were no animals around. There was no sound to be heard. We stood in silence for a few minutes taking it all in. I found it a really humbling experience to be this tiny individual standing in this vast space. It made me think what it must have been like for early man to have found somewhere on the planet. I've never had the experience of being so small compared to the majesty of nature. I don't think I've ever been anywhere else that is so untouched by man. The weather was now starting to close in and we had a long way to go so carried on.

The next few hours would be crossing rocks and wading rivers multiple times always pushing northward. The only sense of civilisation came when we arrived at a remote hut that was receiving a food parcel by helicopter. The food was for those in the Fjallraven Classic that would follow over the coming days. When we arrived at the hut a lady told us to scan our race chips so our progress was recorded and offered to sell us any item – each one would come with a one-hour penalty. We didn't even consider buying anything!

We were soon back in remote territory crossing the remote arctic tundra miles away from anyone, or anything. After a bit one of the two more silent ones in our four-ship said I was pushing the pace too fast so must slow down. Now if someone is not injured, or scared, then racing is racing in my eyes. I had a quiet word with David and said on the next uphill I intended to power off quickly and not wait at the top as I didn't want to slow down. David agreed and when the hill came, we went for it. We knew the other two would expect us to wait but if we went fast off the other side we would be out of shouting distance and what you don't hear you cannot react to! To many this may sound selfish but there is an element of survival in ultras and, at the end of the day, racing is racing.

At the top of the hill David was about 30 seconds behind so I waited and when he caught up, I said 'now is our time to go for it and make a really big gap' and I set off running at a fast pace down the boulder strewn hill. He kept with me for about 10 second and shouted so I stopped. He said he was in too much pain so would take some pills but now was the time to split. I headed on hopeful he would get his pain under control and catch me up. In the distance I could see a person moving so over the next 30 mins slowly but surely caught them up, this carried over the next few hours until, surprisingly, at around 20:30 David caught me up. He was now taking more pills to control the pain but was pleased to meet up – we'd had some really good chats earlier in the day so now we would have some more.

We could see a mountain hut in the distance that had a small lake in-front of it. Walking near this was difficult as there were many flies and mosquitos around all trying to bite us where they could. Out of nowhere a completely naked porcelain white adult female came running down towards the lake. She screamed from being bitten as she ran shoeless down the slope – her long ginger hair flowing behind her. About 1 second behind came a completely naked adult male, also shrieking. They both jumped in the cold lake and stopped screaming when submerged as had relief from the omnipresent omnivorous flies. We could see a tiny tent on the hillside. Whilst they had some relief in the water, I didn't think returning to the tent would be fun. We arrived at the (locked) hut to find a tent outside and a race marshal with a face covered in mosquito bites. She took our numbers and we had a little chat. David decided he wanted to change his T-shirt so stripped off here and instantly got more bites. Just standing there was painful whilst I waited – my only relief being a treat of a jam sandwich I'd been carrying all day to have as my one solid meal. It was so lovely, something to chew, the sweet taste of the jam, my tongue picking food out of my teeth for a few miles to come.

At this point a few things were apparent to me. Firstly, the map we had would not be that useful to navigate by when my GPS watch would run out of battery life as it surely would before the end. Secondly David had done the course before so, theoretically, was a good person to be with only he didn't seem to remember much. Thirdly David was in a lot of pain at times so regardless of everything I could not leave him, even though he was slower than me. Of course, moving slower meant the GPS watch would stop sooner so we'd both have more of a problem as we would be further from the end when we would have to navigate. However, the bottom line was David was not doing well and it would not have been right to leave him so I openly said I'd stick with him until the end at his pace and for this he was very grateful.

As the hours ticked by, I now started to question would I need my headtorch at all and at around 23:00 David took his out. He said last year there had been a lot of lemmings on the next section and we both wanted to see some. Disappointingly David saw only one sheltering under one of the planks to cross a boggy section.

It was about now David explained how his wife was going to start walking back from the end of the course at around 00:00 and we should meet in the wilderness somewhere. I assumed this was his cornucopia of pills talking as the concept seemed highly unlikely so politely nodded.

We knew the next CP should be close and David thought it was by a bonfire on the other side of the river. I could see no fire whatsoever but he was sure there was one over there and we pressed on to a small steel bridge across a gorge. At this point we were both out of water so carefully clambered down to the river – I lay flat to get the bottles submerged, David hanging on to my legs to prevent any accidents. A fall in to this rocky gorge would have been very bad and I remember thinking at the time this was the most dangerous thing we had done in the event. We knew we were close to the CP but where was it? The area we were in was a small forest on the edge of the river and up ahead we could see a tepee. We were unsure if this was the CP or not so decided to approach it to see. We got close to it and there was no sound so tried to find a door – at the time we assumed it was the CP with someone sleeping in it. The ground was rough and I ended up tripping over a support rope and fell on to the outside to be greeted with what sounded like Arnold Schwarzenegger slowly saying 'What the F*** do you want it is the middle of the night?' and I said 'Sorry – we are racing and looking for a checkpoint' to which the reply was 'it is not here'. I asked 'do you know where it is' and the reply was 'go back to the bridge and find it'. I thanked the faceless voice and we headed off. After about 20 minutes we found another tent with three tired looking volunteers outside. They said they had not seen anyone for ages and were looking forward to quitting in a few hours. I said there were still many people behind and they said that is not their problem; they only have to be there for a certain number of hours and they can then close.

Around this point the watch died, just as the terrain got very boggy and a multitude of paths presented itself. It was also sunrise (around 02:00) and I'd gone the whole night without my headtorch which was a first for me. David had no real memory of his previous race but somehow, we managed to keep plugging ahead in the right direction. Most of our chat was on European politics of which David, a Swede, had an amazing depth and breadth of knowledge so I really enjoyed our long chats on Brexit and the like.

It wasn't long before, in the middle of nowhere, we could see a lady standing – David's wife! She had walked out about 10k up the route to meet him. David was really pleased to see her and suddenly our pace dropped right off and before long it went from a three-way conversation in English to a two way one in Swedish. This was no good for me as I knew I'd easily lose an hour but I had made a pact to stay with David to get him home. I decided I'd push on ahead to work out the route and wait so this might either hurry them up or they would release me. His wife quickly read me and asked if I felt OK to push on by myself and I said I did so she suggested I did. I said my goodbyes and headed off running the first km to get out of earshot lest they change their mind. In the distance I could see the remote settlement of Abisko so I knew I was nearly home. Breaking out of the forest a large ore train came past on the railway line – it was around 04:00 and the daylight now was as bright as could be. The path cut under the railway, past somewhere to scan a timer chip, then the final hill to the end. I shuffle ran up this hill to a deserted race village. There were two marshals at the end who said well done. One put a medal around my neck and the medal instantly fell from the ribbon – I said it would be OK but she got me another. As there was no photographer, I asked them to take a few pics then asked about the promised food at the end and they pointed me at a catering tepee. I went in and there was an empty pot of soup and one crust of bread and that was it. I knew I had food in my main bag so went out to see if it had arrived and it had. The marshal suggested I ate the piece of crusty bread and I said I was OK – the marshal then said they had left the hot water on especially late and it was about to be turned off so I should shower quickly.

I'd covered 125k in 22:18 mins and knew I could have done more – I had some disappointment that today was not a 161k race but it told me I could do the distance in a future race. All in I was satisfied with my performance and had experienced a true wilderness with some good company.

I took my main bag in to the Abisko outdoor centre and ate some snacks then went to find the shower. What struck me was runners sitting up in chairs, sleeping in corridors, in a building that appeared to have beds to sleep 100-200 people – most odd. I opened the shower door and went in to the changing room and could see a bench with space for about three people, a few shower heads on the wall and a large C shape which must have been the sauna. On this about 10 naked men sitting tightly leg to leg with various cuts, blisters, friction marks abounding on their skin. A number had moustaches and I didn't recall seeing many in the race so wondered if people a little faster than me typically had a facial caterpillar or whether those with caterpillars were more likely to like a naked sauna. Either way I stripped off and had a shower whilst 10 naked men sat in a huddle looking on from about 5 metres away. Being an extrovert (at times) made me theatrically floss myself with the towel to dry off then I put some clothes on and toddled out and left them in their fleshy heat. Back in the main hall I was pleased to see David arriving – a really nice companion to have spent the day with.

Next port of call was reception to find where the sleeping hall was. I got to the desk around 05:00 and the girl told me there was not one but I could book a room for around 100 Euros a night. Now it was 05:00 and my train was at 12:00 and there was no way I was booking a room. I asked if there were any other options and she said I could sit in a chair however she has to hoover at 05:30 so might be noisy – I said this was fine. I saw it is a good way of training for a 100 miler as would not be able to sleep and all I had to do was to wait until breakfast. She offered me a breakfast or a brunch voucher and I asked about the difference and the answer was none – the food was identical – it was about eating 08:00-09:00 or 10:00 – 12:00. I opted for breakfast then sat and waited. The hoovering was done to a very meticulous level and was a good way of keeping us awake as the hours ticked by and the runners trickled in. Breakfast time arrived and we all went for the slowest and longest breakfast possible as when you left the room that was it! I now had several hours to kill and was feeling a little nauseous as waves of sleep wanted to pass over me so decided to head outside and spotted a giant hammock – I was straight in there to discover it was very wet so was out quite quickly. One regret I have about how I used this time is that I didn't go down to look at the marble river – I could see it from about 100m away but never went close. The issue was a dog who really didn't want me going there and I wish I'd found another way past the guardian of the rocks.

Being really bored I thought walking to the station would be a good idea to check the route and wandered along to the building and wooden platform. The waiting room would sit about 10 and the area behind the counter could sit about two. I say could as it was stacked floor to ceiling with reindeer pelts so was not going to take a ticket seller anytime soon. With nothing more to see I headed back to the centre and after an hour or so picked up my bag and returned to the station. By now about 20 runners were waiting and the train arrived and we all got on. A few miles down the line David and his wife got on and both came along for a chat before settling down in their seats – they had a 24hr train journey to look forward to.

The run from Abisko to Kiruna takes about an hour and is very scenic as it skirts a massive lake. I was quite looking forward to E arriving so I could bore her with my race stories and get some sleep at some point! E was waiting at Kiruna station and we dropped my bag at the hotel (as the camp site was full, we had a hotel for a few of the days) and went in to town to my 'regular' for a coffee and sandwich then back to the hotel. My race socks were fruity and I was all for washing them and keeping them. Not for the first time E sentenced them to a life in the bin so that was the end of them. The afternoon passed dozing over some film then after an evening meal it was time for sleep.

E and I had two rest days and on the first day we did a little walk to the hill with the view of the mine. On the way I bumped in to Johan, one of the four I had run with, who was a bit emotional. He couldn't quite believe what he had achieved and was a bit weepy about it. His partner patiently sitting by his side. When he spotted me, he greeted me like some long-lost friend. I had pangs of guilt leaving him in the middle of nowhere as he was slow but it was a race not a social event. We had a little chat and went our ways.

For our second rest day in Kiruna we had booked a tour down the Kiruna mine. The Kiruna mine is the largest underground iron ore mine in the world producing over 26 million tonnes of iron ore each year; since it opened in 1898 over 950 tonnes of iron ore have been removed. Before flying out we'd gone on-line and booked our morning tour for around 20 Euros each which seemed good value for money. As per the instructions we turned up at the tourist centre at 10:00 to start our tour. Kiruna tourist information has a big model in it for tourists to look at as is often the case in such places – the only difference being this one had both above ground and the mine below. Here the scale of the mine became apparent. The mine itself is measured from the top of the hill that they first started on and this is the 0m reference point. Ground level is at 230m and this is where the railway wagons are loaded. The mine itself is down at 1365m i.e. over a kilometre below ground level. All this detail hung below the table which had the town plan built in miniature with Monopoly-like houses atop.

Our guide arrived and after some introductions about 20 of us caught a dedicated bus to the mine. We were told not to take any photos until we had entered the mine and off we drove. After about 10 minutes we got to a check-in gate where the bus driver showed some ID, then off we went through a hole in the mountain to a subterranean road system arriving at a disused level hundreds of meters underground. Here we watched videos, looked at mining equipment and went in an old miner's café to have tea and biscuits. We were then all given a small bag and told we could have as many iron ore pellets as we wanted that were in an old wagon outside. Here it became a bit like a feeding frenzy at a pig trough with everyone trying to squeeze as many as they could in to their plastic bags. Helpfully more bags were available for those with pressing needs. For my part I took some, about 100g worth or a 1/3 of a bag, thinking they would be good on a model railway. At the end of the frenzy we caught our bus back to the surface and passed one of the long iron-ore trains outside. Our guide was very excited as the golden wagon (number 1000) was there in the sea of blue. She had been a guide for a few years and had rarely seen it so thought it was a good omen for us all. Many on the bus took a picture of the lucky wagon. In my brief time in Kiruna I spent some time watching the trains out of the hotel room window. Each 68-car iron-ore train is pulled by two permanently coupled Co-Co (i.e. two six wheeled bogies with all axles powered, with a separate motor on each axle) diesel locomotives. The majority of trains run on what is known as the northern circuit (11-13 trains per day) heading to Narvik; a minority run on the Southern (5-6 per day) circuit to the port of Luleå.

The trains do not move fast – an 8,600 tonne fully loaded train is operated at 60kmph and an empty one at 70kmph. For the majority of the route to Narvik the heavy train just coasts downhill most of the time, capturing the energy from braking in batteries. 1/5 of the recuperated energy is all that is required to take the train to Narvik, the remaining 80% powers the empty train back up hill to Kiruna. The scale of the railway, and its efficiency, is truly astonishing.

Having the afternoon to ourselves we wandered around Kiruna looking at all the buildings that would be demolished, and the few that would be saved such as one of Sweden's largest wooden buildings, the Kiruna Church that is the shape of a Sami goathi or tent cot. From outside the building is an intricate gothic revivalist structure made entirely of wood, looking reassuringly solid to the point of being over-engineered. Inside there is an elegance and grace about it with a large open area and an art nouveau alter. The church is due to be dismantled in 2025 and be re-built several kms away in the new Kiruna in 2026.

Having stayed at Camp Ripan earlier that week I'd never actually eaten in the restaurant there so suggested to E we did it that night. At the restaurant I again met with one of the four-ship from the race. Johan was still coming to terms with what he had achieved and kept saying what a great time we had all had and that he was still unable to reconcile what had happened internally so was a little bit weepy; his partner still patiently sitting by. I didn't know what to say as, after all, I had abandoned him during the event but he seemed OK about this. Clearly, he'd had an adventure on an epic scale and to still be unable to come to terms with his achievement a few days later must have been close to his edge. I admired him for a number of reasons; his honesty in openly being emotional and not trying to hide it as many men would; and what he had achieved as clearly it was up there in his life experiences. We ate a pleasant fish dish with a cool beer then headed back to our accommodation to pack for our train the next day.

For our final day in Kiruna we had a few hours before the train left and I went in to a mode of 'wanting to see even more' knowing I'd never be back to see this place again as it was all about to be knocked down. It was raining lightly and E didn't have the same enthusiasm so I headed out for an hour powerwalk picking up some snacks for the train. I saw a few more buildings and etched the images in to my brain to reflect upon during the day dreaming moments we all have. Back at the hotel we checked out and walked to the station. There was an old railway wagon on a roundabout here and I couldn't help myself but climb the ladder on it – I could see there were very old bits of iron ore that had fallen off it – not the smooth pellets we were offered on the mine tour but jagged ungainly pieces that would make a perfect souvenir to complement the round balls. Our train was due to leave around 11:00 and we quickly found it would be 14:00 at least. The small building didn't have enough seats for the twenty or so people who were waiting so some stood and some sat. The station had no catering facilities, or shop nearby, so I was pleased I'd selflessly gone out earlier in the rain for some essential train-snacks. In the station a middle-aged woman came in and clocked that E and I were English so came across for a chat. She wanted to sit down so I offered my seat and, over the next few hours, would periodically hover back over to E who was learning all about the lady. The upshot of all of this was the lady said E and her should meet in the UK as she travels there regularly and they exchanged e-mails although, despite the lady making contact, it never progressed to a meetup. Our train eventually came and we headed back up the line to Abisko. Depending on your viewpoint I either educated and enthused or bored E with the minutiae of the route which was stunning – the mountains to the left and the massive lake to the right. Beyond Abisko things got more remote as we headed higher inland coming to some very remote settlements – this looked a very desolate place for people to live. The route then comes out high over a fjord that leads down to Narvik – slowly but surely, we descended. We arrived in Narvik around 17:20, hours later than expected, and now had a worry if our hire car would be available. We had phoned ahead and rushed to the pick up to see it sitting outside with the engine on. We went in to do the paperwork then headed out to check it and the man said not to worry but we should get on our way. E spotted a mark in the car and pointed it out and was told not to worry, we took some pics anyway, then headed off. From my perspective the late start wasn't ideal but there was nothing we could do as we set off for our Arctic driving adventure. As things turned out taking the photos of the scratch on the car was prudent as we nearly got blamed for it and charged for damages but the photos correctly proved the damage existed before we took the car out.

We carried on northward spending about a week touring before ending our arctic holiday in Tromsø. All in it had been a great arctic adventure – Kiruna, racing and our week exploring.

14 TRANSYLVANIA 50 2017

As 2016 started to draw to a close I was looking for fresh challenges in 2017. I'd decided I was going to enter TDS and if unsuccessful in the ballot would find a race where I could aim to achieve my first 100-miler. To get to either of these points I knew I had to start the racing season early so spent many evenings on the internet looking for a challenge around April-May. Ideally, I was looking for 80-100k with >5000m ascent as I thought this would give an early season indication of fitness and let me know what more I would have to do before late Summer to achieve my main goal for the year – be it TDS or a 100-miler.

Deep inside me I have a desire to be in a controlled dangerous situation where I'll have to test myself so I wanted to enter something that had a frisson of danger and edge so whatever race I entered had to meet this need. It can be hard to decide what race to enter as I need to know I'll be getting my excitement fix out of it so I've tended to rely on YouTube videos to see if they give me an instant feel of excitement, jeopardy and edge. My brain quickly reacts to the situation as if I were there and I'll get a release of cortisol and adrenaline and can feel this excitedly rushing through my body. I'll feel my heart pump stronger and have a signal from my sphincter that we need to reduce weight as this is the moment we need to respond and be our fastest and most powerful. I could watch 100 race videos and get nothing but every so often one will grab me like this and I just know it is the one for me. Between entering and the event itself I'll watch it 10 -20 times in part to get a recce of some elements of the route and in part to get my adrenaline fix.

I'd first become aware of the Transylvania 100 a few years earlier and it looked exciting – I was put off at the time as lacked the confidence to try a race in a country where I thought there would be language difficulties and getting to the start would not be possible by public transport.

I didn't want to enter a race where I'd turn up at some foreign airport, drive to the event, race, drive back and fly out as to do so would be to not see the country. This would be to see a sanitised version of the country with like-minded people and I may not get the chance to interact with any local person – this approach was not for me! This meant that any race needed to be possible to be run using public transport alone and this self-imposed restriction ruled out many races however the Transylvania 100 was possible so in Sep 2016 I entered the 100k event.

The event is a series of races of distances 20, 30, 50 and 100k and so the runner can choose, in advance, which one they would be tackling on Saturday 20th May 2017. The 100k race transcribes an (approx.) bat outline on the ground which made it look even more exciting. The bat association comes from the race starting and finishing at Dracula's Castle in Bran in the Parc Natural Bucegi approximately 100 miles north of Romania's capital, Bucharest.

The event itself was going to be a step-up for me. I'd done events of similar difficulty but these had been in late summer so there had been time to train during warmer weather. For the Transylvania 100 I'd have to train hard over the winter months having both the dark and cold to contend with.

About a month or so prior to the race back pain kicked in and the idea of doing a 100k race with around 7000m of ascent seemed a bad idea so I contacted the organisers to see if I could change distance and they were fine with that so I was on for the 50k. I had mixed feelings about my decision; on the one hand I knew it was the right one for health reasons however I was very disappointed that my body was stopping me doing something my mind wanted to do. I was able to rationalise this decision and put it behind me as I looked forward to the event.

I'd looked at the race on YouTube and what really excited me was the snow as I had not raced in such conditions before. I had done some mountaineering in the snow with an ice axe and crampons around Zermatt but that was different – I was largely walking up closed ski pistes. I did this as it was a way of getting some big winter hills in when I was training for the UTMR in 2015. In Romania I would not have an ice axe, or crampons, so things would be different. Reading around the advice was to have 'yak-traks' or equivalent but having large feet (UK size 13.5) I've been unable to find such devices that are available in my size. I thus decided on a pair of Salomon Fellcross trainers and hoped they would work thinking the aggressive tread would dig in to the snow. If things were really bad, I could always turn around on a slope and withdraw. Whilst this would be frustrating at the time, it would be far better to do this than to take a nasty fall.

The race organisers recommended flying to Sibiu as this was the closest main airport to Bran which is served by direct flights from Stanstead. Living in Hampshire I decided to fly from Heathrow to Bucharest.

Bucharest's Otopeni International Airport is situated in a northwest suburb of Bucharest and has hire car facilities so it would be possible to land, hire a car, and be in Bran within three hours. I wanted to see more of Romania so, instead, my plan was to take the bus to Bucharest, spend the night there, then take the 3-hour train ride to Brasov the next morning with a 50-minute bus journey to Bran to finish.

On the Thursday before the race I was going through the security check at Heathrow and spotted a few others with small rucksacks milling around and I wondered if they were Bucharest bound. Shortly after this I spotted them on the plane so guessed we were all going the same way. I didn't really know how to strike up a conversation from a few rows back so sat quietly reading my 'Rough Guide to Romania' to plan what to do on the extra days I planned to spend out there.

We landed around 17:00 at Bucharest's airport and the next challenge was to get to the city. I've travelled a fair bit and there are usually signs for the 'bus to city' or something similar but not here.

I eventually found a small hut in the car park that said 'bus to city' and handed over 20 Romanian Leu (about 5 Euros) as per the sign. I could not see the person inside but a hand came back with a ticket and I was pointed to where to stand. After a few minutes a bus came along and I got on.

On the bus from the airport a fellow passenger was fascinated with my feet and could not help himself checking them out. My bright green Salomon trainers did stand out a little. As hire cars and taxis are so cheap, I suspect I was the only non-Romanian on the bus and whilst I did get a lot of looks, they were always out of curiosity and I never felt threatened in any way.

After about 50 minutes the bus pulled up outside the Gara de Nord railway station and everyone got off. It wasn't at all obvious where I'd catch the bus back to the airport in a few days' time from, let alone buy a ticket, but I thought I'd worry about that then. This station looks like it has seen happier times and is a little tired looking. A feeling of emptiness pervades the station. There are large areas closed off and many cheap looking cafes with people sitting down drinking and smoking. I was quite hungry so went to a sandwich café in the station – my choice based purely on the fact it had a sign on the door saying 'toaletă' and having been cooped up on the bus I needed to go.

From the station I knew the route to the Ibis hotel was about 1km forward and 1 km right; really easy and only a fool would get lost. As I walked along, I was getting stared at by everyone – not in a threatening way but in a curious way as I really did standout with my big rucksack sweating buckets in the heat and humid air. I'd chosen the Ibis for two main reasons; it was not far from the station and it was opposite a building I had wanted to see for a number of years, the People's Palace in Bucharest.

I had early childhood memories of the execution of Ceausescu on Christmas day in 1989, hearing it on the news on Radio 4. At the time I knew little of what he stood for, or why it happened, but since then had taken a small interest in the subject to learn more. I now knew he evicted many people to build a grand palace that was never finished in his lifetime. The building was now the home of the Romanian Parliament, an Art Gallery, a conference venue and a lot of empty rooms many of which are still incomplete. I knew it could be seen from afar, so, as I walked from the station, I was keen to see it and to consider how I would feel if I has been a Romanian national. Turning the corner on to the Strada Berzei I could see it. A large rectangular monolith completely out of scale sitting there ominously peering in every direction. I think if I had suffered the atrocities when it was being built and had been evicted, I'd feel very uncomfortable being near it. It's easy to imagine it being an ever-present reminder of past troubles.

I continued towards it and checked in to the Ibis hotel which is across the road from the People's Palace. After dropping my bag in the room, I went for a walk around the perimeter wall (which was almost 3k) and took in what I could knowing my aim was to return in a few days' time and hopefully see inside.

The next morning my train was at 09:25 and it was about 2k from the hotel so I thought leaving at 08:30 would be fine. I set off with my big rucksack to retrace my route from the day before. I got to a crossroads and recognised a half complete building from the day before so I knew where I was. When I passed this yesterday, I regretted not looking at it in more detail to try and understand what it was. The Casa Radio, as it is known, was to be a 35,000 m^2 museum to communism that was never finished. It looks like two cuboidal shells with a flat area in between. Whilst marvelling at the sheer size of this empty buildings suddenly the main road was closed by the police and a high-speed VIP car came through. Now having had the excitement of watching a road closure and a high-speed car I set off for a quick look at the Casa Radio close up. Unfortunately, it was not two cubes with a plinth between but four cubes with four plinths and I didn't realise this at the time. From above the building can be thought of as a chair with the cubes being the legs and, unfortunately, I'd moved to a different face. As the building is run-down and without any distinct markings, I had not noticed this. I thus turned left instead of right.

I realised I was lost quickly but thought, without a map, I could work it out as the buildings are all huge and I just had to remember which ones I had passed. The trouble was that a lot of the concrete shells look the same. I was starting to get worried as I needed to be on the 09:25 train, so I cut through the university thinking it would help, asking a student who told me I'd done the right thing and sent me on my way. At about 09:10, and around 1k or so away from the station, I asked a man for directions. He said there is no way I would make the train on foot but if I took a tram I might – if there were no delays. I said I wanted to go on foot and he didn't want to give me directions saying it would not work and I should catch the tram. In the end he did give me directions and it was now a full-blown run to the station. About 5 minutes out I knew where I was and I also knew the train was leaving in 5 minutes time. I sped up and got to the station now sprinting through the dilapidated concourse. I could see the clock going from 09:24 to 09:25 and I was out of breath, sweaty, and the bag was hurting but I was in deep at this point so I ran to the platforms. 09:26. I could see my train still on the platform with the guard waving it off. I ran even faster and got on the last door as the train was departing. I walked through the train to my first-class seat (second class was £18 and first was £21) and took my bag off. All my clothes were drenched with sweat. I rubbed myself down (to many stares) then sat down to much relief. I'd made it. What could go wrong now?

After about 2.5 hours of travelling through beautiful landscapes the train arrived in Brasov (pronounced 'Brash- ov') where I had to change to a bus to complete my journey.

As the train approaches Brasov station, the landscape is one of flat empty fields, pylons and sidings with what looks like rotting trains. Upon alighting the station looks quite run down. The back of the grey drab concrete station building is the obvious exit. Looking the other way are many platforms with isolated bus shelters on them which must offer little protection in the rain and the cold. The tracks are overrun with grass to the point of giving the illusion that the lines are not being used. Outside there are rows of taxis and dozens of men, far more than would be needed to drive the taxis, just hanging around watching and staring at those who come out of the station.

It's fair to say Brasov is a functional town with the touristy bits being miles from the station. In my head I'd memorised the map and the turns so set off confidently on the 2-mile walk to the bus stop that I needed for Bran. I'd already got lost today so was not going to make that mistake again. For the first mile things were good but then I got to a junction and was unsure. I pulled out my map but it didn't help as the junction was not on it. It was a 50/50 decision so I went left. After about 30 minutes I knew I was lost. I walked towards the touristy bit and there was a small booth at the side of the road with a lady who sold bus tickets. By way of diagrams I explained where I wanted to go and she advised I catch the number 35 bus and get off near the football ground and walk to a car park behind this. All this information was conveyed to me via pictures on a piece of paper she had in her booth. I caught the bus and was unsure if I would spot a football stadium but fortunately it had floodlights so it was easy to see. I got off and now all I had to do was to get to the car park where I found a small bus drivers cafe, a small shop, a few buses and a few trucks with drivers sleeping in them. The bus to Bran runs roughly every hour and there was one due to go in a few minutes. I paid the driver 5 Euros and he gave me a ticket and I got on. The bus seemed to be a 'locals' service with a number of young families getting on with shopping and pushchairs. We set off through Brasov driving around the car parks of various out of town shops and then hit the road to Bran – the journey taking about 40 minutes.

Bran is really a one street town with everything along it (or on a few short side roads) with Dracula's Castle dominating the scene sitting atop a rocky outcrop about 30m high. I had a room in the Hotel Bran and spotted the sign for it but it looked like a major building site. A large crane was manoeuvring roof trusses in to place. It was impossible to see any window on the front of the hotel as it looked like the entire wall was being replaced. There were builders everywhere. I saw some side steps and went in to the hotel and the first thing that struck me was it was dark. The second thing being there was polythene everywhere to stop the builders getting the carpet dirty. I saw a reception desk (covered in polythene) which was where the main entrance must normally be (doors covered in polythene) and after a few minutes the receptionist walked by. I said I wanted to check in and after some formalities she explained there was no water or electricity during the day as they are having works done but it goes on at night and she showed me my room.

My plan now was to get some food, visit Dracula's castle and register for the race. Due to my roaming in Brasov it was now around 14:30 and so food options were limited, particularly as a pescatarian, but I was able to get a potato and some sort of soup in a local restaurant. I then visited the castle questioning whether it was a good idea doing all those steps the day before a race. The castle was really a long conga line of visitors shuffling up and down stairs and in tiny rooms. On leaving I saw the banners for the race and did have a pang of disappointment not to be in the '100' but merely the '50' instead. I didn't think I'd have these feelings here as I'd made the decision a few months previously. It's a bit like you've ordered a large cake in a café and since ordering have changed your mind and they say 'no problem – you can have the smaller one instead'. When you get to the collection counter there is a large and a small cake there and they tell you to take which ever one is yours. You've paid for the large cake so you naturally want it but walk away with the smaller one.

Race registration was located about 5 minutes' walk out of town, to the west of the castle, and is in a sports hall with space to park cars outside. It felt like I was in the minority walking to race registration (as opposed to driving), carrying my bag for checking.

The kit check was excellent, a really friendly bunch of people who wanted to help and offer advice on the snow and ice we would see tomorrow. They had a very large map on the wall (about 2m by 2m) of the routes and were able to talk in depth about the course. I found this really useful. The organisers spoke excellent English, and some of the volunteers were from the UK, so there was no language barrier for me.

I'd also paid, in advance, 5 Euros for the 3-course meal so picked up my voucher for this. For some reason they had me against a 'meat' voucher but as nothing was too much trouble, they quickly changed it for another one.

After this I decided to head back in to Bran. There are a number of shops in Bran selling touristy souvenirs and one or two shops for the locals selling food and ordinary household products and this is where I headed. I wanted to buy some 'just in case' food for Saturday night as I didn't know what time I'd be back at the hotel and didn't know what the food options would be. I also bought an ice cream for good measure – it was part holiday after all.

As I was walking around, I spotted Ari a fellow runner who I had met on the UTMR in 2015. We both looked at each other in a 'I think I recognise you but I'm not sure' way and carried on peering in to shop windows without making contact. With hindsight I wish I'd said hello and had a chat – I looked him up post event and was pleased to see he had completed the 100k race – no mean feat in the conditions that were to unfold.

I popped back to the hotel to drop off my race kit, and spare food, and there was still no electricity. This was not a problem to me however the hotel wanted to be paid there and then. As paying via a bank card was not an option, I headed back out to the only bank machine in the village to get money then returned to the hotel. As there were many runners in the hotel, they said they would provide breakfast at 04:00 and gave me a voucher for it. I left the hotel and headed out for the three-course meal and it was very nice – soup, potatoes/carrots in gravy and cake. Nice and simple. Other runners were questioning it and asking the restaurant for pasta which they didn't get as pasta is not a known food of this area. They wanted the pasta due to the carbohydrates as would be 'carbo loading'. My take on these things is to go with the flow and be flexible and eat what is provided as every culture is different.

After heading back to the hotel, I put the TV on and found the English language channel was the Travel Channel that was showing back to back shows on American caravans. I would learn a lot about caravans in the next few hours before an early bed.

05:00 came quickly on race day and I headed down to breakfast with my breakfast voucher. In the corridor to the exit were little breakfast bags on a table. I looked inside and there was a large cold boiled potato (which I was beginning to realise was a staple of the Romanian diet), a piece of meat and a piece of cake. There was also a flask of coffee and some cups on an adjacent table. I poured a coffee and carried my potato and cake back to my room. It wouldn't have been my first choice for breakfast but when travelling you have to respect the locals and accept what is provided – I saw some caffeine to help wake me up with slow release carbs and some sugars to get me going. I hadn't left my voucher beside the breakfast table so went down and dropped that off as I didn't want to get anyone in to trouble. I did some final packing and headed off to the start. The 100k had started at 05:00 whereas the 50k started at the far more civilised time of 07:00.

The 50 km Transylvania 50 is described by the organisers as 'difficult' and has 3328 metres of height gain. If successful the runner is awarded three ITRA points. An overview of the race is shown in table 3 below.

Location	Split distance	Cumulative distance	Altitude	Fastest Time	Slowest Time	My Time	Time Limit	Checkpoint
Start	0 km	0	750 m			0:00	07:00	
Malaiesti	12 km	12.0 km	1720 m	1hr46	3hr59	3hr4	11:00	T1
Vf Omu	3.9 km	15.9 km	2505 m	2hr 53	7hr23	4hr37		T2
Batrana	5.2 km	21.1 km	2160 m	-	-	5hr30		T3
Pestera	5.1 km	26.2 km	1600 m	3hr59	10hr27	6hr27	16:00	T4
Poiana Gaura	11.8 km	38.0 km	1520 m	5hr29	15hr12	8hr53		T5
Finish	12.0 km	50.0 km	750 m	6hr28	18hr18	11hr07	22:00	T6

Table 3: Transylvania 50 (Ref: www.transylvania100k.com)

On paper four hours for the first leg seems quite generous for 12k however the route rises to 2250m at the 9km mark before dropping to T1 so meeting the cut-off is not guaranteed. I wasn't worried by the cut-offs as although I'm not the fastest runner, I seem to be able to keep my pace for longer than many. In any race I'm quite close to the cut-offs at the start but, as the race progresses, I get more and more comfortably inside them.

About 300 of us started off down a road that slowly climbed to the small village of Poarta which would be the last village for many hours to come. Like any race most people go off too quickly and I had a fear of getting left off the back of the pack – I knew I was going a bit quicker than ideal but I didn't want to get lost! The first 2kms were fairly uneventful apart from a police car cutting through the runners and heading up the road. At around the 2k point, we saw it again parked near a shop close to where we would turn off to start the ascent of the first big hill.

The field started to thin out and we went up and up through the forest. It was here that I saw the first on-duty mountain rescue person on the course in-case anyone got in to trouble. I've seen people in trouble in races before and typically the rescue person isn't carrying that much as they are near a road or have been dropped by a helicopter. The people out here must have herculean strength to move with what they are carrying – there was a lot of effort involved for them to walk up-hill. I'd guess they were carrying somewhere beyond 20kg in their massive rucksacks.

Eventually we hit a clearing and the path levelled off to about 5% - the relief in the pack was visible. Up until this point we had been moving in silence in a single line. Now we spread out a little and people slowed down to eat their energy foods and admire the open view of the mysterious mountains ahead. The mountains had towers of cliffs rising in to the circling mist, with corries of snow momentarily glimpsed as the mist ebbed and flowed.

Within 5 minutes we were back in the woods on this relentless path. It then got progressively steeper and over the next hour climbed up towards the ominous clouds which engulfed the mountain tops high above. I'd made an error wearing a fleece as it was now drenched with sweat and I needed to get this off me. I was rapidly cooling and heading in to the snow line and I needed to try and get warm.

I stopped at the bottom of a windy ridge at the cloud line and took my wet fleece off and put on my Gore-Tex coat to keep the cold out, and put my fleece in to my small rucksack in the naïve hope it would dry out somehow. We carried on in the mist and the pack thinned. Five of us reached a ridge at Saua Tignaesti – little more than a point on the map, and there was a problem. It was thick mist and the snow was a bit slippery and icy which focused the mind. This was not the main problem though – the main problem was that the path just disappeared. Up to this point there had been regular markers and, as back-up, it was possible to see the footfall in the mud or snow but now there was nothing. We were standing on something the size of a bus and we could not see off the end or the edges as the terrain just dropped away. Worse still in the mist sound was deadened so it was impossible to hear anyone. Clearly standing still was not an option so we had to do something. I had a gpx track of the route programmed in to my watch and it told me to go down to the left on a snow slope that was angled at about 45° that I could only see about 20m of so didn't not know what happened after that. Many years ago, I'd been in a similar position in thick mist on Tryfan and climbed down something to reach a big drop and realised the only way was to get back up. On Tryfan I found this very hard and used all my strength, and four points of contact, to escape the gully. I didn't fancy doing the same thing here so needed to think of something else.

I could see others had continued up along the ridge making me think that the course had changed so I decided to head on up to Vf Scarra (2422m) my thinking that it may then be possible to go on the path to the T2 at Omu (2500m). The trouble was this would miss out the first CP (T1) which is bad practice, dangerous and if a short cut could be cheating. However, I didn't want to slip off the mountain to an icy death. I caught three others and they were very convinced carrying up to Vf Scarra was the right thing to do. I was unsure as every instinct told me going off the route was a bad idea and I should head back to try and work out what went wrong. As the snow was getting worse, I also lacked confidence in the path from Vf Scarra to Omu being passable and expressed this. In the end I said I was turning back and left the other three to continue. I was now alone heading down a snowy spur with no-one within sight or shouting distance and no-one having any idea I was on it should something go wrong. After a few minutes I could hear people ahead shouting below in the mist which was told me I was getting close to where I'd taken a wrong turning. The only people up here would be runners so this was a good sign. When I got closer, I could see a turning I'd missed. At this point those I had been with earlier had turned around and caught me up. They said they were scared as to what might happen on the final ridge as they had no way of knowing if it was passable in this weather or not, and as there was no-one with them things could turn serious very quickly. We all tentatively cut down some snow to re-join the route and we were off again on our way to the first CP at Malaiesti (1700m). I'd describe this CP as a smaller scale of something like Bonatti for those that have done the UTMB or CCC – a mountain hut with enough food/water, and more importantly space for everyone so no pushing or shoving. I knew the most technical part was ahead – climbing up the snow/ice corrie to Hornurile Malaiesti (2300m) and I knew I was getting cold at 1700m so I put on my spare merino layer below my Gore-Tex and headed off. I was conscious that I had to keep moving to keep warm as my fleece was 'out of action' being drenched with sweat. I still had an emergency down jacket on board so would be OK if something went wrong but I knew, having had previous experience of stopping in the mountains, that the cold would be a very serious issue if I stopped so I was focused on just getting up and over the high bit to T2 at 22k. T1 was at 12k so whilst this is 'only' another 10k I knew it would take me at least double the time of a race on the flat!

There is something quite exciting about heading in to the mountains and knowing there is something dangerous coming up that you cannot see. As I progressed up the corrie, I kept looking at the snow gullies above wondering which one we would tackle to reach the top. The path got steeper and steeper and soon we were in the snow heading up a steep gully in both dense cloud and wind. Not being able to see what was coming up added to the overall tension, as did the cold wind that was biting through my clothing. I had on thick winter mountaineering gloves and I could feel the ends of my fingers getting numb – they would be of little use at anything until I was down lower on the other side.

Dangerous situations bring out a real survival instinct in people. I was solely focused on getting to the top and over the other side and this was my target above all else. I knew a slip could be very bad as I could either fall and twist/break something or fall a long way down the mountain. If I fell and needed to be rescued there was no helicopter coming here. I'd have to rely on the mountain rescue men helping me down and this would likely take hours. I had a survival bag, and more clothing, but I knew it would not be good. As we progressed up the steep corrie the man in-front kept stumbling and falling forward. I had a real fear he would slip and start to go back down the mountain and I was adamant he was not taking me with him! I made a real effort to never be directly behind him. I didn't want to see him fall, and if he did, I'd do what I could to help him, but my primary aim was to get me up and over the mountain.

As things got even steeper a rope was lying on the track tied on to something at the top out of sight. Now I was on the back of a train of about eight but we kept stopping whilst the driver caught his breath. Suddenly in the mist on the right a bear growled.

The brown bear population of Romania is estimated to be around 4500-5000 and is the largest population of bears in Europe outside of Russia. The main area they live is in the Bucegi mountains that we were crossing just now. There are cases of brown bears in Romania badly injuring humans but the race-organisers are proud to point out that no runner has ever been injured by wildlife during their races. The advice they gave on bears was to never get between a mother and cubs, and never to startle a bear. To this end we'd all been provided with a bear whistle to blow furiously when amongst bears so they would know we were there. The Romanian bears weigh 'only' 480kg compared to other brown bears who weight about 700kg so although not the biggest in the world they could do a lot of damage.

The path was very steep and no sooner had we started than we stopped again. The cloud was thick and we could only see around 10m around us in a classic white out, the wind was blowing strong, and then the bear growled again.

We quickly got going again and now I could see that our gully was narrowing and I could make out steep rocks on either side. We stopped. The bear growled. At this point it must have been very close as the gully was narrow. I didn't want to make eye-contact as I didn't know if this would be seen as a hostile act and just wanted the person at the front to move on. In several languages we all said 'keep moving' or words to that effect to the person at the front and we got moving again.

It was now scarily steep so I was cutting my feet in to the snow on each step as if I had crampons on and didn't once slip going up unlike others around me. I was mightily relieved to hit the top of the Col and find a relatively easy and wide (well about 20ft) ridge to the summit of Mount Omu. It was very cold on the top not helped by the very thick mist that made visibility, and navigation, quite tricky. I pushed hard to get in front of the others on my train as I wanted to be down in less cold conditions as soon as I could. On the ridge line were a few race volunteers who must have spent hours up there in the cold. I didn't really see anything at the top of Mount Omu. Someone asked if I was on the 100 or 50 and I said 50 so he pointed the way. He also asked me if I wanted a warm drink. I had no idea where I'd be able to get a warm drink as it just seemed a wind-swept snowy summit so said I was fine and headed on – it turned out there was a building on the summit that they had opened for shelter. Throughout the race I was always impressed with the dedication of the volunteers spending hours and hours out in the bad weather.

From this point the 50k course took a 90-degree right turn and slowly but surely descended from the clouds. After about 10 minutes visibility improved and I caught a couple up ahead. We hit a windswept forest where the trees were about 30ft tall but so badly bent they typically only came to 4-5ft off the ground. The three of us stayed together for about 30mins talking about what we had just been through and working together at the junctions to determine where to go.

As there had not been a marker for a long time, and we knew we were on the correct route, we now started to think someone had removed the markers deliberately. Sadly, this sort of activity goes on in some races and puts competitors, organisers, and local rescue services potentially at great peril. It's not the first time it has happened to me and in these situations the best thing to do is to work out where you are with a paper map and keep checking and if you see someone go off track to advise them so they don't get badly lost. As the terrain is quite remote, and the weather was not good, the lack of markings increased the general tension. For someone to go to all that effort of removing markers they must have done it for a reason as there was the very real possibility of people getting lost in the mountains. One worry is that some people are going to mug you and rob you so you just want to keep moving along the course. We got to a junction and had differing views as to which way to go as we could see that runners had split and gone different ways. I decided to stick with the gpx track on my watch so we went our separate ways – I never did see them again.

The mist thinned and before long I was down at T3 at Refugiui Batrana (2200m). I'd done it. I'd tackled the snow/ice wall and the hard bits were behind me. This CP had plenty of food, water and some big dogs roaming round which presented no problem. In many races, pasta is the staple food provided at a meal CP, and this was what was provided here. I didn't expect pasta having not seen pasta so far on my Romanian travels so was grateful of getting some here. I sat down on some nearby logs and shovelled the tepid pasta down – it was so good! Those on the 100 double back up to the previous summit from here which must be mentally tough knowing how inhospitable it would be up there heading back up through the mist and in to the snow.

Feeling quite pleased with myself I thought a mere 28k to the end on some undulations should be fine. I'd got a bit wet in the snow but I'd dried out in the wind so now a pleasant trot back. A nice evening meal in a restaurant in Bran then bed. Easy.

By now my left big toenail was starting to hurt, the self-inflicted injury caused by cutting snow steps in the steep bear gully with my shoes. I thought I'd snapped it and didn't want to take my shoe off so pushed on.

This next section was quite pleasant, the way to T4 Pestrana (1600m) at 26.5k. There was snow on the ground and I spotted both bear and wolf tracks so they had been here recently. I took some comfort having had no problems with the previous bear so now wanted to see one, preferably on the other side of the river. I knew wolves did not present a problem and last year runners had met wolves on narrow sections and passed each other safely so quite wanted this experience if possible. Alas I saw neither during the race - just their tracks. The view was great so I took many photos of the rocks and the mountains. The path slowly descends a valley and at the bottom was a river crossing. Those in front were making heavy weather of rock hopping whereas I always wade the reason being that a fall can be really bad and in races you tend to get wet anyway! Pestrana felt like it was on the edge of civilisation as from here it is possible to get a cable car from the nearby town of Busteni. Some runners had friends/family here to cheer them on and the whole area had the feeling of an off-season ski area that would have many blue runs.

After more food at Pestera it was time to head off again. The path passed both small roadside churches and what looked like a world class underground cave attraction. I made a mental note if I ever came here again, and E came with me, to recommend the caves as a possible thing to do when I was racing. Trotting down this road a few specks of rain came. Never mind I had my waterproof coat on. After the first few drops came a few more, you could sense it wasn't going to end any time soon, and then it happened – a thunder clap! Almost as soon as the sound hit my ear drums, the heavens opened.

I quickly put on my waterproof trousers and headed off – in the time it had taken to get my waterproofs on I'd got cold so needed to get moving and was pleased to see the next section was uphill across a barren farmers field. At the top of the field the route joined a small path that contoured along the side of a mountain. This next section, from about the 26k mark round to the CP5 at Polara Gaura, can be best described as a remote alpine trail – a lot more remote than something on UTMB and more like something on UTMR. At CP5 I met the two race volunteers I'd seen at Heathrow and on the flight out – incredibly friendly and helpful standing out in the pouring rain. They had their work cut out as several of the races met here so were constantly scanning the mountains to spot people and check they were OK. People like these two are the real heroes of such events as without them so many would never have the pleasure of discovering such places. We had a little chat and I then moved on agreeing we might meet up in Bran for a beer later. I knew I had 15k in the woods to come then down in to Bran and job done. I carried on down and could feel my left big toenail hurting a lot as I continued through a very dark forest. I caught up some Americans in the race and in chatting followed them the wrong way to the point where we had dropped about 50m, and gone about 500m, off the track. We'd stayed on a nice wide inviting track which was the wrong one. When I spotted this, I told them saying I was going to head back up and work out where I'd gone wrong. They said they just wanted to get off the mountain out of danger and would work a way back in the valley. I later learnt I got in around 4 hours before them as they got badly lost and had to phone the organisers. I found where I had gone wrong and eventually reached a road. In my head I thought this was the run in so sped up and started to catch and overtake people. Unfortunately, it was not the end as about 5k from the end a marshal told me we had 5k to go and pointed up a slippy track. Hmmm. I carried on and was able to overtake every person I caught – perhaps I was just more comfortable taking bigger risks than others on some slippy bits. I came to one very steep downhill and found someone frozen at the top out of fear. I couldn't leave them there getting colder and colder so close to safety at the end. I know from skiing that if a slope looks bad just looking at it doesn't change anything – all it does it build more fear. I'm a believer in being sensible and making slow progress when the consequence of failure is high. I was comfortable tackling this as a reverse crab walk so deliberately went for the steepest bit and got them to walk on a less steep section beside me to get down. I then wished them luck and headed off along the course. About 200yds from the end there was another steep adverse camber and I advised three people here how it was best to cross it using three points of contact as I couldn't just leave them there. I ran around the corner and could see some open sheds to the right that had race supporters huddled in them. They all looked expectantly as I came along hoping I was their runner, so they could be released from their cold vigil, meet their loved one, and head back to their accommodation. They had probably been there for hours and probably some had hours to go still. They were dry but were standing huddled, no chairs and no prospect of a toilet as they waited. I could see the end banner ahead and ran under it quite pleased with what I had achieved. Ahead about 6 volunteers stood under a canopy and called me forward and gave me my medal – I thanked them then asked would they take my picture with my medal, the gantry and the castle behind.

There was a canopy over food with a few volunteers staying dry under it – I went over for some food and was served in the pouring rain – my side having no shelter. They invited me in to the dry and I ate a few bowls of cold pasta then thanked them and went on my way. It was only about 5 minutes to walk back to the hotel now and the chance to get dry!

When I got to the hotel, I was conscious I was very wet and muddy so stripped off outside to my base layers, put everything in a bin bag I'd been carrying, and went in to the dry.

On entering the building, the realisation of the epic nature of the race kicked in – there had been adventure throughout the race and

I'd loved it. I'd not been injured, had a good time, and wanted more. I feel at some level I'm addicted to the risk element and entering these events gives me my fix and makes the mundane nature of normal life worthwhile.

I looked at my left big toenail and didn't give it much of a chance of staying on – if it came off it would be one of nature's trophies. As it happened it came off about four weeks after the race and took about a year to grow back but wasn't really a problem.

I had a shower and put on some dry clothes and realised I now had a problem. My coat was absolutely drenched so I could not go out in the pouring rain for food. Time for my emergency bananas I'd bought the day before. I got colder and colder and ended up in bed wearing every dry item of clothing under every blanket I could find watching more caravan review shows. Through the night I could hear dogs barking whenever a runner came towards the end. The next morning, I went out and runners were still coming in. It had been an epic night for some as it turned out someone had been deliberately moving markers which was investigated by the authorities post-race. The organisers did everything they could to keep people safe some staying >24hrs in remote cold areas until everyone came off the mountain. As an organisation they are second to none and I'd recommend any of their events to anyone. I'll definitely be back as it was a well-run race by very friendly organisers who did everything they could to help people succeed.

Post-race the organisers sent an e-mail to everyone explaining that someone had been tampering with the course and the local mountain rescue were investigating as it was a safety issue.

Sunday saw me catch a minibus back to Brasov where I left my large rucksack in a left luggage in the station (down a staircase below the town side platform) and explored the town. The km or so around the railway station is just as one might imagine an Eastern Bloc town to be – very functional but not necessarily the most picturesque. Today the Brasov International Marathon was taking place. This large running festival had full marathon, 1/2M, 10k, 4 x 10k relay, 5k and a race for children so a lot of variety. If you had a partner who was interested in road running then this could be the ultimate weekend for both of you – the trail on the Saturday and the road on the Sunday!

Brasov is situated on the edge of a plain with some hills rising abruptly behind it. In case you forget where you are, the word 'B R A S O V' has been installed on the hill, not too dissimilar to the famous 'Hollywood' sign – I knew I had to get up there! I managed to find the cable car and bought my ticket. The fare was something like 6 Euros and I handed a 20 Euro note in so a simple 14 Euro change. Either the ticket seller was unfamiliar with their currency and made an innocent error or they introduced lots of theatrics with giving me my 14, then asking for it back, then giving me it in small change but the outcome was I was 10 Euros down. I've found whenever such scenarios go on the person fortunately has whatever I'm missing just sitting there beside them so can quickly pass it across. I pointed out the error and my change quickly came. I'm always super cautious when such theatrics start as over the years have nearly been short changed several times. I hopped in the cable car and went up to the sign. It was huge. It was a great viewpoint (955m ASL) and well worth the visit as could see far across the plain. The trouble was the path didn't lead to the very top of the hill and I just had to get to the top so clambered through prickly bits to get there following a path that had been made by others of a similar persuasion. Not sure it was worth it for the view but it was worth it for knowing I'd reached the top!

From the top it was possible to look towards the mountains from yesterday but I was unable to sensibly work out where I'd been. The mountains did look mysterious and inviting and I was pleased to have visited them.

On the plain ahead I could see some very high-density housing rising out of the fields of crops. These buildings had been constructed in the late 1980s and were the start of the mass moving of people. However, with the fall of Ceausescu they now remain just there in the middle of large fields so are very isolated.

From the road Brasov station looks modern and functional situated on the edge of the concrete quarter of town, a mile or so from the quaint old quarter where the tourist buses stop. Inside the station building has the feel of somewhere that you would not want to wait at quite times for fear of being pick-pocketed. At the station I had two occasions where 2-3 young men would run at me as if trying to get me to move and one would brush past tightly – like a pocket drive by. Now I'm wise to this one so my strategy is never to run or show fear and never have anything in an outside pocket. I thought it to be safest to head out on to the platforms outside and await the train there. The overgrown deserted tracks, and the many unkempt platforms, had a feel of what might have been at some point in time.

I caught the train and enjoyed the ride back to Bucharest. Like the first time I arrived, a few days ago, everyone around the station stared at me but gave me no problems.

I checked back in to the hotel and read some of the rules. It seemed you were allowed one 'masseuse' in your room at no extra cost – basically you could phone up for one to come however if you were going to use two at once you had to pay an extra fee to the hotel to cover any mess. This struck me as interesting. How on earth would someone go to the front desk to declare this. Also, to get around the hotel you needed to use your swipe card so how did that work when your 'friends' were leaving? Not feeling the need to hire a masseuse I didn't get in to any of this but it was intriguing none the less. There were also leaflets advising on what was, or wasn't legal and advice on such matters. From the various leaflets it seemed possible to have two females, or a male and a female, if going for the double option but there was not a 'two males' option; this struck me as not being equal. However, it could just be market forces around supply and demand. The leaflets all explained when travelling on business it was important to have a clear head and any helping hand that could be had was worth it if it made your decision-making abilities more focused the next day. The hotel staff were very friendly when it came to ordering food and a good main meal, and a beer, could be had for around 14 Euros.

Always liking a walk, I decided to explore a bit after my evening meal and headed off to the back of the Parliament to explore the streets that way. There is a grand Marriott hotel that was originally a hotel built for the ruling party – its grandiose architecture standing out with its columns and huge rectangular frontage. Beyond this are row after row of concrete flats interspersed by large empty roads that are definitely off the tourist trail. I was used to being looked at by everyone but it was now dark so I thought it sensible to head back to the Parliament building and headed to the front of it to admire it at night. The large square was now deserted apart from the occasional car who would park up, the driver gets out and take a photo of the car and the building and move on. They would spend less than five minutes here and I thought they were really missing the opportunity to feel the atmosphere of the square, take in the Parliament building, look at the huge government buildings across the street, peer down the 4km boulevard of unity. Look closer and spot the stray cat being given stealth cat biscuits at the police station on the corner. See the crumbling concrete due to fast construction and subsidence issues.

The next day was the day I'd intended to visit the Parliament. I'd done all the on-line paperwork weeks in advance and part of the rule was to phone up 24hrs before your scheduled visit (mine was 10:00). I'd tried this repeatedly on the Sunday and whenever the phone was picked up and I spoke it was put down. In desperation I hatched a plan. I'd basically walk up to the security gate, flash my passport, say I had a visit booked, and continue to walk in without awaiting an answer. Obviously if the police shouted, I would stop as I didn't want to be shot! I knew the Parliament was the most popular place to visit in Romania and I knew the first tour was 09:30. I thought, to play it safe and increase my chances, I should stroll up about 08:40.

Now the Parliament sits on a large island surrounded by fast wide roads and then a wide pavement. Beyond this there are about 10 entrances around the 3km boundary. Of these there was one gate that had 'official tours' written nearby so this was to be my gate of choice.

The road leading in is the width of two cars and there is a small security shed with armed police standing outside. I was feeling a little nervous but thought if I tried to explain what had happened in that I'd booked a visit but had not confirmed I'd be turned away, that is if they were able to understand English and there was no guarantee of that. I held my passport in my right hand and walked up the drive and showed it to one of the policemen and said I had a visit booked (which was true) and kept walking whilst making eye-contact. He gave me a quick nod and I kept on walking in.

I was surprised the police didn't say anything to me. My next problem was where in the complex to go? I thought it made sense to walk up to the building as if I knew where I was going so as not to attract attention and work it out from there. I carried on and saw a sign saying 'visitors' so this felt good. I got to the building and saw a door. I thought best not to hesitate and went for it. Inside people stopped and stared at me. It appeared I had come to the entrance for the members of parliament – I deduced this from the attire of the people and the way they all stopped and stared straight at me – even the guards did this. I said 'sorry' and reversed out quickly. I carried on to another door. At this point I realised that it didn't seem to matter if I got a door wrong so opened it. Inside was an art gallery and I could hear staff talking and so I went in. In the back of the gallery there was a tour desk with a sign that said 'opens at 09:15' so I was in the right place at least, albeit early. Oddly none of the staff seemed to mind so I perused the art. I went to the desk at 09:15 and asked to book a tour and was told they were busy and asked how many people. I said just me and got on one that started at 09:30. Our small group set off and our first stop was the x-ray machines. Beyond this was a drinks machine and two of the group bought a coffee. We moved on about 10 metres and were told no drinks so they had to either down in one or bin in one. The tour of the palace is well worth doing – all the grand rooms with their finery. I really wanted to get on to the main balcony if I could and it was unclear if that would be possible. Our guide was very nice but liked to keep us close in together in each room and sometimes he would want to go somewhere but change his mind as someone else was in the room. We got to a big room and I could see a door open about 50m away that looked like it would be to the balcony. This was my moment. I was confident that the worst he would do would be shout me back and I'd have had a quick look out by then – I may even be out of hearing range when he was shouting but a risk worth taking. We were listening to a description of the fine chairs and like an errant child I was accidently on purpose drifting away. He called me back and I came. He carried on talking and this time I drifted further and did not seem to have been spotted. Another member of the group drifted and was between me and the guide. This was my moment. I was out that door quicker than he could say 'stop' and took a few quick pics. I cut back in and think I did it unspotted and joined the group. He now said 'we can now go on to the balcony through this door' and off we went so my stealthy look had been in vain! It was worth it for the view tempered with the oppressive nature of what it represented. It's not a theme park. We carried on our tour and in one room a BMW i3 was being photographed – most odd. Part of me wondered how it got there but with the scale of the place it could easily fit through the doors. The tour was well worth it and with that we headed back to the start. Time to explore the city. Bucharest has plenty to see from ancient churches through to Parisian buildings of the 1800s and on to the vast 1980s concrete structures and finally even more modern architecture. There are also a number of museums and art galleries, parklands and churches. There are also buildings and streets where bullet holes can be found from the 1989 revolution.

I'd decided I wanted to see a bit of everything but on top of this I wanted to measure some of the roads and squares. On the face of it this may seem a bit odd but I'd read somewhere that the main Boulevard Unirii from the Palace of the Parliament was 4km long. Having a good GPS watch I decided one of my walks would be to measure it. As well as measuring I wanted to see how looming the building appeared from 4km away and if the style of architecture changed as I walked along the road. This road was tricky to measure due to both the width and the variety of street furnishings it contained. From left to right there is a pavement, some trees, another pavement, more trees, a 2-lane road, a linear fountain, a 2-lane road, more trees, another pavement, more trees and a final pavement on the right-hand side. It seemed best to walk along the linear fountain down the middle. There was no real risk of getting wet as it wasn't very powerful. I set off down it and my next challenge came at the Piatta Unirii. Here the road slaloms for some reason around another fountain that has been put in. Being Bucharest, the slalom was on a grand scale, so I kept an eye out in the traffic and ran for it to try and stay straight. This fountain had not operated for a long time and had homeless people sleeping in it. The road carries on now with the apartment blocks now featuring large advertising hoardings on the roof. At this point the baking hot sun was getting really draining and part of me questioned what I was doing but at 2.5k in I was over half way so had to continue. I kept going and the Piatta Unirii ends at 4km at a large roundabout. I struggled to get to the centre of this due to the traffic but wanted to do it to look back. On the roundabout a man was cutting a grass area about half the size of a football pitch with a small mower and there was a lot of rubbish around. I looked back and could see the Parliament looming oppressively in the distance.

Over the next two days I covered over 60km in foot in the city, further than I had raced on the Saturday, but was determined to see as much as I could of the real Bucharest. I visited the former Communist Party Headquarters building where Ceausescu's speech to the crowd on 21st Dec 1989 had gone so badly wrong for him and he had to escape via a helicopter on the roof. The square holds a number of monuments to the revolution.

I visited the historic quarter where the buildings all look like they belong in Paris and the streets were thronged with tourists and there were touristy cafés on every street corner. This seemed to be about the one square mile where tourists would come to 'see' Bucharest with a lesser number additionally stopping outside the Palace of the Parliament in their tour bus or an even smaller quantity going inside the building. There is absolutely nothing wrong with this approach, all very safe and relaxing, I just feel there was a whole lot more of Bucharest to see.

In a northern suburb of Bucharest is the Village Museum which is a village made up of 300 historic buildings; houses, windmills and the like; that has been collected from all of Romania. After a short while they all start to look the same so I sat down on a bench and a stray cat ran over to me. It had clearly been in a fight as one of its ears was bleeding a little. It looked very underfed so I gave it some of the plain biscuits I'd been eating. It then jumped up on my knee and wedged itself facing forwards between my legs. My new-found feline friend put its head on my right knee and its right paw cupped around my knee cap. It looked back at me and started purring so I gave it a stroke and it was happy. It was almost as if it were saying 'you're mine now' and was so relieved to have found someone to love. Now I like cats so was fine with all of this but after a few minutes wanted to go. My new feline friend dug its front claws in as I went to stand up so I sat back down – it looked back at me and gave me a kitty smile. I gave it a bit more of a fuss and thought this time I need to get up more firmly so it will jump down. I did this and it jumped off and gave me a real sad eyed look as if I'd done something really bad. No sooner than this happened than a donkey ran up to me like a long-lost friend. I thought it a little odd and started fussing it scratching its chin and nose. It was loving it. We took a few selfies together (with my camera) and I thought what do I do now? Has the donkey mistaken me for someone? I could see a number of ladies with straw brooms watching me from around the corner of a building. The donkey was now super friendly loving the fuss. I didn't think I knew the donkey but perhaps I was wrong? Nope – I definitely did not know this donkey. I walked a little down a path and the donkey followed me. More fuss. I walked a little further and it turned the other way. Suddenly the ladies ran at it with their brooms and it ran off down a path being chased through the village. I turned a corner to where the donkey had come from and could see what had happened. There was a pile of straw that was being used for thatching and there was a big hole where a donkey had taken a bite out of it. The cat was also sitting atop it so perhaps the cat was the wing cat for the donkey or vice-versa. The ladies came back and I wanted to go down another street but was worried my donkey friend may come back and the ladies would get angry at me or the donkey so I left the museum. Overall the buildings were average but the cat and donkey well worth seeing!

I'd seen a lot of Bucharest so now it was time to head for home. I went to where I got off the bus from the airport and crossed the road and spotted a sign 'airport' so waited there and after about half an hour the bus came. I didn't have a ticket at this point so hoped to buy one from the driver. I was holding my original ticket as I got on and he put it in and out of a machine to 'clip' it. I had not known it but I'd been sold a return which was good.

At the airport I met some of the race marshals and we had a good chat about the race as we flew through the evening landing back at Heathrow around 21:00. I was really glad I'd entered the race and really glad I'd travelled the way I did as I'd had some adventures along the way.

My mind was now focused on the next big challenge that was only months away – the Ut4M.

15 Ut4M 2017

Whilst surfing the ITRA website one night I'd come across a series of races grouped as the Ultra Tour Des 4 Massifs. These events take place in August each year in Grenoble and there were a number of different distances offered and the whole race weekend looked like a viable alternative to the UTMB weekend i.e. a series of races centred on one place that was easy to get to. The main event is 169k and 11000m in one go and I knew this was not the one for me – I would be aiming at something similar in Oct and this was supposed to be a warm up. The two options that seemed best for me were either the Master (100k and 5000m ascent) or the more appealing Challenge (still 169k and 11000m, but split over four days). In researching the race, I realised I could fly in to Lyon and take the 1-hour TGV journey to Grenoble where the race was based. It was looking like this was definitely going to be possible. I read more on the race website and learned that for 600 Euros I could get my race entry, accommodation for five nights, transport to/from the race start each day by bus and all meals. This was exceptional value so I completed the paperwork and secured my place.

I arrived at Grenoble station at 13:00 on the 15th August quite excited by the whole adventure. At Grenoble station it was 1 Euro to use the toilet and all I had on me was several 20 Euro notes which were no good. I decided to go to the McDonalds and get some food as I'd discovered when travelling they always have good clean toilets. This one didn't have one; worst still the change I had did not contain a 1 Euro coin so I was back at square one. I thought I'd find a shopping centre in the town to use so pushed on. Grenoble in August is like a ghost town – everywhere was shut. I got to the park where the 'bib collection' was to be hours ahead of time. My bag weighed about 15kg and my back was drenched with sweat as I settled down on a bench to wait for time to pass. I considered going to the toilet in the bushes but thought best not to as didn't want to get in to trouble – how I wished I'd had a 1 Euro coin at the station! I clammed up and drank nothing which is not really a good strategy the day before a race. The 'bib collection' was in the Palais des Sports in Grenoble – a covered sports centre that sits behind a high metal fence. I was outside on a bench at around 14:00 with about 2 hrs until it opened. Lots of official looking people seemed to come in and out of a gate that was policed by a large security person. Slowly but surely other runners arrived and most just had their running bag for kit check. I had a 60-litre bag with all my belongings in it. As 16:00 approached people started to mill around the security gate. After a few minutes it opened and I was about 20th to be checked by the security man. Each person had their bag gone through in depth. I was fearful of being sent away with my massive bag so had it on my shoulders to look small, well as small as a 60-litre bag can be. I did feel a bit like a tortoise with a massive shell on my back. I was now next in line to the massive security person. He said open it. I did. He motioned me to empty it on a table and I started pulling out pants, socks, maps and the like. After about a carrier bag of stuff had come out, he put his hand in the bag and poked around, pulled it out, and told me I could go in. He then went back in to detailed searches of the tiny bags. I headed on in through the door and could now see it was a velodrome. Along the edge of the track were various running related posters and small pop-up shops selling running bits. Everyone who had got in to the centre before me was perusing all of this so I strolled on by following the signs to 'kit check'. I was first! Kit check was done very efficiently with me putting everything I wanted to declare in a grey plastic crate that was then examined by two staff. After some more processing I was out and straight to the loos!

Next challenge was to get to the accommodation. I knew it to be a military barracks in a compound but had no idea which side of the compound was the gate. The recommended route was to catch two buses and pay the driver on each and then walk the last 10 mins or so. As French is not my strong point, and I had a massive bag late afternoon, I thought it best to approach the accommodation from the South on one bus and have what looked like a short walk in. The other advantage with this idea was I could buy a 10-ticket carnet from a machine so would not have any awkward language issues. I did this and caught the bus and got off at the destination. Now I had a problem. Where were the barracks? I headed in the direction I thought and came to a fence that surrounded the barracks. It was unclear which way to go so I elected to go clockwise as this would be the direction those that caught the desired bus would come from. I set off and before long realised I'd taken the long way around the base. I got to the front and after showing some details was let in to a deserted military camp with just a small map showing me where to go. A French soldier approached asking if I knew where I was going and I said I thought so. She asked did I want her to come with me and I said I didn't mind. We did small talk for a few minutes as we walked through the camp and after a few minutes she peeled off. As I approached the building, I could see every window was shuttered up. I went in the only door to be met by two volunteers who told me I was in room 167. I asked where breakfast was the next morning and they said they didn't know. Up to this point I had assumed there was no bus to take us to the start on day 1 and I was pleased to see a sign up saying they had put a bus on for us. My other three roomies arrived and we chatted briefly – as they were all French the conversation quickly became something I could not understand. One had been to the brief and told me it was mandatory to wear a long-sleeved top so I made a note to do this. All that was left now was to sleep before breakfast at 04:30 and the bus at 05:30 to take us to the start for 08:00. The adventure was about to begin.

Day 1 Vercors

In our room our alarms all went off at 04:25 and we quickly got up and headed to breakfast. The building was easy to find as it was the only one with lights on. Inside were rows of tables with one big food table at the front which had on it bread, cheese, ham, cakes and a big cauldron of coffee. Coffee seemed to be being taken in polystyrene bowls so I did the same making a mental note to take my own mug tomorrow for ease. Breakfast was a silent affair possibly due to the early start, many not knowing others, and everyone focused on the enormity of the next four days ahead. For many, myself included, this would be one of the biggest physical tests of our lives.

I headed back to the room, put Bodyglide on my feet, picked up my bag, and headed down the hill to the entrance gate thinking the bus would pick us up there. As there were no instructions as to where to go for the bus this seemed obvious. I met two others at the gate who had been told the RVP was back in the camp at the basketball court so we three headed there. En route we met someone else who told us the RVP was the corner of the road near an anonymous building so we headed to there and slowly but surely, we massed – all in about 50 runners. At this point the accommodation leader Michel, a friendly man who clearly loved the area, arrived and took his phone out as he wanted to register us all as getting on the bus. To take part in the event we all had to wear a tabard with our name on it that contained an RFID chip that would be scanned throughout the race at various points. We also had to carry a complicated looking 'bus ticket' that was A5 in size and contained two barcodes – one would tie in with the RF chip on our tabard and record our progress getting on the bus each morning so they knew who had left the accommodation – the other barcode would withdraw us from the event should we be injured, timed-out etc. In the dark it was hard for his phone to scan the main bar code but, after several attempts, he accidently scanned the 'withdrawal' one and I hadn't even done one step! Everyone had a good laugh and after a few minutes he fixed it and we were all scanned and got on the bus. All of this took 45 minutes so it was now 06:15 but it didn't really matter as the start was at 08:00 so we had plenty of time.

After about 15 minutes the bus dropped us by the start and we all got out to do final kit re-adjustments, use the toilets etc. Whilst waiting a French photo-journalist came up to me and asked where I was from and took my picture which was a first for me. Although she used a digital camera, she had an old-fashioned camel coloured sleeveless jacket on with pockets for film, lenses and the like. It was still dark with her face hidden behind large framed sunglasses with a very long camel brown cigarette hanging out of the corner of her mouth as she spoke to me. At the start of each days racing the same music was played – a cover of 'Mad World' by Jasmine Thompson and a traditional French song by, I think, Edith Piaf. Juxtapose this with armed soldiers patrolling due to the current security climate and it made for a strange experience. As with many races there is a 'start pen' that we all needed to get in to, after first having our RF tag on our tabard scanned so they know who was in there. Unlike most races there was a last-minute kit check for everyone upon entering the pen. What happened was the person states an item and you are supposed to show it. They seemed to be asking everyone if they had a mobile phone on them and everyone was saying yes without showing so when it came to my turn I said 'oui' and carried on through.

There is an organisation in France called Run Handi Move who aim to help People with Reduced Mobility (PRM) to experience some amazing races. I'd first seen pictures of them in a race in Madeira and was hugely impressed to see what they were doing, using brute strength to open events and areas to those who are unable to do it themselves. They do this by having a team of 26 runners, and 7 chaperones, who work with the 6 PRMs to get them along sections of the course. Each PRM will get to cover about 5k or so each day and each team has two PRMs with them (so each get half of what is offered that day). The way it works is that the PRM sits on a chair that has two long metal poles attached (a bit like a stretcher) and directly below them is a single mountain bike wheel. The runners push and pull the chair along and the runners/chaperones also help trying to clear the course so they can get through as momentum carries them downhill and brute strength carries them up.

At 08:00 the Run Handi Move teams departed, to a big cheer, heading along the edge of the park and on towards the Vercors massif. The Vercors massif rises above the plateau and is often referred to as the French Dolomites because of this. Standing on the start I could see a series of high cliffs (about 800m) and I knew we had to get on top of them. Whilst scenic these mountains have seen a lot of deaths during World War II and there is a memorial to the fallen in Grenoble. The Battle of Vercors ran for two weeks in the summer of 1944 and saw 4000 members of the French resistance fight 8000 German soldiers and the losses were heavy. The French lost 693 (and 201 civilians) and the Germans lost 65, had 133 wounded and 18 were never found. I hadn't heard of this battle until the race when a fellow French competitor started to explain it to me. Grenoble next comes in to recent history with the winter Olympics of 1968. Thirty-seven countries took part (compared to 92 in PyeongChang in 2018) and amongst other things, these were the first Olympics that ordered drug and gender testing of competitors. Grenoble decided to split the sports around the area and was the first winter Olympics to do this. Ut4M starts at the Palais des Sports which was known as Le Stade de Glace during the Olympics and was used for figure skating, ice hockey and the closing ceremony. Half of the Olympic budget was spent on this building and it is good to see that it is still used today for both sport and concerts. The Ut4M route also visits the site of the ski jump in Saint-Nizier-du-Moucherotte but more of that later.

The minutes ticked by and at 08:06 the race started. The organisers advised for 'reasons of security' to move swiftly through the city. I suspect the reason is that the main roads have been closed in rush hour and they want to disrupt traffic as little as possible. I slipped in to the back third of the pack as we headed off down the roads at what was, for me, about half marathon pace so for the distance felt a little fast. I spotted a fellow Brit, Bob, and we had a chat. Bob has entered each day individually as opposed to what I was doing and was going to take each day as it comes. The advantage for Bob was he can record four finishes (and four T-shirts and four medals) and can get 3 ITRA points a time so can earn 3,6, 9 or 12 points. I was doing an 'all or nothing' approach and would only get anything if I got through each day and finished on day 4 to be rewarded with one T-shirt, one medal and 5 ITRA points. It's a bit odd that he can get 12 for the same course however made even more unusual by the fact that he has an extra hour each day to complete the course that day in! We chatted for about five minutes and Bob explained he had done many of the big races, like UTMB, but now that he is in his sixties, he has to slow down a bit and may not be able to start each day so the approach he was taking seems sensible. I realised I needed to get up the pack a little for the first hill so we wished each other good luck and I moved up through the field starting to sweat a little as the temperature was in the 20s and it's not even 9AM. After a few k the road ended and we started on a trail. I overtook two Handi teams on an ascent and the trail was now wide enough to take an off-road car and it stayed like this for the next 30 minutes. Suddenly a member of the Handi team came running through telling us to get out of the way as they charged down a hill with their momentum. It's impressive on two levels – firstly the brute strength of tackling the hill with the weight – secondly to trust your team to carry you, and not drop you, as the PMR does get bounced around a bit high up on the chair. The Handi team slowed up so I passed them now sweating profusely in the heat. It was now my time to slow down and get a drink as I thought I'd made a sufficient gap – how wrong I was. The Handi team came charging through so I had to get off the course. It was now starting to affect my flow so I decided to try and push hard to get in front so charge after them down the hill and when they come to a stop push hard to make a gap.

Before long we came to a large clearing and I could see, in my 2 'o' clock, what looked like a long string of runners bent double going up an enormous staircase. I carried on, having a quick snack and a drink trying to work out what I'm seeing. I could also see a drone filming the staircase and what looks like real suffering from the heat on it. I changed down from my ultra-shuffle to a walk as needed to keep some energy for this horror that was only about 10k in! It was hard to work out what it could be but it was a narrow concrete staircase that was going up and up in a single flight built directly on to the hillside. No handrail just up and up and I could make out the top or what it could be. To the right there were overgrown concrete bowl shapes – each looked large enough to sit 30 plus people in them comfortably. The penny dropped and I realised we were walking up a ski jump. The heat was building and people were stopping and sitting down. On we continued plugging up the hill and I could now hear cheering which must mean we were near the top which was the CP at Saint-Nizier-du-Moucherotte. I was drenched through with sweat and suddenly got the shivers. This happened to me in the Lakeland 100 in 2012 and I did not know what it meant so I withdrew voluntarily thinking it was some sort of heat stroke. I've since learnt it is down to how my body manages temperature so if I do a very quick stop, and keep moving, I should be fine. I caught sight of my eyes in a mirror and could see they looked like they had hollowed in to my face and were red. I've done 13.2k and 1030m and this is how things are now – how will they be at the end of today at 39.9k and 2670m? Only one way to find out so off I went. We slowly climbed up to the summit of Moucherotte (1900m) which was a cluster of aerials with far reaching views over most of the Ut4M course. There cannot be many 100-mile courses where from one spot you can see everything. There were a lot of official photographers on the course and one asked me to re-pass him again so he could take a better picture and I did. In my head I imagined an amazing image of my gazelle like form hopping on to a precarious rocky crest, that will be a picture I'll treasure forever. A memory captured to reflect on when I'm no longer physically able to enter these races. I'm hopeful when the time comes that I'll still get to the Alps and look at things from below whilst my mind drifts off to those distant places and memories of what actually happened as opposed to what might have been.

After a short rocky descent, we continued to drop to the CP at Lans-en-Vercors (1410m) before climbing up towards the highest point of the day. The path now turned rockier with a need to be a bit hands on at times. It then gives way to very small stones on a very steep path where grip is minimal. A family going up were in trouble and feared falling so decide to watch my progress. I powered past them using quad strength and walking a bit like Donald Duck and kept going giving a friendly 'hello bonjour!'. At the steepest, and narrowest bit, my luck ran out and I face planted as my duck legs lost traction so the only way was to fall forward. The family made lots of 'ooooh' noises and threw in a 'zut alors' for good measure then realising I'm not French asked if I was OK, which was nice. Being fine I got up and pushed on up to the top of Pic Saint Michel (1960m) at 25.5k. The view was amazing and I've a slight regret we had to go down to the left as I'd much rather continue in to the wilderness on the right. That's the thing with summits, the more you go up the more you see that you want to go up! The path dropped quickly to a col and then dropped through the forest to get to a CP at the small village of Saint-Paul-de-Varces (370m) - water refills were done directly at the village fountain. A fellow runner was a bit wobbly on her feet and fell in the stone fountain but was OK. There was now a 400m hill to cross then it was down in to the finish at Vif. I knew it was early days so decided to walk the last k at about 5kmph to really wind the legs down for resting. I could have been quicker and save a bit of time but thought it was a good idea - I'm not sure the race commentator did as I strolled in across the line - he asked me if I were going to run and I said 'no - saving the legs!' There were three buses back that night separated by an hour each - I'd missed the first one by 15 minutes so had a bit of a wait but that was fine. On each day we never knew what time the bus was going until the end. Due to drop outs for the remaining three days there would only be two buses.

Day 2 Oisans

Today was set to be the longest day on the course - 48.3k, D+ 3370m, D- 3140m and, because of the length, we had an early start and were all ready to board the bus at 04:30 for the 05:00 departure which went smoothly and took us to the start of the Oisans massif. At Vif (310m) I looked around at the start and could not spot Bob from yesterday so wondered what had happened to him. Today's course started with an easy k along a road before heading up to the Col del la Chal (1180m). We all knew this was just a warm up so made slow and steady progress and were greeted with a pleasurable descent down grassy tracks and meadows as we made our way towards the next CP at Laffrey. As we got closer it was obvious this was an easy one for supporters to reach as many lined the road which was nice – all cheering everyone who came through. Laffrey (900m) came quite quickly and after stocking up it was time to head to La Morte (1370m).

Before coming to the race I'd never heard of Laffrey but I was aware that Napoleon had marched from Golfe Juan to Grenoble in 1815 in an attempt to regain power. I'd looked at the map in advance and spotted the course came very close to a monument of his progress. There may be good reasons that our course avoided it but I always think when travelling to a race if at all possible, items of cultural interest should be on the route. The monument I didn't see is of Napoleon on a horse. Our route continued on around Lac Laffrey and then our hill started. It was a relatively gentle affair heading up through trees that opened out in to a huge bowl that we contoured round. To the left I could see what would be the main hill of the day sitting high in the haze and I was starting to try and spot the line we would take. Before very long we dropped down to the CP at La Morte (25.3k). The road heading through the valley is known as 'The Col at La Morte' and has featured in the Tour de France (TdF) most recently in 2015 and is classified as a Category 2 climb. Quite often in the Alps there are small signs that explain when the big races visited there.

The CP had a bin outside that said poles must be placed in it and are not allowed in the building. I had no idea how I'd get my poles back as so many look the same so collapsed mine, put them inside my bag, and headed in. Here it was nice to get a break from the heat and I took on a lot of fluids and food for the climb ahead. The room also had three beds for those in the extreme version of the race. I left the CP to find someone distressed as their poles had been taken and they now had the problem of not knowing which ones to take as someone had obviously taken theirs in error. It had the potential for many people to have their poles taken erroneously.

I crossed the TdF route and could see the path zig-zagging up in to the sky. The heat was baking. It was ideal conditions for me to overtake others as having done many treadmill inclines, I am used to coping with the tedium of such hills. I've also used the gym at odd hours and put the heating up, and fans off, to make things harder so this hill had my name all over it. It's odd to get real pleasure in physical suffering but there is something that is really addictive about such hills for me. I set off and slowly but surely caught small groups, or trains, as I like to call them. I'd latch on to the back, or ride caboose, then slowly make my way up the train to take the engine. I'd then ease off and go at the pace of the train to get some energy back and breathing back to normal. After a few minutes I'd accelerate off to ride caboose on the next one. At one point the path was wide and suddenly I had my first chat of the race. 'Do you think it is easier with such large feet?' was the conversation starter from Pierre. We chatted a bit about shoe types, grip, weight distribution until eventually I pulled off and moved on up the course. Pierre was great and we would chat on future days and, as it turned out, in Spain later in the year. It was really nice to meet someone so friendly.

After many zigs and zags, we reached the top at the Pas de La Vache (2350m). This was a landmark for everyone as we were at the top of today. There were a few dozen runners lying out in the sun but I wanted to press on so headed down the course. Up ahead it said 'danger' and I could see people slowing down on a rocky ridge. To this point we'd only ever had one 'danger' sign and that was at a waterfall yesterday that was quite benign but I guess they play it safe for changing conditions. The 'danger' up ahead had a marshal. As I approached, I could see that it was just a single rock step on the ridge, nothing like Crib Goch in Wales for those that know it, so I quickly got over this and headed on down to the next CP at Lac du Poursollet (1650m) at 36.3k. From here it was only 12k to go and most of this would be downhill. Upon leaving the lake we started our last uphill of the day and this made me feel like a hot lizard climbing on hot rock in the baking sun. It was roasting – people were stopping and sweat was pouring off everyone. The heat and humidity felt like being in a sauna, with red and sunken eyes from the dehydration. People were getting lightheaded and having to sit down. If we crossed a river, we would dunk our hats or head in it for anything to take away the suffering of the heat. This was one of the most satisfying days of my life as there were many challenges to overcome to get to the end of it.

Pierre caught me up and we chatted for a bit and then I left him again as it got steeper. At the top (2075m) was a beautiful plateau with far reaching views to the north to big mountains with snow on them. Running on this plateau was amazing – running on narrow rabbit tracks through luscious grass – all fresh and as nature intended. It ended all too soon as the route cut down to the last CP at Les Chalets de la Bariére (1870m) at 42.9k. There were two other male runners there who didn't seem to want to depart in a hurry but I thought they would catch me before long. I'm slower than many on steep downhills due to my height so wanted to get down as far as I could before anyone caught me so headed off alone down the trail. The route would drop 1300m in 6k so was a series of relentless zigs and zags along very narrow trails in the forest. Each path had tree roots to trip on and big rocks to stumble over. A trip up here could be quite nasty as it could result in quite a fall or a nasty impact with a tree.

Suddenly a few hundred metres below I heard a scream. Then silence for about 2-5 seconds. Then another scream. Then silence. Nothing. This didn't sound good as if someone had fallen, I thought I might have heard more. My guess was that someone had fallen off something and the first scream was the fall and the second them stopping – due to the length of the gap I guessed they had fallen off a small cliff as the path often came close to some big drops. The path was dry, and we had lots of daylight, so a fall wasn't to be expected. As there was nothing after the second scream, my guess was they were unconscious. There was also no cry for help from someone else so they were probably alone. A quick calculation in my head told me a vertical drop could be of tens of metres and could end really badly. I knew there was nothing I could do until I got to them so headed on down the course now thinking what sort of drop there could be ahead. On the one hand I wanted to move quicker as if it was someone in a bad way, I may be able to save them with some emergency first aid then get help. On the other if I went too fast, I may make the same fall and then there could be two serious casualties. I've seen some people in bad ways in races in my time and know how things can turn bad very quickly – I also know ultrarunners always look out for each other and I now had two priorities. Firstly, was getting down safely and secondly, was doing what I could for the screamer when I found them. The path took a right turn as the slope decreased slightly and I headed down this seeing a runner up ahead. He suddenly screamed, his arms shot up the air and one of his walking poles was flung up in the air, he then ran on about 10 metres screamed and fell on his back and lay there. The scream was a bit like a man consumed by night terrors screaming in his sleep in a very troubled fashion for those that have ever seen someone like this. I had about 10 seconds until I would reach him and a lot went through my mind. Firstly, if he were now unconscious, I needed to get to him quickly to check airways, breathing and circulation then get him in the recovery position and use my phone to call for help. As I was using a GPS watch I could give our position quite accurately. As we were in dense woods a helicopter rescue would be unlikely and he would need to be carried. The next thought I had was to try and work out what had happened to him – he had not been attacked by an animal so what could it be? I thought it could be a deranged sniper with a gun so no matter what I was vulnerable so I may as well keep going and get to him.

I carried on and then it hit me. It was like an invisible force field that stopped me in my tracks, but realising I was in a crowd of very angry hornets I pushed through holding my arms in-front of my face. As I approached the collapsed runner he shouted 'did you get my pole?' and I said no. We could see the pole below the hornets.

I'd been stung badly and started to pull hornets off me that were still in the process of stinging. Two runners came around the corner and we shouted at them about the hornets and they stopped. One of them considered cutting through the woods to find another path but it was unclear how wide the hornets stretched so in the end they ran forward and flicked the walking pole from the ground to the first runner. All four of us stopped around the corner and examined each other to see how we had fared. The last two runners had done remarkably well with only a few stings each which was similar to the first. I'd come away with a few on my arms but my legs had been well and truly done around my ankles and knees. I could see some stings still hanging in so pulled them out. The first runner said 'are you allergic to that?' and I said I didn't know so would get down quickly and headed off – I left the three of them and would not see them until the end. It was now a solo run for me as the stings in my knees were swelling up as if someone was pushing drawing pins in to me. I got to the bottom and reported the hornets and there was now a big gap until others came down – about 20 minutes later the runners were reporting no problems which was good news. I found some pasta, cake and biscuits and ate my meal then caught the first bus back to the accommodation. It had been quite a day and we still had half the course to go!

Day 3 Belledone

It was another early start to be on the bus to head to La Saligniere (540m) for the start of today's challenge with the billed highlights being a vertical k at the start and a visit to the highest point of the course at the Grand Colon (2390m). The run would be 39.1k with a D+ of 2420m and a D- of 2670m. This is annoyingly just below marathon distance of 42.64k as, like many, I'm in the process of collecting my list of marathons, aiming to achieve 100. Before coming to this area, I knew Hannibal had crossed this region with some elephants in 218 BC on an epic march across a large part of Europe with the goal of taking Rome. History is unsure (GPS watches were not around in those days) as to the precise track he took but today the course would cross it at some point, as there is no doubt that he headed up the main valley that holds the river Isère. It would be nice to think there might be a sign somewhere so I was going to keep my eyes out. I had no interest at all in cricket but knew Ian Botham had done something similar in the late 1980s, although this time the elephants only walked a mile each day and were taken by road between stages – the elephants were there to raise publicity for the trek which was raising funds for Leukaemia Research. I thought it pretty unlikely there would be a 'Botham line' but I similarly was aiming not to miss it if there was one! The Belledone massif is huge and we were really just skirting a corner of it. There is a famous race, L'Échappée Belle: The intégrale, that covers the 144k from Vizelle to Aiguebelle and from a difficulty point of view is reckoned to be harder than UTMB. Their race website contains a lot of useful information for training and competing in mountain races so is well worth a look.

 The bus dropped us at yesterday's finish but it was not clear where the start was. A number wanted to go to the bathroom and on previous days there had been many toilets at the start. There was a tiny wooden shed and one runner opened the door and the rancid stench hit our nostrils and he didn't have the stomach to enter. We looked around to work out where to go and spotted a staircase dropping off the road to the right and leading to a road over the river. We all knew we had to cross the river to get to the main hills but were all a little reluctant to go down lest we needed to come back up and it was wasted effort. Suddenly a few went down and with collective group think we all powerwalked over the bridge and up the other side and found the start area – a very small square amongst some houses hemmed in between the mountains and the river.

 I spotted Bob, from Day 1, and he explained he had been timed out by 30 mins so did not finish. He had decided to rest on Day 2 so now was back for Day 3 to give it his best shot. I wished him good luck and hoped he did finish and would also finish Day 4 as he was a nice friendly person. The announcer gave a long speech in French that I didn't really understand but I thought he was talking about the weather and a possible route change. He said he'd do it in English and I could not hear as the silent French masses who listened intently to the last speech now spoke dix-neuf à la douzaine to each other. I spotted Pierre and he told me that thunder was expected from 14:00 so we would not be going up the Grand Colon and the route diversion would be marked. No sooner had he said this than we were off.

The route card said a D+ of 1090m, and a D- of 0m, in 4.1k to L'Arselle (1630m). I know I'm faster on the uphills, so I ran in the middle of the pack to get a good place for the hill. Unfortunately, we seemed to be running away from the hill and I realised, horror of horrors, that we were starting with an 'out and back' run in the valley. Now as the route was due to change today, I had no idea how far we were doing this for, so eased up and slipped in to about the back third to take things easy. We soon reached our turn point and started to double back so now I had to overtake to make some spaces on the flat taking about 20 on the final 50m before we ground to a halt at the narrow bit at the bottom of the hill. This hill, as may be expected, was relentless and kept going up and up. I slowly but surely moved from caboose to driver on various trains settling as a caboose about 800m up. The train I was on was a little too quick for my liking and on one section which had a supporting rope I fell forwards but caught myself on my hands. There was a significant drop to the right, the sort you can imagine a base jumper launching from, and my instinct threw me in to the hill as opposed to away from it. Others on the train asked if I was OK and I said I was and we continued up. Of course, I could have slowed down and joined a later train but that's not really in my mindset – you have to commit to a pace and keep to it to succeed right to the top and make no excuses to yourself, but you can learn a lesson about believing a little too much in your own abilities!

The route levelled off as we approached L'Arselle (1630m) and I loaded up at this CP. The next push would be to the Chamrousse (2240m) in about 5kms time. This next section was an absolute delight – undulating interesting terrain, trees, mountain lakes, a good rocky path that became what looked like a blue ski run to Chamrousse. On this were many spectators, and others, out for the view. For me it was tinged a bit with sadness knowing we were not going up the Grand Colon (2390m) but I can understand why the organisers would not want us out there in a thunderstorm. Approaching the CP, I could see the top of a ski gondola and the ski station and there was a canvas tent outside that was our CP that contained all the usual food and water. Upon leaving this there was a pan-pipe band playing on the edge of the piste. As this was so surreal, I took a small movie with my camera and set off on the new course. I asked the marshal how far to the next CP and they said it would be the same as planned and this struck me as great planning to keep the CP distances the same even with a route change. We now ran down a red run to the village of la Recoin. This was a pathless piste so had lots of potato size rocks to trip on and various rivers to cross that would not present a problem to skiers in wintertime. At the bottom we crossed the road then headed under a road and on to a narrow path that joined a forest track. The heat and humidity were now really building as the route contoured along. I was now on my own with no-one around and all I could do was to watch intently for the markers which were easy to find and spaced every few hundred metres. Whoever had marked the entire Ut4M route did a good job as it must have taken ages. As the hours passed by, I ran out of water and realised the next CP was a lot further than I had been told. At one point the track tangentially skimmed a road and there was a water stash for the runners there – about 2/3 of the bottles were empty. Other runners were there filling up and pouring water over themselves to cool down. I filled up with 2 litres and poured about 1 litre on my head and down my back to try and reduce my temperature. Suitably refreshed I pushed on and about an hour later reached the CP at Freydières (1120m). The official distance in the route guide was 34.1k but my watch made it 40.8k. For me it was now just a question of getting down before the thunder if I could so I shuffle ran the next few k to the side of the main valley that Hannibal, and Botham, walked up. I could now see the most amazing thunder clouds building over Vercors to the South and knew it would be touch and go if I could do this dry. The route cuts down some quiet roads then heads along the river through tall reeds then crosses the main road and it now looked about 2-3 k to go and I was still dry.

To this point I'd been battling with another runner, Norbert, who always seemed frustrated when I overtook him saying it was down to having long legs. It's a bit of a bugbear of mine when people say this to me as I think they are really trying to justify their pace to themselves by saying I've some sort of physical advantage. Whilst it is natural to feel this way about others, I've never seen the need to verbalise it to someone but I seem to get it a lot. I decided to have a bit of fun with him so whenever he stopped running, I'd walk past him to irritate him a little. I did this a few times so each time he'd mumble at me then run off. All of a sudden Pierre appeared friendly as ever and said we three should run to the end. I said I was OK so Norbert had no choice but to continue (as otherwise Pierre would beat him!) and he ended up stopping again very quickly as he was out of power. I did my annoying thing just to push him along a bit and at the very end he ran in. I didn't mind that he'd made 30s on me as I reckon my legs would be fresher tomorrow so I'd easily have him there! Wherever you are in the pack it is always possible to get some friendly racing going so it was good to have him on the course. Within 5 minutes of arriving the heavens opened so I was glad to be inside tucking in to my pasta and cake as was normal now for me. The end, at Saint-Nazaire-Les-Eymes (290m) has a large sports hall and is geared up to have many of the full course racers sleep here. They also have a postmistress who had letters that friends/family had written to the CP to give out to runners when they got there to encourage them along. Whilst most runners in that race had support there where a number who did not so I thought it a really nice touch to lay this on for them. Many runners were in tears reading their letters, their emotions stretched to breaking point with the physical pain they were pushing through.

It would have been easy to miss our bus back as sheltering inside we didn't have a view of the road outside so, along with Pierre and a few others, I went outside and sheltered along the edge of the building only getting rained on a little. After a few minutes it stopped completely so we went to the bus stop and waited. The group slowly got bigger until there were about 40 of us here. A bus came along and the group went to it as to get on. The driver said something and the group were still keen so, along with others, I moved forward thinking it was our bus. An organiser came out and stood in-front of the bus door in a slightly comedic style saying 'not this one' but still people persisted to try and get on. It slowly dawned on me that we were actually looking at a scheduled service bus that happened to come where we were all standing so, along with others, I got back on the pavement. Someone undid the boot at the back so it drove off with this large door swinging in the wind exposing the drive belt on the engine. A few minutes later our bus arrived and we all piled on – I was somewhere near the front. It was about a 10-minute drive to the military barracks we were at and as the bus arrived at the gate I got up and suddenly from further back I head Pierre and some others say 'Daa-viiiiiiiiiiiiiiid – sit down' so I did and the bus drove right to the gate and the driver said something to the guard and we went in and we were dropped off at the pick-up point. The bus then left with the remaining passengers for Grenoble. This was all a bit odd as the camp was very keen to know who was coming in and out and we would normally have to show ID but today many came in that were not controlled. I asked the others did they know this was going to happen and they said from the angle he drove at the gates at they suspected so and didn't fancy the walk so thought best to keep quiet and see what happens. One of the people was Simon, a Frenchman in his 50s, who had done days 2-4 of the course last year so I'd spoken a little to him during the week. He had really bad blisters so was going to give up tomorrow – in his words he had enough points for UTMB so there was nothing to be gained. I didn't like to see him defeated as he had been a very reasonable person going out of his way to have a chat with me each day so I really wanted him to succeed. We had a chat and I said I really hoped he would start tomorrow and offered to look at his blisters but he was feeling low and declined. He was going to phone his wife but he said the trouble with that is she will say to continue but she doesn't know what he is going through. For me Day 3 was over and it was now just a question of getting back, resting, and getting ready for Day 4.

Day 4 Chartreuse

The last day in a multi-day can be odd. It seems like the end of a routine and newly found friends are often lost over the coming months. Only those who have been through everything with you can really understand what it takes to do these things. Sure, you may have family/friends who know something of it but I feel unless they've actually stood on the start line of something that has tested them, they will struggle to understand what it actually takes to see it through. I like meeting people at other races so we can reminisce on how wet the 2010 CCC was or how bad the weather was at the 2011 CCC etc. It's an odd thing as there is this common event that will link you with other racers forever. Today was to be the Chartreuse massif which would be 41.9k with a D+ of 2540m and a D- of 2610m. Breakfast was chattier compared to previous days – Norbert and I spoke about our feelings of the last day having got this far and knowing short of injury we would finish. There was lots of talk of 'what next' with others as we were all thinking of the future. I think in our heads it was already finished hence we needed to have a goal lined up to look forward to those moments of excitement and real peril that can be faced and conquered in the mountains. We only get a few days a year for these adventures but these days make the months that lead up them, when times are low, endurable and worthwhile.

After a quick bus to the start (yesterday's finish checkpoint), it was time to start the last leg of the adventure. At the CP were some of the runners tackling the full course in one go, having just had a short sleep. At the time I thought the full course was a step beyond my capability but in the intervening period (I'm writing this on the 1st Jan 2018) my views have changed and I now think I could give the extreme race a serious go. If I had not been accepted for TDS in 2018, I'd have probably entered. From Simon I knew the first hill was muddy and slippy and his advice was to get as far up the field as possible. I was very pleased that Simon was starting again today – he said he had spoken to his wife who had convinced him telling him when he has pulled out of other events, he is really miserable around the house, so he has to complete this one for the good of both of them! We had our usual music for the last time and there were some tears amongst those of us who were starting our fourth day. As with other days there were about 200 who were just racing this single day who were all clean shaven and rested and were interested in how we trained for these things. I was pleased to see Bob had made it to this day – he had been timed out twice this week and had not started one day but he was going to give this day a go with a view to finishing. It takes determination to do what Bob was doing so I wished him well and hoped to meet him at the end.

For the first k or so from the start at Saint-Nazaire-Les-Eymes (290m) the course is flat heading up a road and across some farmers fields before it starts to climb. The path then started on long zigzags heading higher and higher through a forest until it crested the top of a large cliff face about 1000m above the plain below. The top was spectacular as we were on a very narrow rocky section with lots of rock, slippy from the engulfing mist we were now in. Upon leaving this the chilly mist made navigation a little tricky as we headed across high alpine pastures to the CP at Habert de Chamechaude (1570m), 12k in. I'd been keeping something in reserve on the first few days so now found myself about mid-field which was a great place to be to tacking the main hill – the Chamechaude. Before entering I'd watched the official race video and had been hypnotised by the beauty of this hill. It looks like a large limestone block, about 2km long by about 500m by 500m, that has been tilted through 45 degrees so presents this large surface about 2k by 500m. On closer examination this surface is all loose rock with nothing growing on it but has some small very steep paths on it. It's an absolute monster of a hill where there is nowhere to hide and no descent on the ascent. To someone who likes hills it's a top-drawer hill – there is little that could be done to make this uphill even better. I'd dreamt of this hill many times. I'd seen myself conquering it with a smile. The excitement I felt when watching the videos came back as I knew this next 45 minutes would be it and would be an amazingly positive memory, whatever happens in life, that I'd take to my grave. When you tackle a hill with such a clarity of success you know it is going to be a fast one so I set off, my only disappointment being it was in the mist.

The path traces a lasso shape on the hill with the initial ascent, and descent, being on the same course. As I headed up these very fast runners, at the front of the field, were bombing down against me at such speed I had to keep side stepping them as they couldn't stop as they propelled themselves down. This wasn't too pleasant for me so I got up as quickly as I could, running when the gradient was less than 5% (rarely), and speed walking the rest. The path quickly split so I headed onwards and upwards in to the eerie mist. After not that long I reached 3 marshals in the mist who scanned my RFID tag and I asked which way now to the top and they told me this was it, I'd reached the top at 2000m so the only way was down. I was a little disappointed as in my head I was on for more and was full of adrenaline to climb higher. I wanted to go to the summit but that was in the mist so instead started along the scree trail they pointed me at and started running down. I was absolutely on fire on this descent catching and overtaking and was soon at the bottom of the lasso. I barrelled my way down looking for gaps to get past those coming up as opposed to forcing them off the track. I saw Norbert and Pierre coming up who could not believe I was so far ahead today – we'd done about 4hrs and at this point I was at least 45 mins in-front of them as that is how long it had taken me to conquer the mighty Chamechaude.

The route down to the next CP was easy going underfoot and Le-Sapprey-En-Chatreuse (990m) at 24.4k came very quickly. This was a large hall with plenty of chairs inside and more food to stock up on. I did my usual trick of eating a bit there and then and taking a small bag of food to eat over the next 2k and headed off on what was to be the last hill of a mere 400m ascent on forest tracks. The descent was a bit tricky as the forest track had suffered a lot of erosion so was a bit muddy and 'steppy' - it was hard to get any flow on the way to Fort du Saint Eynard (1300m) at 28.4k. This fort sits right on the edge of the cliff that overlooks the plain below. At the time I didn't head to the edge to look down and take some pictures as I didn't quite realise where we were at – I've some regrets but will hopefully get back there in the future to do this. Now there was only a half-marathon to be done and that would be it! The next section was just long zigzags of descent in the woods – all runnable with some potential to have a drop on the bends if something went wrong. Far below Grenoble could be seen in the haze. It struck me that Grenoble had a massive cemetery that extended over the river that was very close to the centre – I've never seen such a big one in a city.

The route cuts to the Bastille (500m) that is a castle area full of tourists who will have taken the cable car, walked, or driven from Grenoble below. For a runner it gets exciting here as you run through castle passages to drop height much to the amusement of tourists. Upon exiting the Bastille, I knew I had about 4k to go and caught up a fast runner. There was no way I could match his pace to the end but I thought I'd hold on for as long as I could and thoroughly enjoyed running 3 road zigzags behind him. Very quickly I was out at the bottom and here the markers had gone. Simon had told me when you reach the bottom to head left along the river, further than you may think, then double up to the end in the stadium.

I set up left along the river a little unnerved that I could not see a single runner, or marker. I asked a few locals from time to time who all just shrugged their shoulders at me. A runner caught me up, John, and asked if I knew the way and I said I didn't but told him what we were doing. He said OK then did the classic trick of pulling back about 10s and keeping me in sight so I could do all the nav work and he could wait for his moment. I got to the point where I thought we should turn off and could see the heavy footfall of off-road trainers on mud so went for it and saw a marker just after this – I pointed it out to him and at this point he accelerated past me as we both knew we had about 800m of the park to go and then we'd have done it. Neither of us knew who was really winning, as we'd been at this for four days, but it was clear to me he wanted the place today. It was also clear to me he was not going to have it! We carried on and overtook someone from the 100k 5000m race who was slowly walking in towards the stadium. This was the first runner I'd seen from that race so must have been a back-marker but good effort for sticking in there.

There was a small crowd lining the street and John from the river was now show-boating a bit running to either side to high-five people. He also had some family there and was waving to them and getting his photo taken. Suddenly the crowd started to cheer louder and John was show-boating all the more thinking it was for him but it wasn't. I could see we had less than 100m to go so this was my moment. I accelerated hard and flew past him before he knew what happened as we turned the final bend with the finish now being within half the width of the stadium. I knew the finish was inside but where was the door as I could see two ways in? Get this right and I've beaten John. Get this wrong and John has beaten me. I shouted to a marshal who pointed the way and I bolted in to the dark then came out in the light having to decelerate very quickly as there was no run off. I'd arrived. Everyone cheered. I looked round and my fellow competitor came in. Everyone cheered. I went up to him to say well done and have a chat as always goes on in these things, and he completely blanked me and walked off. As there was no official race photographer, I got someone else to take my photo then went through the building to get my medal and finishers T-Shirt. Next came some food and general race chat as one does in these things.

I'd bought my ticket for the pasta party which was due to start at 18:00 and this was only an hour or so away so I thought I'd wait. Slowly but surely some familiar faces came over the line and we chatted about the race and future ideas. Pierre was going to take part in the South de France 100 in October so I looked forward to seeing him there as a familiar face in a race is always a good thing. The arena got busier and busier as more runners arrived and 18:00

quickly became 18:30 with no sign of the pasta party starting anytime soon. Next came a long drawn our medal ceremony that took ages for many reasons one of which being that each winner needed to kiss each other winner on each cheek and as there were many categories this really dragged on. Still no pasta. The Run Handi Move teams arrived about 19:30 and at this point everyone was standing on the chairs either cheering them in, making a movie on their camera, or wiping grit from their eyes. I kept an eye out and never did see Bob finish so I hope whatever happened to him he was not injured. There was still no movement on the pasta party. The staff had eaten as we could watch them eating pasta whilst tapping away on their smart phones. It was now getting near to 20:00 so rather than continue to wait I decided to head back to the accommodation. This journey takes a good hour and I knew the buses became less frequent after 21:00 so I had to make a move. I headed back passing a number of take-aways wishing I'd thought of these at 16:00 to get some food in! At the accommodation I had some of the snack-food I had left then chatted to my roomies for one last night when they arrived back.

Day 5 Heading home

Today was departure day and it felt like a last day of a university term with everyone clearing out their rooms. As I'd arrived by public transport everything fitted in a big rucksack so I was travelling light (well 15kg). Others had enormous quantities of food/clothing/shoe options with them in plastic boxes with detailed labels loading them in to their cars. We said our goodbyes and I set off down the road to the camp gate for one last time. Outside the camp is a great spot to view the four mountain ranges. Over four days I'd tackled 178k with 11795m of ascent/descent in 36:09 which gave me an ITRA cotation score of 453. The cotation score of the extreme challenge is 420 so, on a good day with the right training, I should be able to do it as my score was higher. Something to remember for the future.

I caught the bus in to Grenoble then walked its deserted streets surprisingly bumping in to my hornet stung friend from day 2 – his stings were going down but we both had a good time chatting about the experience in depth, not just being stung but the four-day adventure we had just taken part in. Doing a big event, like the Ut4M Challenge, changes a person for ever as you never look at hills/distances, or even yourself, in the same light again. I knew this race was just a training step on the way to the South de France 100 so now all I needed to do was to not over train in Sep so I'd be ready to take on the biggest physical challenge of my life on Oct 5th 2017.

16 SOUTH DE FRANCE 100 2017

It's now the start of June 2018 and I've still not fully unpacked from the South De France 100 (SdF100) race I started on October 4th 2017. When I got home, I emptied my rucksack in to a box and the box has remained unpacked - an untidy mish-mash of clothing, food, head torches and items that should have been used but were not. I've a bit of mental block with tidying it as what should have been an amazing finish on October 5th turned out to be an ineluctable withdrawal on October 4th. The crowning glory of years of racing was not to be. The dream of completing a 100-mile race would remain unfulfilled for now.

Having been unsuccessful in the TDS ballot for 2017 it was time to try and achieve my other main racing goal – completing a 100 miler. I'd already bagged a DNF at the Lakeland 100 but that was only my first attempt and it takes a couple of goes for many people so it seemed good to have another go. A 100-mile race for most people will involve the need to be awake, and moving, for 2 consecutive nights. The fast may be able to get away with 1-night but even being awake for 'only' 36 hours is fatiguing. Races start at different times of the day with 18:00 being extremely common. In this case the runner has already been awake for 10 or so hours and many will need to be awake for another 40 to complete so it makes for a long 'day'. A few races start in the morning so I decided to find one of these and discovered the SdF 100. It starts at 10:00 at Fort Romeu in the Pyrenees and had between 8000m and 10000m of ascent/descent (depending on what you read) finishing on the Mediterranean coast where the sky meets the sea. Each CP had a cut off but, based on my previous performances, it all looked 'doable'.

I entered the race around March 2017 and in the intervening months had a few questions that the organisers replied to quickly each time so things looked good. At Ut4M I'd met three runners who would also be taking part in the race so I knew I would not be totally alone during the experience.

The race finishes in Argeles-Sur-Mer so the first challenge was to get there. I flew to Barcelona airport and caught the metro to the city centre and had 3 hours until my train to Argeles-Sur-Mer departed. On the flight out from the UK I started to have doubts about whether I'd packed enough layers for the potentially cold night before the race as I'd be staying high in the Pyrenees in the remote village of Fort Romeu. I decided to try and get to Decathlon in Barcelona knowing it was on a side street off the right of Las Ramblas – I thought when there I could ask someone for directions to the store. The idea of finding a shop, without even a street name, was somewhere between naïve and ambitious but, perhaps surprisingly, I did manage to find it by a process of elimination. I bought a pair of Merino leggings for about 20 Euros which seemed a real bargain, all I had to do now was to get back to the main railway station within 90 minutes. As I'd managed to find the store without a map my navigational confidence was high so I decided to walk back on the roads using my metro map to navigate – all I had to do was to spot stations and take turnings until I met the next station. I quickly realised that this was flawed and got lost and started to think I may have to get a taxi. Couple all this with the lively political situation around Catalan independence at the time and it made for an interesting walk – lots of calm protesters out and TV crews waiting to capture some action that never came.

I was pleased to see the station as I turned a bend, and with about 20 minutes of time to spare, I made my train and settled in my seat for the 2-hour train journey. The train had no aircon so my watch told me the temperature was in the mid-30s. I'd paid a little extra for 1st class (for the leg room) and slowly but surely people left and moved to standard class where they could cool down a bit. Always being ready for a pointless contest I, and two other random blokes, sat it out to see who would blink first and get up. We gave each other steely stares as our clothes got wetter and wetter. One man got up and left and it was just me and my friend in the striped shirt and black framed spectacles. We carried on like this all the way to Perpignan where I had to leave to catch another train. The contest was fun but utterly foolish 2 days before a race as all I was doing was dehydrating myself and making a set of clothes wet. After a 20-minute wait in the station I caught my connection to Argeles-Sur-Mer and walked about 2km to the hotel for the night. Argeles-sur-Mer has one of the biggest campsites in Europe but in Oct is as quiet as can be. A beautiful place to watch the sun set on a deserted beach.

It was tricky to work out what to do when it came to accommodation before and during the race. The organisers offered two options for getting to the start. One option was a bus at 06:00 on race day from Argeles-sur-Mer that would take about 3hrs to get to the start in Font Romeu. The runner would register, then pretty much start the race straight away. The advantage of this was that a runner could leave all of their non-race gear in a car (if local) or in a hotel room (if they were keeping one open for the entire race weekend). The disadvantage being the early start as it would mean getting up at around 05:00. The other option was to get a bus at 14:00 the day before that would drive to the start so the individual could register that afternoon before finding their accommodation in the small village of Font Romeu. The advantage of this was that on race day it would not be that early a start. But they would need accommodation reasonably close to the start, and this was in short supply.

I'd decided early on I wanted to get to Font Romeu the day before so booked my bus but, from the organiser's website, it was quite tricky to work out where the start actually was. I booked a B&B close to the start on the map and had visions of, maybe, getting a taxi to the start. As nerves started to kick-in in the lead up I decided to look in detail where the start was and, to my alarm, found my accommodation was about 5k and 200m in height drop away i.e. a reasonable walk in the morning bearing in mind I had not found a taxi firm in the village. I needed to try and find somewhere closer. I got lucky and found a room in accommodation about 5 minutes from the start that had been booked when I was originally looking but was now available. This accommodation, that I'll call number 4, e-mailed me about 1 month before the race and asked would I like a meal on the night before and, if so, could I confirm and then transfer some money. As Font Romeu is small, and there are no restaurants/cafes near the start, I was quite pleased and wrote back saying this was really good, asking is it OK to get something vegetarian, and how much should I pay. They wrote back saying 'forget it' and no meal would be possible for me. I assumed this was down to asking for a vegetarian option so rather than let this get me down moved on and decided I'd take my own food when I got there.

The day before the race I got up and headed to the beachfront and watched the waves to pass the time before I caught the bus to the mountains. A few other ultrarunners milled about the place all looking a bit lost also. I had nothing to do until the bus left at 14:00 so sat there fantasising about coming along the seafront in a few days' time and meeting E at the end. The plan was E would travel out on the Saturday and I'd finish late Sat / early Sun and we'd meet at the end of the course then have a week's holiday travelling up France. In my mind I was finishing and insisting I wanted to wade in the sea and E advising me not to as I was wobbly/tired but with sufficient stubbornness I was going to go in – I'd already decided that.

I knew the bus left from the tourist office but which side? Was it in the car park? As I mulled this over in my head who other than Pierre and Jean from Ut4M walked around the corner – Pierre as friendly as can be and they told me exactly where to wait for the bus.

Slowly but surely more ultrarunners turned up and the bus came and we got on for our drive in to the mountains. It really was a lovely route with great scenery all round – at times we all looked intently at part of the mountains we would face the next day. There was a metre gauge railway, 'le petit rail jaune', that followed a lot of the drive and I thought it would be excellent to take this mountain railway at some point in the future. The 63km line had a number of impressive looking bridges and clearly passed through many tunnels to work its way to Mount Louis, which happened to be the first CP on the race.

16 SOUTH DE FRANCE 100 2017

After about a three hour drive the bus dropped everyone at a lay-by near a sports centre and my plan was to drop my bags at the accommodation and go down and register. I'd banked on the streets having names and obvious house numbers but, unfortunately, they didn't. This presented a bit of a problem. After about 20 minutes of walking around trying to find a name or number on something, I decided to have a change of plan and register for the race and ask the organisers for help. At the sports hall there was a small queue and after about 10 minutes we shuffled in to a small room to show our kit to the kit checkers. One item was a 'foil blanket' and I showed my 'foil survival bag' which is far better and this was declined. I tried to explain what it was and, after a minute or two, was accepted by another kit checker who explained to the first person that it was actually better than a 'foil blanket'. Little did I know it would not be long before I'd be using it. As I progressed around the 'kit check' room I was given three bags to put bits in to be taken forward to CPs. I'd known about this in advance and planned for food, clothes and batteries for my head torch to be in them. They told me if I left anything at a CP it would be disposed of if I did not collect it– this was news to me and not good news at that. I asked another kit checker and was told the same. This had big consequences on my whole plan. At the final table I picked up my race number and a free bottle of local wine branded 'South de France 100'. I picked this up and was a bit disgruntled about the drop bag news so went to another part of the hall and left it behind. I headed out to find my accommodation and decided to turn back to pick up the bottle and try and get it back after all. In the hall I asked for directions to my accommodation and a local pointed out the house on the road above so things were starting to look up a little. Next stop the B&B!

I found number 4 relatively easily – it was a small B&B that had about eight runners staying there. The landlady was friendly and asked what I was doing for my evening meal as there is nowhere to eat in Font Romeu. I said I'd brought some food so would be OK as I had bananas and bread. She said she was not happy with this and very firmly said that when the others are eating their evening meal I would sit on a stool at the end of the table and she would find something for me. I said I was OK (it was the same person I'd been e-mailing pre-trip who had not been helpful) and she was very insistent. She said if I were in my room she would come and get me at food time and bring me down to eat with everyone as that is what she wants. I said I was really OK and would not be coming down. As nerves are a bit stretched before an ultra none of this was very helpful. As things turned out I ate my bananas and bread very quietly whilst they all ate at the main table downstairs and she did not come to get me. Pre-race I often like to watch foreign TV channels but this room had no TV so I spent the evening reading a three-day old copy of 'The Times'.

I was starting to have some pre-race nerves about the race and asked myself the question 'have you done enough training?' and convinced myself the answer was 'no'. I thought I'd reassure myself with some internet searching on my phone and this went from bad to worse. Every page I read was from someone unsympathetic saying things like 'you should have thought of this months ago and if you fail it is down to your lack of prep'. My heart rate started to increase a little with the nerves and I tried to control things with a few texts to/from home; naturally not letting on to my bought of pre-race nerves. Knowing what I know now I'd advise not to search for such things the day before a race and stick with your plan. After all most will have done months to get to this point so if things have worked so far keep with the plan and it just might see you through! If a 100 miler was an easy distance every runner would be doing it – the whole point is it is a challenge where failure, or success, often hangs in the balance and that is part of the attraction.

The next morning, I went down to breakfast and the other runners were there. The landlady gave me a detailed tour of the table pointing out the various breads and jams on offer then left and I tucked in to a reasonable amount of food. Race start was 10:00 so at 08:45 I went to check out and could see there was a piece of paper with my name on it sitting on a table. I picked it up and the other runners told me it was the details to pay. On it the bill said 'cash or bank transfer only'. Now this was completely news to me. I did not have cash, or the ability to do a bank transfer, and there was no cash machine in the village. I was also 75 minutes away from the biggest race of my life so I did not need this. I found the landlady and explained I didn't have cash and she asked me if I could do her a bank transfer there and then. I explained I could not and offered to pay on a bank card. She said she would not take a bank card as did not trust them. I then said I needed to be getting going and would pay by bank transfer as soon as I was back in the UK which would be about 9 days and she accepted this. I left and was pleased to be walking down to the race start to get away from number 4.

At the start the sports hall was filling up and I left a drop bag that contained spare batteries, toothbrush/toothpaste and some food and planned to collect this about 100k in to the course. The organisers had laid on what appeared to be a limitless supply of cake and coffee which was great. Pierre and Jean arrived like long lost friends and we chatted about the challenge ahead. Roman, from Ut4M, came on the early bus and talked about how he intended to finish about 09:00 -10:00 on the Sunday and had to catch the 12:00 train ultimately to Paris as he was working on Monday. These three had lots of clothing/food in the drop bags and were sure they would not be thrown away and agreed I'd been given incorrect information.

The minutes ticked by and at around 09:45 we headed outside into warm Pyreneesian sunshine. These last 15 minutes passed very quickly and after a race brief (in French) we were off. The first few km circumnavigated the 'Pyrenees 2000' ski station and can be thought of as running on flattish grassy terrain the main purpose being that supporters can see their runner off at the start then see them a few kms in to the course.

The route then turns and heads eastwards towards the coast the first highlight being Fort Mont-Louis (1585m) which is the French National Commando Training Centre. This is a large fort from the 1500s that has a dry moat attached which the route descends in to and circles around before leaving it. Within the moat are large scale climbing frames that are used by the military – our route just ran along the middle avoiding everything. Running through the fort was a real highlight and something unique to find in a race. There was a CP at the exit and we'd now covered 10k. No sooner out of this the route crossed a road and headed to the second CP at Planès (1530m). Before the race I'd spent quite a bit of time working out target times for CPs to pace myself and my target for here was 12:30 and I was about 30 minutes ahead so everything was going well – 13.8k done – only 150km to go!

The village is pretty with a church and from here a lot of the course covered so far could be seen. Beyond this the route started to get more interesting and rugged as it headed in to the mountains with the trees dressed in autumn brown leaves. The path rose to 1911m at the 17th km. I'd read about vultures in this area and wanted to see some and was not disappointed as several griffon vultures circled around for the next few hours. The route here is nice and narrow within woods – one minute a view up the valley and the next minute none – every corner giving excitement to the eye. At one point I could see the path several kms ahead on the other side of the valley so made a mental note to look back from there to see if people were still behind me as this would give a feel for where I was in the rapidly thinning pack. The turning in the valley was easy to spot being an unguarded bridge over a river and now the route went back down the other side of the valley, I looked back and could see the spot I'd looked from 30 mins earlier and could see people still coming so I knew I was in a reasonable position in the field.

Cab Aitèque (1671m) was the next CP which was a small table with two soldiers and a guard dog in an isolated location at the bottom of a hill and when I got there the water had run out which was not good news. The temperature was heating up and I knew it was a hilly section ahead so whilst disappointing I just headed on through. In the space of about 500m the trail rises to 1895m then continues to rise until the summit is reached (2367m) about 24km from the start. At this point I'd ascended 1336m and descended 740m and knew I had so much more to go!

16 SOUTH DE FRANCE 100 2017

The scenery on this part is absolutely stunning – lonely silent mountains with birds of prey circling overhead. I was looking forward to the Ref Caranca CP (1845m) as was quite thirsty and I as approached it I could see a gathering of cattle outside a stone farm building. Next to this I could see a soldier in a 4x4 vehicle and, when I got there, I took on some more water and some snacks. It was now 14:00, one hour ahead of my target time, and I was already starting to think about the night ahead hopeful I could get to the first Life Station by then. The course has 3 Life Stations (where the drop bags are sent to) that are larger CPs in sports halls. From Caranca the course climbs again through the trees and up in to the mountains and here is where it all started to go wrong. The sun was beating down through a cloudless sky and I was wearing some CAT3 sunglasses and a sun cap to keep the sun out of my eyes. This was good for the most part but in the dark sections of trees not so good so I was constantly having to take my sunglasses off.

On one steep ascent I was bent forward using my hands a little on the ground for stability and suddenly I hit my head on something which turned out to be a very sturdy branch, of about 40 mm diameter, that was perpendicular to the tree trunk. The impact knocked me backwards and I was lucky not to fall over. I knew it was a bad hit and touched my hat and could feel blood. I needed to assess the damage so took a quick photo and could see I'd taken a cut above the left eye just inside my hair line. I knew I was carrying a wound dressing in my bag so took it out and bound it tightly round my head then jammed my cap on for good measure to hold things in. Whilst doing this another runner caught up and asked if I were OK and I said I was. He asked if I was going to head back to the last CP and I said I wasn't but was going to push on. I didn't feel the need to withdraw at this point and the idea of going back to a soldier in the middle of nowhere to ask for a lift didn't seem great as I had no idea where he was based and thought it best to head for the Life Station and work things from there – it was only 28km away so seemed sensible.

Freshly bandaged up I managed to make some progress and caught up some other runners and overtook them. In my head I was amazing. I had this bloodied bandage tied around my head with a blood patch on my hat (as it was still bleeding a little from time to time) and I was still going – OK I could not put my sunglasses on as I'd put the bandage tight over my ear but I'd be fine. It was just another challenge to be overcome. Who needs stitches when you can just bind your head tightly!

After about 30mins a different feeling came in to my head. My stupid cut kept opening up and bleeding and spending another 35-40 hours with it bandaged was a bad idea – it needed to be checked. If it rained, I'd be in a bad way with a soggy bandage. My head was throbbing from the wound or the tightness of my bandage or both. I didn't think I could wear a head torch. Hundreds of hours of training had been for nothing. Internally I had tears of frustration which occasionally showed their head in the baking heat. I was frustrated with my stupid tall body that causes me so many problems – I hate not fitting properly in many cars and seats, hanging my legs out of the bath and having to duck under doorframes. The ducking thing got me again as everyone else went under that pesky tree but not me – I had to hit it.

The view was great as I crested the Col del Pal and I was feeling invincible with my cut head. I knew I was going to conquer and succeed and was hopeful of getting some bad blisters as this was too easy – I could handle another injury – bring it on – I'll heroically push on to the end. I was the nearest thing to ultra invincibility. At this point I was completely unbeatable and no amount of physical hardship would stop me reaching the end. The mind controls everything and my mind was completely blinkered to the reality of the situation.

The balloon burst. It wasn't long before I was asking myself if I have to stop at the Life Station where will I go? I've no accommodation booked for that night. If they drop me back at the beach at the start I'll try and find some bushes to sleep in but not sure about the local wildlife or if there are any nasty snakes. Maybe the safest thing would be to sit out on the beach as whilst I may be vulnerable to a mugging the risk seemed minimal compared to the risk of snakes.

Things were not looking good.

I'll just have to try and get through the Life Station without being stopped – try and bluff it as if nothing is really wrong – pull my hood to hide things. If they don't see all the blood, they will not know it is there, so there is no way anyone can stop me. What's a cut head compared to all the pain that cannot be seen? My left foot had inexplicably swollen – it does this from time to time in races and last did it in the 70-mile race 'The Wall' in England in 2015. What happens is that the foot swells up and is a little too large to fit in the shoe so painfully presses up against the inside of the tongue – this means the lower leg slowly but surely starts to swell up until it can get to double its natural circumference – it really hurts when it does this. My lower back was hurting in the discs around L5/S1 – a bit like someone had a screwdriver and was gently trying to force the joint apart and they kept getting their screwdriver in to the nerves. The rucksack straps were really hurting around my collar bones – the one disadvantage of not having much body fat is there is little natural padding when carrying things. All these pains were internal and hurt far more than the pesky cut on the head.

I cannot wear a head torch. This is terrible. Who am I kidding? Game over.

In the distance I could see the Mantet (1517m) CP at 36.2km and the two opposing thoughts were intensely competing in my head. It was now 16:20 and I was only 40 minutes ahead of my target time so had lost some time. The cut off for this CP was 19:30 so I was still fine but I had slowed down a little. Here was the first CP with some seats and a large amount of food. Along with about 10 others I ate quite a lot here. The CP staff asked if I were OK pointing at my head and I said it was nothing. I was concerned so sent E a text saying what has happened and might pull out and would read any replies at the Life Station at Vernet-les-Bains at 51k. My thinking around the texts was to firstly seek some external advice and secondly to expectation manage a potential DNF. I felt I would be letting E down if I did not finish – after all I'd persuaded her to come to the bottom of Europe to see me complete my first

100-miler. I had to deliver the goods and complete otherwise I'd let her down also.

The route out of Mantet is very steep – where the road zig-zags up the mountain the trail goes straight up to the Col de Mantet at 1761m. Here a marshal pointed to the route ahead, an overgrown trail that would stay close to the road to the next CP at Py (1044m) at 41.8km. This trail was quite narrow and I could feel the temperature dropping as the sun set. Py CP had two elderly ladies behind a small picnic table and they very nicely said I could have one of something – a biscuit or a cracker that they had spread out on a small table etc. They didn't have much so I took a biscuit – my hunger could have taken everything. Lack of food now started to play on my mind as I was about ¾ of the way to the back of the field and I was starting to get worried about having nothing later on arriving either after the food has run out or if the stocks are severely rationed. It was now starting to get dark and the path was very indistinct as I thought through the rest of the race. I tried to catch up three runners in front as this would make route finding easier but could not so settled in to my own company doing my own route finding which was hard at times in the failing light. Coming through the Col De Jou (918m) at 46.2km I knew I would not reach the Life Station in daylight so now had my head torch on as the rain started. The head torch strap was at a really annoying place when it came to my head wound as was half on my head and half on the bandage. What this meant was the head torch was slowly but surely pulling the bandage down my head.

At around 48k the trail joins a quiet road and I managed to pick up some speed and catch and overtake a runner. Then I was back in to the inky darkness of the night on my own in the rain. I was quite pleased to see Vernet-les-Bains (684m) and I knew my race was over. Even if I could get patched up and get a head torch on the prospect of doing two further nights, with no sleep and being unclear on food, just didn't seem appealing. Although the mind rules the body on this occasion the body was using a rarely seen 'overruled' card. Part of the problem was I knew tonight would be sub-zero. I knew

I'd be heading out pretty much alone and going up high and if I ran in to problems with the headtorch not being able to sit on my head what would I do? I could carry it in my hand but that would mean no walking poles and progress would be slow. As I headed in to the checkpoint all these thoughts were going around my head as to have come so far and only done about 50k was bitterly disappointing. On entering the CP several people gave me a good look as I had a bandage wrapped tightly around my head and blood had come through it. I asked one of the organisers if there was a first aider and he said there was someone who was more than a first aider but less than a paramedic who would have a look. I went to the medic in the back of the hall who cleaned up the wound and with his assistant holding my head still put some stiches in. I asked his view as to whether I could go on and he said I could but he would not recommend it as the wound could open. At this point I didn't really have a choice. I went to a table and ate some food and texted E back in the UK looking for a mix of sympathy and advice. E's take was not to rush anything as I was about 4hrs ahead of the cut-off and have a think about things. After a bit of thought I decided to pull out and handed my number in to an organiser. Having put in months of training this was a big deal handing in this little piece of paper as that meant game over for not just the race but getting to 100 miles in 2017 as there was no 'plan B'. I asked what happened now and was told there would be a bus around 00:00 to the end and there would be a hall to sleep in. The hall was good news - I was regretting not having a hotel room in reserve but I'd not booked anything on the Friday night to save some money! It was only about 20:00 so there was plenty of time to wait to watch other runners come in and then disappear out in to the very wet night. The hours ticked by and slowly the CP closed down and we were told there was a bus outside and about 10 of us went to it – all with our tails hanging between our legs. I was first on the bus and asked the driver a question about how long the journey would take and he explained he did not speak English so could not understand me. As the only non-French person on the bus I thought it was going to be a lonely night drive until a fellow competitor, Victor, asked the driver the question in French then told me it would be about two hours. For the next two hours Victor and I talked about all sorts of things – he was a very friendly person. He had previously done the shorter 112k version of the race and now having done the first 51k had done the complete course, albeit in two different years. His problem had been excessive vomiting and not able to keep anything in so he had no energy to continue.

We arrived in Argeles-sur-Mer around 02:00 and the bus driver stopped near the race end. In front a van was turning down a road that would lead to the race end. Somehow Victor recognised the van from Font Romeu and asked the driver could we follow it and get our bags. The driver said yes, so Victor and I left our running bags (passport, bank cards and all) on the bus and set off jogging after the van. All the others runners came behind us walking. The van stopped at the race end tent and the driver got out and Victor explained we would like our main bags as we had withdrawn. The driver was OK with this if we took all the bags out and put them in the tent until we found them. We had little choice and, along with the driver, started to empty the van. Other runners stood back and if their bag came out, they took it and left. Victor's bag came quite quickly but he was not going to leave me so we carried on. In the end it took about half the van to be emptied until we spotted my bag. Grabbing it quickly Victor said 'quick, back to the bus' and we jogged back to where we had left it on a roundabout. We got on and I was surprised that all the other runners had gone – our race bags remained which was a good sign. Now it was time to drive to the sports hall. I tried my best to look out for landmarks as I'd have to work my way back in daylight and after a few minutes the driver dropped us off at a hall. The hall was locked and empty. Victor asked the driver to wait while he phoned the organisers. The driver said he would and the bus slowly moved forward at walking pace on its way back to the main road. Suddenly it accelerated and it was off in to the dead of night. It was now around 02:40 and Victor and I stood outside this hall having been unable to contact anyone. We talked about the prospect of sitting on the step for the night as this looked a distinct possibility. Shortly after this Victor got through to the organisers on the phone and they told him they would send along someone 'busty with a large chest' to open the hall for us. We both thought this odd and waited. After about 10 mins a man turned up, opened the door, and left. He was neither busty nor large chested. We went in. Now it turned out Victor had been here before so had a feel for where things were and we went to get gym mats. There was the main hall and a side room and Victor joked we could have a room each and said he would take the side room. I've seen many sports halls in races and bearing in mind this was for those who had withdrawn I expected food/water to be available and there was neither. For food I was OK as my main bag (thanks Victor!) had this in it. Water was a real problem. My throat was as dry as I had drunk nothing from about 23:00 and I now had the prospect of a night in a sports hall with no shops opening until around 10:00 on Sunday morning. It was also really cold in the unheated hall. I took two gym floor mats and put on all my clothes and got in to my survival bag and got some warmth and drifted off in to an uncomfortable sleep. My mind whirring with feelings of failure and asking why I'd quit. My mouth and tongue really dry and sore. I woke up wet having overheated in the survival bag so took a lot of clothes off and got back in the wet foil bag. I had an uneasy sleep and woke up around 06:30 no longer alone in the room - about 10 other runners had arrived in the night. What really irked me was I'd been sleeping on two mats and I was now on one with a random man snoring on the other about 2m from me. How on earth he had got the mat in the night from under me I don't know. Also, why he didn't take from the big bundle I don't know. I can only assume I must have agreed in a semi-sleep state to the arrangement but if I talked to him the dark and gave up a mattress what else had I done in the dark? I checked and could see I still had my passport etc. so all seemed good. At this point my throat was really sore from dehydration so I decided to drink the water from the showers. My thinking was I might get sick but it would take several hours and at least I'd have quenched my thirst until then.

Drinking tepid water in a communal shower from a shower hose is not the nicest thing to do.

From the night before when I was having problems E had contacted the hotel we had booked (Hotel Beau Rivage) for the Saturday (and several more nights) explaining my predicament. They were nothing but helpful saying they would let me in the room as soon as possible on the Saturday. In my head I thought 11:45AM was acceptable so now just had to get to them.

I went to the toilet in the sports centre and left about 09:30 to walk to town to buy some food/water. The shops opened at 10:00 so with some food I headed down to the course end on the sea front and had my breakfast. It was hard to sit so close to the end thinking what might have been. The minutes ticked by and I started to need the bathroom and this feeling only got greater. It was as if I had a large balloon full of water inside me that wanted to burst but not in a good way. In the end I decided to try and check-in and arrived at the hotel around 11:00. The person who checked me in, whose name I regretfully cannot remember, was amazing both on that day and throughout our stay. He let me check in and was so helpful in every possible way. I made a mental note if ever I come back for this race, I'm definitely staying at the Hotel Beau Rivage. Now that all remained was to pass the time until E arrived which would be around 19:00.

After a well needed shower and some proper food I decided to head out to recce the end of the course and walked along the sea front and up in to the mountains, about 10k in total, to the last CP. I enjoyed telling runners they did not have far to go and they seemed grateful for this information. After admiring the view from the CP, I headed back down and after more food headed up to the station to meet E. This meeting should have been so much more. It should have been in the early hours of Sunday morning at the race finish and should have been amazing as I paddled in the sea against, perhaps, better judgement. I headed up to the station feeling very sheepish as I'd dragged E all the way to the bottom of France for nothing. I say for nothing but it was the start of our week-long France holiday so whilst the start location was clearly my choice there were going to be good things to come. It was good to meet E then walk 3k back to the accommodation and check-in. I need not have worried about feeling sheepish as it was what it was.

The next day we again headed back up the course seeing the back-markers from the 100-mile race. We went high up in to the hills and the views were amazing. We then headed back to the race end and I collected my drop bag that had been returned. That evening we went out to a local fish restaurant which was most pleasant – out of season the area is warm and very quiet so it makes a great location to visit.

All in the race gave me mixed feelings. On a good day I could have done it. From now on I'll use photochromatic sunglasses (CAT1 to CAT3) in races and have bought a pair from Decathlon for £24.99. I know it would have been cold heading in to the first night but without the head injury I would have left the 51k mark and pressed on.

For a race to be a challenge failure has to be distinct possibility and I'd experienced this on my two 100-miler attempts. 2018 was hopefully going to be TDS year so the next 100-mile attempt would be 2019 or 2020. I just need to find the right one to target in 2019 and give it my best shot.

17 ECOTRAIL PARIS 2018

The really good news for 2018 was that I'd secured a place in TDS in August – all I needed to do was to select some warm-up races and keep on top of my fitness and training. At some point in 2017 I'd decided I wanted to do three French races within 12 months. I'd gone for the Sud de France 100 in October 2017 as my main race, Ut4M in August 2017 as my warm up and the Ecotrail Paris in March 2018 as a fast one to get things going in 2018.

The Ecotrail Paris takes place on Saturday the 17th March and, for me, would be hard with a 12hrs45mins cut off for the 80k course which is listed as (4,2,350). The difficulty is compounded with a 12:15 start as this means a lot of the race would be in the dark. The race is billed as being 92% off road, on trails cutting through parkland and forests from Saint Quentin-en-Yvelines in the south eastern outskirts, and finishes on the first floor of the Eiffel Tower. When I entered, in November 2017, I had visions of running through lush parkland on woodchip trails admiring the handsome bulbs flowering in the spring air. As well as the 80k race there are shorter races of 45 and 30k and the additional race up the Eiffel Tower for a lucky 100. To enter the Eiffel race runners first had to set a pre-qualifying time in the past 12 months over another distance (e.g. sub 1:50 half marathon) then enter a ballot – if successful they would get to race on Wednesday 14th so would have time to rest post-race before the main event on the Saturday. I'd entered the ballot, and been unsuccessful, but was glad to have tried as to climb right to the top by stairs is something that members of the public cannot do. I'd first seen the staircase in the Tintin book 'Prisoners of the Sun' and had been interested in the structure ever since. On Weds 14th March I received a text with a hyperlink telling me to download a form I would need to get my race number- the link didn't work so I decided not to worry about it. This would become more of an issue when trying to register in Paris later in the week.

The Eurostar to Paris proved very convenient and within 45 minutes of arriving I was in my accommodation at the Eiffel Rive Hotel very close to the finish by the Eiffel Tower. I put the 'minimum kit' in my race bag and took the metro to Ballard which is the nearest station to Port de Versailles where the race numbers are distributed. It's about a ten-minute walk to the Port de Versailles which turns out to be a series of seven buildings that could host concerts, sporting events, expos and the like. I got to security at building 1 and showed my paperwork – a lady behind a desk told me I was at the wrong place but did not know where I should go. I started to fumble in my bag to see if I had anything else and they waved me through their barrier and told me to go inside building 1 to seek help. In the building itself hundreds of people had tickets and were getting them checked to go in a door – there was a 'help desk' nearby so I went there. The help desk lady told me I was in the wrong place and I should leave the building, turn right, and go up the stairs and it was all up there. I left the building, turned right and realised there were no stairs but met another security guard. At first, he told me he spoke no English but after a bit we were able to talk about what I was trying to do and he explained I needed hall 4. I left the area around hall 1 and walked back through security on to the pavement outside i.e. outside the complex. I then walked along to the next security area and could see some people were stopping to get searched and others just sailing through. Feeling as if things were taking ages I decided to sail through and had no problems. Now I was in an inner sanctum with several halls including hall 4. I passed a man who was selling bus tickets to Vladivostok – it would take 49 days and would be the ultimate Atlantic to Pacific adventure – and kept walking. In the distance I could see an 'Ecotrail' sign on a building so was getting close. I could then see a smaller 'Ecotrail' sign on a door and went in. I'd arrived at the Salon Destinations Nature where I knew I had to register. This time there was a turnstile and security and they would not let me in as I did not have a copy of the form they had sent me a hyperlink to on the 14th. They sent me to an 'Ecotrail' desk to the right and the man there asked if I had my dossard paperwork that will have been sent to me via a phone message. I explained that the hyperlink had not worked and he asked to see the message on my phone. I showed him and it said my race number was 1640. He asked me to type '1640' in to an 'Ecotrail' app on a PC and this returned a 'number not found' message. Undeterred he said not to worry and gave me a pass for the exhibition which I presented to the turnstile man and got in. All I had to do now was to work out where to go. There were about 200 booths selling all manner of outdoor related holidays from extreme outdoor sports to fruit tasting trips in the sun. I eventually found the Ecotrail section which was well organised in that all I had to do was to join the '1600-1699' queue with one person in front and no-one behind. The man in-front was given an envelope of bits and, in French, he asked what every bit was and was told. They chatted a bit about the pack and he left - now it was my turn. I showed my passport and was handed an envelope and was given a 'merci' and he looked away. I asked could he go through it with me and he said 'it is obvious – it is all in there'. At this point I'd found many things non-obvious so asked could he still go through it with me explaining the bits and he did. I'm glad I asked as many things were not obvious e.g. the red wrist band – was this for my bag or me? There was a tag with my number on that was for my race bag but what was the additional red tag with my name and number on for? The wrist tag was for me and the second red name/number tag was for a drop bag should I want one. I headed out in to the expo and the only person who approached me was someone from Ut4M asking if I wanted to talk about their races as I might enjoy them. I've no idea why he selected me, and not others, or why no other race tried to chat with me, but it did seem an odd coincidence at the time. Fully registered it was now time to head back to the accommodation to sort out my bag for tomorrow – all in it had taken 2hrs45 of which only 30 mins was on the metro train - registering really can take time.

It was now time to double check the cut-offs on the 'road book' that had been provided at registration. Although it was called a 'road book' it was only a postcard sized piece of paper with key information. In it I could see the distances were not the same as the distances on the paperwork I had from the website. Basically, the race had grown by 2k. Coupled with this I could see that although the race started at 12:15 everyone had to be through the start gate by 12:30. This may not seem much of an issue but if you are a marginal candidate in a fast race this sort of thing counts. Still information is everything so time to do some calculations. When I looked at the cut-off times, I could see things were even worse as making the first cut-off by a small margin would mean being timed out later down the course. E.g. the Entrée Parc St-Cloud was at 63k with a cut-off of 23:00 and St-Cloud was at 67k with a cut-off of 23:30 i.e. the runner needs to average 8kmph when ¾ way through the race. Compare this with the cut-off at Buc (22k) of 15:45 i.e. 3hrs 15 so 6.29kmph. Now if someone is only just making the first section within the cut-offs (say they are doing 7kmph) there is no way they are going to get faster later on in the dark. Taking all of this in to account I decided to generate my target times based on completing the event – I needed to cover these first 22k in 3hrs to have a fighting chance of getting around the course. As I drifted off to sleep, I kept telling myself I needed to cover between 8 and 9 k in both the first and second hours and as long as nothing went wrong I could do it. I also told myself I needed to be cautious and not go too fast as the start as this would mean I'd get timed out later on.

Upon waking on Saturday, the first thing I did was to check the weather – it was saying rain at 12:00, 14:00 and 20:00 with 20-30% chance of rain for the rest of the day – this wasn't that bad so I sorted my bits out and walked to Montparnasse station (about 2k) to catch the train to the start. We'd been told to catch a 09:05, 09:35, 10:05 or 10:35 train that would take 37 minutes using the free train ticket that had been provided at race registration. At the station an army of brightly coloured runners were staring at the departures board. It was 09:00 and the first two trains were not up there. Suddenly a train was advertised on the board departing at 09:14 that would take 24 minutes so we all went for that. Before long hundreds of runners were boarding the train and sitting down – either lost in their own thoughts or talking with their race buddies. I knew the drop-out rate was about 11% so I looked down the carriage wondering who it would be. Would it be those in road running shoes who would have no grip? Would it be those with minimal clothing who would suffer in the cold? I found myself doing this then stopped it as I thought it was bad – of course I wanted everyone to realise their dreams and who was I to judge others based on no knowledge of who they were or what their journey had been? I'm sure others had the same thought looking at me – would the man sitting on the flip down seat by the door make it up the Eiffel Tower? We arrived at a stop for Versailles and about 2/3 of the passengers got up and left – their race was going to be 45k and would start from here.

Before long we arrived at our destination and now all we had to do was to get the shuttle bus to the start. We all exited the train and dropped down to an underpass with both ways saying 'Sortie'. Unsure what to do some went to the right, while I and some others went to the left. Slowly we had a greater number of people so now everyone was walking to the left and wherever that would lead. Truth be told I didn't have a clue but sometimes it pays to be decisive as the direction was never going to be resolved until we left the confines of the underground station! Outside there was a paved courtyard and I could see a bit of 'Ecotrail' marker tape tied to a lamppost so walked over to that and pointed it out to the others – dozens followed. In my mind it was now just a question of looking for tape and that would take us to the shuttle bus to the start. I spotted the next bit so, quite pleased, walked over to that and about 60% of those who had got to the first bit followed. A fellow competitor walked in completely the opposite direction and shouted something and, all of a sudden, everyone followed. We crossed back over the railway (so the other exit downstairs would have been better) and then turned right along a road and, about a few hundred metres away, four buses with an 'Ecotrail' sign on them were parked - result! We got on and before long set off on the 2-mile drive to the start. I had considered walking this but was glad I had not as there was a nasty junction with no provision for pedestrians. We pulled up in a lay-by and the bus driver put his warning lights on and out we got. We passed what looked like a seldom used fairground and came to a trellis table and two men with 'securité' on their jackets. They said something to me that I did not understand and I thought they may want to see my race number (that I had tied to my rucksack) so turned around and showed them this and they waved me through. Ahead I could see a few tents, a few curtainwall trucks with the curtains open and the toilets. In the spirit of being eco-friendly the urinal was a plastic pipe of around 200mm diameter and about 4m long that had been fashioned in to a trough. It was inclined so it poured in to a black bin. I needed to go but as it was right on the path it didn't feel right to be peeing with people milling around a few feet behind me so opted for a cubicle. These were in-situ pine builds that had a hole for a seat and a pile of sawdust – the one I entered had already had someone splash around the seat hole and as there was no toilet paper or anything like that, I did feel sorry for anyone who wanted to sit down. Fortunately, I only needed to stand up so did my business and left with my unwashed hands to the breakfast tent. This had cake cut in slices, cups, instant coffee in a jar and water containers. I'd banked on the breakfast tent having more but this was it. I needed to drink so decided I'd have a cold coffee if needs be. I grabbed a few slices of cake from the bundle and put some coffee powder in the cup and filled up the water – it was good to see it steaming! It was now around 10:15 and the next challenge was to work out what to do for two hours. The ground was wet and it looked like it was about to rain heavily. I could see a small tent on the right and headed in there – about 25 people were sitting down on camping benches and I could spot two spaces near the door and one down the far end between two people – I thought I've got two hours to kill and need to stay warm so would go to the far end and squeezed in next to a woman called Nadine. It was only going to get colder so I took a few layers of clothing out of my bag and put them on – each time elbowing Nadine due to the limited space. Outside we could hear pop music playing on loud speakers whilst the rain started to patter on the canvas roof. It now dawned on me I was in here till the start so there would be no more food, or toilet trips. This was it. Over the next hour more people would come in until we had 28 sitting and 25 standing and the space was tight for all. Of the stand-ees many came in to rub anti-friction lubricant on their bits – you would think people were in the comfort of their private homes as they rubbed themselves up – both male and female. One chap came in with a casual holdall and stood in-front of me. He took his coat off and had a tight long-sleeved t-shirt on below. He took his shoes off and stood on the coat in his socks. Next, he took his jeans off and below he was wearing very tight briefs – blue with green rectangles on them. Mr Left was well and truly outside the barracks and hung there looking like the head of a mad-scientist who was touching a Van de Graff generator. It's hard to believe he didn't know Mr Left was doing this about two feet from my face. Next, he took his shorts out and pulled them over everything and put his shoes and coat back on. Now it was time to lube. He pulled his anti-friction cream out– it looked like toothpaste. Another man spotted it and asked could he have some and the owner of Mr Left said 'oui'. The other chap squeezed it on to his fingers – rubbed his nether regions then squeezed more on the same fingers for good measure for another go and passed it back. This man was a deep vigorous rubber playing it all out about four feet from my face on the left. Mr Left then took the cream and squeezed it on to his fingers and then gave himself a good two-handed rub, grab and adjust. Job done everyone was back in silence trying not to make eye contact.

'Nathan' was the next to strip off and what struck me as unusual was the tattoo he had on his calf. He had a shark with massive teeth jumping out of the water and over some palm trees. The shark had arms extending forward. On the back of the shark was a naked busty lady that looked like it had been touched up to draw a bikini on it at some later date but the lines looked all wrong. Above this it said 'Nathan' and below 'Sabine'. I wondered if he were Nathan and saw himself as some sort of tree jumping shark with arms or what did it mean. I was really cold in the tent and had lost feeling in my toes but it was now 12:00 so time to head outside in to the rain for one last toilet visit. Outside about 2000 people were amassed sheltering where they could – most standing looking miserable and cold. It was now time for the mass urination session as lots of people were peeing in the parkland around the start. I knew time was going to be tight in the race and estimated it would take about 5 minutes for everyone to cross the start line. I thought I was about a 'back quarter' finisher but didn't want to miss out on vital minutes on the gun time and get timed out later on down the course. Based on this I estimated where about 1-minute back was and joined the pack there. Normally when you get in the pack you can feel the warmth emanating and get some shelter but everyone was cold in the rain so it was not warm at all.

First to set off were some 'Run Handi Move' runners who set off with a cheer from the crowd. The minutes ticked away then it was our turn. Two horses led the field as we set off – it took me 40-seconds to reach the start line from the gun time so in my head I knew I had to go that bit faster to complete without being cut-off. Of the 2500 entries about 2198 had turned up so it was a big field at the start, bigger than most races I'd entered. After we ran under the start gantry the pack widened out as we ran down a muddy field towards the shore of a lake – as soon as we got there the pack slowed to a walking pace as everyone seemed to want to keep their feet dry. As it was pouring with rain and we were in for a strong soaking this seemed a bit pointless to me so, along with two others, went through the water everyone was sidestepping around – this one move of about 50m made up a good 50 places – back to the running. At the next section like this a man came hopping towards me with one shoe on – his other was sinking in to the mud – I've no idea if he salvaged it as I was just focused on trying to get some warmth in and completing 8-9k in the first hour. The rain was quite heavy and, with everyone running in close proximity, the only sound was a crinkly noise of raindrops hitting 2000 coats. For the entire race there was never any random chat going on between strangers – I put this down to the pace we moved at. I've found in races the nearer you get to the front the less sociable things become and everyone is just focused on moving quickly.

At about the 8k point we left the lake and headed towards the railway station from a few hours ago – to cross the tracks there was a concrete bridge and again everyone slowed to a stop to queue for the stairs. As so many were running on this long bridge it started to bounce in a most unpleasant manner, particularly near the end as the concrete came up and slapped the base of the feet. Down the steps and back to the railway station this time taking the markers I'd nearly followed earlier in the morning then off in to some woodland for many more kms. I was now worried my pace was a little fast as I predicted I'd cover 20k in under 2 hrs. This was balanced against a few thoughts though. Firstly, although CP1 is at 22k what if it was actually 22.9k in to the course – this would mean everyone would have to go even quicker so as not to be timed out. Balanced against the 'am I going to fast' feeling was the contradictory feeling of 'this course is going to get more and more slippy so I need to be as far along it as quickly as possible'.

From about 500m out I could see CP1 that sat slightly lower than the trail in a valley to the left. I crossed the timing mat in 730th position and it was 14:29 with an official distance of 22.7km so things were going well – completing the course within 12hrs was starting to look possible. There were numerous tents serving snack food and water and there were lots of runners milling about. I saw a fellow British runner so had a quick chat – he told me the course gets far worse from this point on so it is important to have something in reserve. I took on a few snacks but in taking my gloves off my fingers got really cold, no feeling down to the second knuckle, it would be about 30 mins after I got my gloves back on that feeling would be restored. It now started to snow and the rest of the day would be either snow or rain. My fellow Brit was correct in that this next section was km after km of short steep up/down hills the trail getting really churned up now with the passing of so many runners. I was wary of going too fast so on any wide section I'd slow down to let other runners past.

At about 43k I was getting really cold and started to see what looked like some sort of chateau and we entered a side gate in to a very posh formal garden. We carried on through the estate and I had visions of the CP being in a nice dry stable block. How wrong was I. The CP was at 46k (1km further than the road book stated) and it was now 18:02 and I'd slipped back to 1072nd place. As I stood at the CP, on an exposed terrace in front of a grandiose large building, I pondered how nice it would be on a warm day. Realising it would be dark soon I quickly left my daydream and now pushed on as hard as I could to make as much distance in daylight as possible. This next part was quite impressive as we cut through the grounds of the Meudon Observatory – as well as the large building housing the telescope there were extensive manicured grounds that the course ran through. There was a small crowd here cheering everyone along which was a nice touch. Leaving this we went back in to the woods and the slippy muddy trails. A number of people were falling off the track to the side but I managed to keep going OK. The next worry was darkness as things would only get worse so I decided to push really hard until it was time to get my headtorch out at around 48k. To try and save weight I'd consciously not packed my heaviest, and brightest, Petzl NAO torch. Instead I had a lighter torch that was not as bright. As the woods were really dark, I regretted this. Slowly but surely a singing French runner caught me up who had a Petzl NAO headtorch – this suited me fine to have her behind me and she did not seem to want to overtake. We carried on for a bit together but I ended up pulling away and catching a group in front.

Suddenly on a downhill it all went a bit wrong for me. I think my foot caught something under the mud and I tripped and fell face forward landing with a pained 'huuuuuuuuuuuuuuuh' noise. Everyone behind me stopped and a fellow runner said 'are you OK?'. Whilst he said this, I checked my teeth with my tongue to see if they were all there (they were) and looked round over my right shoulder and said 'I'm OK'. My right walking pole was off to my right and I went to reach for it and my right lower leg went in to a spasm. He said 'are you really sure you are OK?' and I said 'I'll be fine' and he said 'let me get your pole' and he passed it over. I now got up and he looked at me again and asked 'do you really think you are OK to continue' and I said 'I'm fine thanks – perfectly OK – thanks for helping me' and I headed off a little surprised that no-one had overtaken me when I was down and no-one was overtaking me now. The first pain I could feel was around my left eye and it seemed to be swelling a bit. Now I've had a few black eyes in my time so know how they feel and thought it was a possibility but I'd have the right eye so would be OK. Next, I could taste blood on my lips and no matter how much I cleared it the blood kept coming – this was down to a cut nose and a minor nose bleed. Being cold, and it being in heavy rain/snow, I didn't want to stop so just kept pushing on. Eventually the bleeding stopped and now it was about getting some food/water in and continuing along the course to the next CP due at 57k. It's fair to say these were not the best kms I've ever run. I was cold, injured, the weather was terrible and the path a quagmire. It would have been easy to have got miserable about this but I refocused and at each hill wished we would go up-down-up-down (as we often did) and would be disappointed if a simple single up-down. I'd re-framed the experience to be harder than it was and mentally it was working for me.

At the next CP, which was at 57.7k, I was running in 1077th and it was now 19:57. Despite having a fall I had only lost five places which is nothing really. I took a photo of myself to assess the damage and could see I'd cut my chin quite a bit and a few other cuts to the face – looking at my legs I could see my knees had also taken some damage. I felt pleased that I did not have my expensive Gore-Tex trousers on at the time as they would have been ripped! The next 10k were really just twists and turns in hilly parkland with the occasional road crossing. Everyone was really wet and cold at this point – rain was a positive as it was slightly warmer than snow so brought a tiny sliver of relief. The final CP was stated to be 67k but was actually 69.3k and I was still 1077th and arrived at 22.05. This was a series of trellis tables under tents that had food and drink laid out. I had two small cups of warm soup that went down a treat. Putting some cubes of cheese and chocolate in to a small plastic bag I headed out across the churned-up quagmire to continue down the course munching on my newly sourced fuel. Now all I had to do was to get to the Seine at approximately 72k and the danger would be over. These last few off-road kms passed very quickly and suddenly there was traffic and a hard-paved surface underfoot.

I knew I was sub 12hr and my target now changed to sub 11hrs45 so I'd finish by 00:00 on the Eiffel Tower. I plugged hard on this last 8k walking around 6.5-7kmph. The rain just kept driving down and I just wanted to see the tower to know I was nearly there. It was 76.93k before I could see it so now knew it was going to be less than 30 mins to the end. Near the tower the course leaves the riverside path and crosses to the tower where crowds had assembled to cheer on their loved ones. I got cheerful shouts of 'International' as I came through and headed to the base of the north leg. The stairs took no time at all and I managed to overtake five people on them – I could have taken a sixth but he wouldn't let me past which was a bit annoying but it made no real difference on the overall time finishing in 1079th in 11:31:54. At the end a man in a large green hat gave me my medal and said 'well done, it was tough out there, you did well' and after a few photos I picked up my t-shirt and looked around the snowy first floor of the Eiffel Tower. I'd made it and it felt amazing! There was a barrel of beer that the organisers were offering up to people who had their own cup but I was so cold I just wanted to get down and back to the hotel. Catching the elevator down was some respite from the weather then it was back out in to the cold and damp. The minimum cotation for the race had been stated as 350 and I thought my effort was the hardest I'd ever pushed myself (previous contender being CCC 2011) so I was hopeful of a cotation score of 450-470. It would be a few weeks before I found I had a score of 431.

On the 15-minute walk back to the hotel I tried to clean the mud off me and thought I'd done a good job. I arrived at the hotel and buzzed the night porter who came and let me in – I quickly said 'room 426' and walked straight past him and in to the lift. At my room I saw how covered in mud and blood I was and knew getting clean and dry was going to be a problem. I decided to change over the toilet so I could drop mud in there. This mostly worked except when my foot fell in and I managed to jam it just out of the water but it came out quite quickly. I needed some food so had some snacks and water and it was now time for bed, but the trouble was despite being physically fatigued I was mentally very alert. I went to bed around 02:00 and dozed off around 02:30 for a restless night getting up at 06:00. There was blood on both pillows and the sheets from my legs despite being fully clothed. As I'd pushed myself very hard during the race my legs now had limited power and I realised I could not pick things off the floor. I put my quadguards and calf-guards back on so now had the ability to bend to do things! After a large breakfast I left the hotel for a long slow walk around Paris ultimately visiting the empty zoo in the rain.

Next day I checked the results and found out that in my race 487 starters pulled out before reaching the end – the weather conditions had been very challenging. Despite the hardships of the race it felt really good to have completed it in a good time, particularly with the weather as it was. I knew I could have been a little quicker on the day, and a lot quicker if the course had been dry. The feeling of satisfaction grew over the coming days and it seemed like a long time to the next race, the Transylvania 80, even though it was only two months away.

18 TRANSYLVANIA 80 2018

Having completed the Transylvania 50 in 2017 I knew I wanted to come back for more. I wanted to try the longer 100k race and I also wanted E to come to the area as I thought she would really like it. Around Sep 2017 I entered the 100k race and we sorted out a plan to have a week's holiday out in Romania. We'd spend a little time in Bran (the race venue) visiting the castle then head back to Bucharest to see the sights.

For 2018 the organisers included an 80k option so now they had races of 20, 30, 50, 80 and 100k which makes the event really inclusive. After a few weeks I realised having entered the 100k race I'd be starting at 05:00 on the Saturday and finishing 24ish hours later. This presented a bit of a problem for our holiday as I'd need to sleep at some point on the Sunday, so E would have several days waiting around. I changed to the 80k as thought better for both of us.

Getting to the start in Bran was really easy having done it before (!). Flight from Heathrow to Bucharest airport on the Thursday then the bus to the Gara de Nord station staying that night in the nearby Ibis. After some food we headed out to see the parliament building lit up at night. The next day we caught the 08:07 train from Gara de Nord and arrived at Brasov at 10:45. From here it is a 3k walk to 'bus station number 2' where we caught the 12:00 bus to Bran arriving in the Hanul Bran hotel at 12:45. After a short rest I packed the race bag for kit check then we walked past Bran Castle to the sports hall to register and collected my race number. Back to the hotel to drop the race bag off and then we headed to Bran Castle to sightsee. Next it was time for an early evening meal at around 17:30 then back to the hotel to rest. All very easy when you've done it before!

For a 05:00 race start we thought it best to get up at 03:30 so set two alarms and went to bed at 21:30. Often when travelling we put in ear plugs to give a peaceful night's sleep but with the early start was wary of doing this. It quickly became apparent there are a lot of trucks going through Bran at night so after about 20 mins the ear plugs were in! The trouble now was I had a nagging doubt I'd not hear the alarms so repeatedly woke up to check my watch, at one time reading 02:35 so told myself time to start to wake up and be ready. 03:30 seemed a long time coming but I'd actually misread it as I'd seen 22:35. I knew this as the next time I spotted was 00:05. I carried on checking my watch about every 30 mins and got up just before 03:30 for my banana sandwich breakfast. I paced around a bit as I wanted to defecate but nothing was happening down there so, reluctantly, got in to my race kit and we headed out at around 04:30. At the last minute E persuaded me to carry a small packet of tissues lest I see a toilet later in the day. Sometimes at the start of a race I look around everyone else and see that I seem to have the biggest bag and I question myself as to what I'm carrying noting there is nothing that can be done about it now. I'd decided to carry three pairs of gloves thinking this would mean I would have a dry pair for the night – was this overkill?

The start was very dark with hundreds of people waiting in the shadow of Bran Castle. About 200 runners were taking on the 100k and there would be 67 in my 80k race. Both routes follow the same course for the first 27k then the 100k people do an extra bit before re-joining the 80k course to the end. At the start the organisers gave a warning about thunder saying that the 100k runners may be changed to the 80k course dependent on the weather but would see how things played out. Around Bran castle are a number of stone lined ditches about 1m deep that have no fence next to them. I was taking a pic of the castle and dropped right in to one cutting my knee and elbow – bleeding before we had even started! It wasn't long before 05:00 came and we were off – everyone slow running the first few kms from the castle. I gave a wave to E on one of the early bends hoping she would have a good day out at nearby Rasnov Castle, the location where the film 'Cold Mountain' was filmed.

Knowing something of the route has distinct advantages as I could pace myself going up the first major hill. Bran is at 750m ASL and the first summit is around 2200m at 10k in to the race. Compared to last year there was a lot less snow so finding paths should be easier. Before the race I'd set myself target times for each CP and at the first one I was 40mins up which was a good sign. Quickly eating snacks at CP Malaiesti, I could see the route highlight, the snow gully far ahead. This is the gully where, in 2017, the bear had been growling whenever we stopped our snowy ascent. The rain had really set in now (before long it would change to hail then rain/hail most of the day) so it was time to put on my waterproof trousers before heading on and up. I took a small bag of food and set off with gloves and poles in one hand whilst I ate my bag of cheese/raisins/chocolate slowly but surely gaining height. I've done this eating/moving approach for years as over a long race it really saves time. Food finished I went to put my gloves on and saw I had only one. What an idiot to have lost a glove. I was carrying three pairs just in case but decided to go back to look for it and found it after a few mins which was good. I put it on and headed back up the course. This year the visibility in the gully was good and suddenly to the right of the track I saw what I thought was a dzo (without horns). This would seem very unlikely but it is what I thought I could see having seen many in Nepal. As I got closer, I could see I was wrong and it was a large brown bear. My first response was 'hope it stays there' then on closer examination I could see it was spread-eagled on top of a large rock and was not moving. I then realised it was dead having taken a fall and landed there. Was it the bear I'd heard last time in this gully?

Carrying on past this we kept going higher and higher the trail now getting slippy. I managed to overtake a few others by sidestepping round them in the snow then back on to the 'staircase' that had been created by every runner stepping in the same bit of snow on the way up the ever-steepening gully. Coming near the top we all kept stopping as the final exit was steep and slippy and everyone needed to use the rope that was hanging down. My turn came and I put my poles in my left hand and gripped the rope with my right and tried to power up but I ended up just churning snow. Not good. Next, I gripped the rope with both hands with my poles in my left hand and ended up spinning under it. Still not good. Finally, with some brute quad strength, I powered on up over the top on to the ridge that would lead to the summit of mount Omu (2534m). As per last year the top was shrouded in mist and this was the case until we dropped below about 2000m but this would be a little further ahead. In the mist the path clung to a narrow ledge on a small cliff face and I could hear what sounded like a pained goat ahead – not sure what creature it was. Suddenly on this very narrow path a mountain dog came towards me and squeezed past – no idea where it was going. The goat noise came again. I had no idea what creature was around the bend but carried on as it was on the path. It was a marshal with a vuvuzela! When we eventually dropped out of the mist it was now just a question of getting to the next CP at Pestera (1700m) that is 25k in to the course. This is a lovely section that is like running a remote valley in the French alps. There is a river at the bottom that has to be forded and other runners were hunting for an invisible bridge – no idea why anyone would think there would be a bridge here as the only way is to get in and ford the icy water!

Pestera is a good stop as it has warm food, benches and some friendly mountain dogs (this time with two puppies). It also feels as if you are 'down off the mountain' and is sheltered from the elements so there is some respite here. I took the opportunity to use the toilet – it is a single cabin built adjacent to a river in a beautiful spot. I opened the door to be treated with a disgusting mess – someone had defecated all over the toilet seat as if they had been trying to ice a large ring donut with their anus. The floor was covered in urine. I feel this is truly awful as this is someone's mountain hut that we had stopped at and some inconsiderate runners had done this to them – these local people who open their houses to help others do not deserve this. I used the tissues E had given me to remove a lot of the poo in to the bowl then squatted and did my business. There was a sign in Romanian saying 'do not put paper in the toilet but in the bin' so I did this but not sure others had as whoever had iced the toilet seat had left paper in the loo but I was not going to fish that out before I started. When you see this sort of thing your thoughts extend further to the food – we are all dipping our hands in to bundles of crisps, nuts etc. to select items to eat – what germs are lurking from dirty individuals in there?

Time was ticking so before long I was heading back up the mountain. This time everyone was in silence as we went up a rough rocky track that would gain us about 500m height in about 3k. At the top of this was Babele (2200m) where our routes would split. The 100k people would head back up Mount Omu on their extra loop and the 80k people would head straight to Piatra Arsa (1900m) which was about 5k away. It was very misty and all the 100k people peeled off in line and took a left. Another runner and I took a right and I quickly got lost in the mist. I could see one marker but could not find the one beyond that so started zig-zagging the mountain side for it. I had the route on my watch but it was of little use in this rocky misty area – I really needed to find the way off the mountain. The other runner clearly knew where to go as ran off in one direction with confidence. Then a pair of runners followed suit. I decided to catch them up and was quickly back on track. It frustrated me that they would not shout to catch my attention here, as if someone is lost, I feel it is the sporting thing to do. Once on route this next section is short and easy to follow and I caught, and passed them, at the next CP. The next 5k is crossing high fells where there is no path at all so it was important to try and keep on the 'track' as much as possible as it would help with river crossings. At one river the marker was on the edge and there was a drop of about 3m-4m to the water. I could see the bank was collapsing and had no real idea how to get down to the river but thought I may as well go to the edge and drop down the bank. As I stood on the edge a bit of ground, about the size of a coffin, broke off and I had two conflicting thoughts. My first thought was, environmentally, I'd done a bad thing and had contributed to the erosion. This was quickly followed by a second thought of 'can I surf this in to the river and stay dry to cross?'. As I slid down, I managed to stay upright and as we hit the water, I threw my weight one way to push my bit of earth in to the water, and it ended up making a new stepping stone for everyone. I still had to get wet stepping off it but I'd tried.

After about 10 river crossings, and one road crossing, the race route joined a real path as we headed on to Bolboci lake. I'd really wanted to see this as knew it was bear/wolf territory so had high hopes of an interaction on this next section. Back at Babele I'd passed two runners who knew where they were going and they now caught me up and overtook me. After a bit they started to irritate me as they were not any quicker but whenever I overtook them, they would overtake me back and run about 100 yards then revert to their slow walk. I think what irritated me the most was on one of these occasions they did their hundred-yard thing then both stopped, threw their running rucksacks off their back and faced each other on either side of the track. Next, they decided to have a simultaneous pee as I walked between them with their flappy bits watering the trail from either side. They in no way splashed me or anything like that but I thought it pretty weird. For the next few kms I had a bit of fun toying with them as I could force them to go faster than they wanted as they always wanted to be (just) infront of me. All this fun passed the time to Bolboci CP (1450m). My target time had been 15:20 and it was now 15:10 and the cut off was 21:00 so I had everything well under control. At this point 6 of the 100k runners had been through and about 30 of the 80 runners so it was quite quiet at this CP as the CP staff waited for the main pack who would arrive in 4-5hrs time. Here I had table service(!) of pasta and a cup of coffee. All very nice with a great view of Bolboci lake. The humidity was building and it looked like a storm was in the air so, before long, I set off on the trail. I could see two other runners up ahead so thought I'd do my own navigating and check I was on their route also as this was a 'belt and braces' approach to keep on track. As we gained height, I could see a storm building on Mount Omu far off to the right – at this point all the 100k runners should be off there so no-one was going to get caught out which was good.

The temperature started to drop and the wind pick up in a way that meant only one thing – there was an epic storm coming. I took a quick photo then put my camera away for the storm to come. In the distance was a massive rumble of thunder and the heavens opened. It was now around 16:00 and we had a large whaleback of a mountain to climb with several false summits. The path was indistinct at best – the organisers had put out a bike light every 200m as most would be traversing this in the dark so it was relatively easy to head in the right direction along the course. The rain was now torrential and the thunder getting closer so I caught the other two up and ended up overtaking them. For the next hour I led the route and they followed me the whole way. Next came the lightning – first to the left, then behind, then to the right. It was always between 2 and 5s before the thunder so striking between 500m and 1500m of our path.

Living on edge like this for a period of time is really mentally draining as it feels as if, at any point, a direct lightning strike could occur and there is nothing that can be done about it but to keep moving quickly on the mountain. In my head I started to think about withdrawing on safety grounds at the next CP. I had a similar feeling in CCC in 2010 that the risks were too high and when I decided to pull out then the organisers had decided to stop the event for safety grounds. The Transylvania races have more inherent risk than the UTMB ones due to the remoteness of the terrain and every runner who takes part is made well aware of this and signs a long waiver against all manner of things happening. It really came down to a personal assessment of risk and whether to stop balanced against here was the chance to take part in a grade A adventure. It's back to the moth and the flame – how close do you fly?

All the time we kept heading upwards on this mountainside being the three tallest things on it. I was about 30cm taller than the other two so started to ask myself questions about lighting and does it really go for the highest thing or is that a generalisation. I had no wish to be struck up here so sped up even more and we all kept plugging away in the rain and hail all the time wanting to be off this mountain. I really wanted the other two to lead on some of the navigation as having my left wrist exposed (to see the watch) meant my left hand was getting really cold but they were content to follow. I did a few illogical routes to see if they would stick to an obvious path and they did not - they just followed me very closely. I slowed down a little and they slowed. I sped up and they kept with me. No matter what they wanted to just follow. The only exception was about 1k out from the next CP when one of them passed me and headed off. He actually made good time arriving at the CP a few minutes ahead of us.

I was pleased to reach the CP at Bucşa (1700m) which comprised of a tent and a small fire, somehow burning outside in the rain. In the tent was a table with some food and I spotted a few flasks. I asked if there was a warm drink and was told 'yes' if I had a cup which I gladly took out of my bag. I was told it was coffee but it tasted like a fruit tea but it was warm! There was a medic in the tent who looked at me and said 'you are really cold'. I knew this as despite wearing Gore-Tex gloves my fingers could not bend and were bright red in contrast to my white hands. Of the other two runners the same could be said – we all had a bit of a problem. One of the runners said he would withdraw at the next CP so headed off - the reason for not withdrawing now was we were not on a road so noway of being picked up! The medic asked about the other runner and I and we both said we would continue once warm. My fellow runner was in a worse state than I was as his one pair of gloves were drenched and he had done the last leg without waterproof trousers. The medic managed to get some latex gloves on him so now it was my turn to get sorted. I pulled out my third pair of gloves and could not get them on – I asked the medic if she could check the fingers were good inside the gloves and she put them on no probs – clearly my fingers were the issue. With the help of someone else they managed to get some latex gloves on my hands then get them in to my dry Montane alpine guide mountain gloves. The warmth was amazing. When I entered the tent, my watch was recording an inner wrist temperature of 8 degrees and whilst staying in the tent it had risen to 12 degrees - over the next hour it would rise to a toasty 27 degrees - I was very pleased to have packed three pairs of gloves as I needed them. Without these gloves I would have withdrawn at the next CP and my race would have been over – thank you Montane!

This next section drops a lot of height through the woods and the relief of being out of lightning roulette was immense. As we were now in bear territory my fellow runner kept shouting so the bears would hear us – this is the recommended approach so as not to startle a bear. The rain stopped and the scenery was truly beautiful. I wanted to get my camera out but dare not remove my gloves as I was still warming up. It was a Romanian pasture with traditional buildings, bales of hay, cows and an amazing vista of storm clad mountains. The stiles were traditional ones that looked like two logs standing up like a large 'X' and were crossed by sliding them out of the way. This was new to me and I quickly came to realise crossing them was not quick as there was the dismantling and rebuilding each time! The CP at Moieciu de Sus (950m) came quickly – my target had been 20:00 and it was 19:50 so all on track. Here I sat down in the village hall and ate quite a lot of food and thought of the course ahead. It was really about pushing on as far as possible before it got dark and then the final wooded descent to the end.

It was now just my fellow runner and I with no-one around in any direction. We set off and he spotted a black and orange salamander on the trail – we passed many green/white slugs that must have been grateful for the rain as it made it easier to move. The path here slowly climbs up through the woods to around 1500m and it was now starting to get dark. We could see the last CP ahead on the left but the markers were gone. At this point a 100k runner came though and asked the way and I said it was a hard left to the CP. The CP staff seeing us stopped about 500m out started shouting 'over here' and shining torches and we got there quickly. They were surprised the markers had gone as they had checked them only 1hour ago so went out to check. This CP was manned by, amongst others, Danny and Pete. I'd met them about here in 2017 and people like them are the true heroes who make running in remote places possible, selflessly staying awake in remote spots helping others. It was nice to have a chat and a cup of coffee with them. My target time here was 21:30 and it was 21:31 so I thought things were going well!

It was now really dark for the final 15k to the end and I set off with my fellow runner following me. The underlying rock here is bright white and blocky so I kept thinking it was snow when it was not. I also saw some rocks that I thought was a sleeping white poodle. My fellow competitor sat on my tail so I asked did he want past and he said 'no – sore knee so damage limitation so happy here'. We carried on in silence until my watch ran out of power at around 17hrs. The stated life is 40hrs so now I had a bit of a problem. I knew my fellow runner also had a watch so asked could he navigate and he said 'sorry no – due to an error don't have route on my watch'. We came to a junction and I asked him what did he think? I said left due to the footfall and he said he wasn't going to give an opinion so left it was! At this point I thought he is not adding anything to my race and is a bit slower so I'll accelerate off so on the next uphill this is what I did. If he had called me back, I would have stayed with him but he didn't so that was OK. I now had a very slippy long descent in the woods on my own. At one point there was thick smoke and I could see little – who was up here in the dead of night with a fire? In the woods I kept seeing eyes watching me – mainly rabbits but your mind does play tricks at times knowing there are wolves and bears out there. Over the next 3hrs two of the 100k runners passed me and that was it. The path is overgrown so trees would spring back behind me and I'd snap round to see what was following or gaining on me to see nothing. I did not want a wildlife encounter up here. It was with some relief that the road came and I headed down this knowing there was a twisty section off road to come. The road passed quickly then it was up in to the twisty bit.

I had some conflicting thoughts about E – on the one hand I wanted to see her at the end but on the other didn't want her to be bored waiting. The target was 00:10 and now I was on for 01:00 so later than planned. As I approached several dogs barked from gardens but, fortunately, they stayed on their side of the fence. On the final section I tried to dismantle my poles to run in but being in gloves and tired could not so ran in to the end – E was on the right of the course so I said hello as I ran in and went under the banner. An official photographer took my pic as did some random person next to him. In races random people often take my photo so I'm used to it. It was only after about 30s I realised it was E who had quickly moved. Now this may seem odd but with fatigue, and bright lights, it was hard to see anything. After collecting my medal and diploma we headed back to the hotel for food and rest. Of the 67 starters in my race 53 would finish and I'd come 32nd finishing in 20hrs, 0 mins and 45 seconds and was quite content with my middling position. Although called an 80k race (with 4979m of ascent) the organisers say it is 82.9k however those with watches that lasted made it more like 90-91k so it is reasonably long but good training for other things – I didn't mind the extra distance.

The next morning, we were up at 07:00 for a quick breakfast before catching the bus and heading off to Brasov. As was the case in 2017 there was a large road race taking place with 10k, ½ marathon, and marathon distances – the Brasov International Marathon. It would be perfectly possible for one runner to do the Transylvania 50 on the Saturday and the other the marathon on the Sunday which may appeal to those couples who have differing views as to the best terrain to run on! We walked around Brasov to look at the historic buildings then caught our 14:25 train back to Bucharest to spend the remainder of our week in the capital. All in a great race full of adventure and far harder than any 80k race I've done to date.

19 ZUGSPTIZ ULTRA 2018

As my racing plan developed leading up to TDS I was convinced I needed a race about 100km long with about 5000m D+/D- in June as this would a be good test of fitness and kit. Look as I might on the ITRA website nothing quite fitted the bill – for sure there were races of that distance/height in that timeframe but there was always something that didn't quite work – typically, finding accommodation. The problem being that as soon as the races opened for on-line registration all the keen runners had entered and got the accommodation so there was nothing left for anyone applying later. It's really how a lot of races work now – you have to enter as soon as you can and secure accommodation/transport otherwise risk either missing out or having a very non-optimal arrangement such as staying >10k from the start necessitating a long walk before and after the event.

Undeterred my next approach was to do general web-surfing for non-ITRA accredited races. I know there can be some real high-quality events that fall in to this category such as the Lakeland 50/100 or the Andorra Ultra Trail series of races. In doing this I came across something called the Zugspitz Ultratrail which is Germany's biggest ultrarunning weekend. They have five races running over the weekend ranging from the Basetrail of 24.9k (with 1595m) right up to Ultratrail (102k 5480m). All races used the same course – the shorter races just starting a little further along the trail. The race is based in Grainau, which has a campsite and railway station, so logistically it was looking possible so I entered the Ultratrail and booked my flight.

As the days approached, I got more apprehensive in my mind about how intense the race weekend would be. I'd be leaving home at 05:00 on the Thursday to walk 3km to my local station then catch a train then a bus to Heathrow. At Munich I'd have two trains then a 2k walk to the campsite and I'd get there about 19:00. I'd then have to get my tent up and head to the local Aldi that shuts at 20:00 to get supplies. Friday would be relatively easy with race registration and sightseeing. On Saturday I'd have to get up at 05:00 and leave campsite by 05:30 for my 3k walk to the race start for kit check at 06:30. The race would start at 07:15 and I thought I'd finish about 05:25 on Sunday morning. I'd then walk the 3k back to the campsite and wait a few hours then dismantle my tent to catch a bus then two trains back to the airport for my flight at 17:40. At this point I'd have been up for about 36hrs. I'd then land at Heathrow and catch a bus and a train then a taxi to get home about 22:00 to then go to bed to be up at 05:20 the next day to go to work. The lack of sleep in the plan was what was bothering me but I kept telling myself it was all stages and all I had to do was to aim for one stage and complete it before considering the next.

Thursday went to plan but my bag just seemed so heavy. The big rucksack on my back, with tent, sleeping bag and all the trimmings, was as comfortable as carrying a sleeping sheep – its bony legs digging in to my shoulders and waist in a most uncomfortable fashion as I walked in to the campsite in Grainau. After checking in I had a choice of three areas to pitch my tent. The first was near the road and was an area about 10 m by 20m that also contained a kids climbing frame so I thought this could be noisy so would skip that one. The next one was on the far side of the campsite but near the toilet block so, again, I thought it could be noisy so decided against it. This left the final one that was next door to the coffee factory – I thought a factory is bound to be quiet at night so it seemed ideal and I wasn't disappointed. I arrived at the area and was met by a friendly man from the Netherlands, Matheus, who was in a group cycling from the Netherlands to the Vatican covering about 100km per day. He was very friendly and offered me half of his giant sausage he had cooked in a pan – being pescatarian I declined but it was a nice gesture. I quite enjoyed Friday night talking to Matheus about what he was doing and we chatted about possible routes to get to Italy. As well as the pilgrims there were five other runners in the campsite and we exchanged tales about other races we had all completed.

On Friday morning I headed off to register, walking the 3k to the race village which is in the centre of Grainau. The race village had the feel of Chamonix on a smaller scale – lots of stalls selling race gear, lots of people wandering around in various race t-shirts. I'd planned on taking the aerial tramway to the Zugspitze mountain post registration so had a small rucksack containing waterproofs, gloves, water and the like. At registration I was slightly surprised to be given a quality 20litre rucksack of race bits along with my race number. A lot of the content was leaflets which I removed and I broke the packaging down on the food items to the bare minimum then stuffed my original rucksack in the new one and headed off to look around the stalls. There were actually some good deals here – more obscure items but at good prices – I bought an XL 'Lawrence of Arabia' style sunhat and some Compressport socks as a gift for E.

It wasn't long before I was at the railway station to make my way up Zugspitze. The return ticket is 60 Euros which is a lot of money for a few hours but the view is spectacular from up there. I'd been to the top twice before and was keen this time to see the new infrastructure that had been put in. The aerial tramway now has a much larger gondola and it was not long before we were gaining height to cross the tallest pylon anywhere in the world (127m). As we crossed it the gondola rocked and a man behind pushed quite hard in to the small of my back to hold on – not good! Once we had stopped wobbling, he continued to press in there until I shook a bit and he got the hint and moved. To the left I could see a works cable lift going to the top so knew building work was still going on. It wasn't long before we entered thick cloud only to exit at about 2600m and see the view opening up around us – a peak jutting out of a sea of cloud. At the top it was very much 'work in progress' with various bits being rebuilt. The view to the Eibsee Lake about 2200m below was spectacular.

Zugspitze itself has a large building on the top that connects two aerial tramways and a cable car and the actual summit (2962m) is not much higher and less than 100m away. On the way up in the gondola I had a small idea that, if it looked safe, I'd go for a summit attempt. I could see what looked like normally attired people up there along with some real climbers with harnesses. To get there I first had to head down three flights of metal stairs to where the goods cable lift joined the mountain – workers busy removing building materials for the construction work going on. Climbing down the stairs was a little tricky as the headroom was low with the problem further being compounded by no handrail on the inside so a drop if things went wrong. Finally, there was a further complication being the vertiginous view on each turn over the valley below. As a child I had a real fear of heights, perhaps brought on by living in a bungalow and going to a small primary school that was only on one level. The first time I came across stairs was in secondary school as one building had four floors. I found going up a very scary experience but, in early adult life, I tried to expose myself to drops and mostly got over it. I find the fear comes back when I'm either tired or nervous about something and it does come back during races, hill walking and visiting tall buildings from time to time. In this case I wasn't tired but I was a little nervous about what lay up ahead.

Soon I was down on the small flat col – about 10m by 5m – and felt safe as I was standing on a solid piece of rock. From this it was just a matter of crossing about 10m of snow, climbing a ladder, traversing on a wire then, what looked like, a walk along a small summit ridge to get to the top of Germany. If there was no-one around it looked like 5mins to the top. The trouble was that there were lots of people around who lacked the experience to be up there. The first problem was climbing the slightly angled snow bank. There was a via ferrata cable to hold on to and this was fine when no-one else was using it – it was all about finding a gap. Getting to the top of this the next challenge was the ladder. Here I met a man who was really scared coming down it and taking ages and this meant the queue was building behind me. Eventually he came down so I shimmied up and traversed the next via ferrata wire to turn for the summit which was now about 5m above me and 30m away. I was behind another chap so I patiently crouched there. The reason for crouching was that to my right was a drop down to the col (and beyond) and to my left a drop of hundreds of meters in to the cloud. The only thing to hold on to was a via ferrata wire that was about 30cm off the ground that led to the summit. Whenever someone came down, they would carefully pass the queue going up as a trip or slip could lead to a fatal fall. This was the first time in my life I had experienced a queue to a summit and I didn't like it. The trouble was that to go back was to run the gauntlet of the various hazards so I thought I'd just stay put and wait my turn. Up ahead there were lots of selfies being taken with various cameras in various groups and the man in front of me was getting irritated, eventually telling those up ahead they had to get moving. Nothing happened so he said it even more directly and they did. I felt really vulnerable without a harness but I eventually reached the summit, took a few pics, and started now to head back against the line of people. Going back, the drop to the right, through the clouds, looked enormous so I was really careful getting to the cable and to the top of the ladder. The group in front were day trippers who had no confidence or skills at all and were terrified. They kept wanting photos to be taken at each hazard so I spent about 5 mins holding on to the first wire as they manoeuvred down the ladder. As soon as they left the ladder I was down and on to the rocks that led to the 10m snow bank. At this point the last member of the group started to get terrified so random climbers were helping her with foot and hand holds and words of encouragement. A climber coming up put one of his climbing harness attachments in front and one behind on the wire so she could not fall and eventually she got down. Now it was my turn to pass this man and he decided he was not going to unclip his harnesses to let me through so I had no option but to step over his harnesses which is risky when on snow/ice/rock. Safely over, I grabbed the final via ferrata cable to head down. Now this climber was obviously frustrated having stood for a few minutes so he grabbed the same cable to go up – the upshot being I grabbed it really tightly (so as not to fall off the mountain) and the wires cut in to my fingers. There is an unwritten rule that there is only one person on each wire section and he well and truly broke it out of impatience. Worse still as I didn't want to fall, my left leg, which was steadiest, pushed really hard in to the snow to the extent I pulled a muscle in my quad. Cut fingers and leg strain are not good things to have before a race. I headed back up the metal staircase then caught a cable car down to the glacier to buy some food. I was really frustrated that each step hurt my leg and I was worried the cuts on my fingers would keep opening when I used my poles the next day. I'd been foolish to head across when it was so busy and the view was no better than at the actual summit station. Suitably fed I headed back to the top to head to the Eibsee thinking a boat cruise would keep me out of trouble and it did! I then headed back to the campsite to rest for the big day to come.

The campsite was now even busier with more people arriving for the race – I got chatting with a friendly couple (he was from the Netherlands and she was from Germany) who had entered the 40k race and had a long-term ambition of completing Marathon des Sables (MdS). I mentioned the X-NRG Druid race in the UK as a lot of MdS runners tend to complete this in November prior to MdS the following spring and suggested they consider it and they said they would look it up when they got back home. A few runners had mobile homes with them and I'm always slightly jealous as they have everything they want and have arrived relatively refreshed.

The tent sat right in the sun and those in the camping field typically had their tops off or were wearing as little clothing as possible – it was around 37 degrees in the sun. I tried everything but there was no escape except to head to the bank of a nearby tree covered river. By about 20:00 the temperature had dropped about 10 degrees so it was time to pack the race-bag and settle down for the night. Fellow runners had some pre-race nerves and spent a long-time packing, unpacking, repacking and packing bags and this carried on towards 22:00. There was also another group who had arrived (not runners or cyclists but people just staying there) who were a bit high-spirited so it was time to put the earplugs in and try and get some sleep.

I woke up a few times in the night and properly woke up at 04:12 with cold water dripping on my face. Despite leaving my tent partially open it was soaked on the inside from condensation. The air temperature inside the tent was 12 degrees and I was really cold – I shuffled out and headed to the toilet block to get changed. I popped back to the tent and had my breakfast of 2-bananas, 2 slices of bread and an energy drink (for the caffeine) then left for the start at 05:15. I was a little ahead of schedule but thought I may as well get moving. On the way there I passed a bench where a fellow runner had been sleeping – he must have been really hardcore!

The event start is at a horseshoe shaped music venue that probably sits around 500 people but, today, all the chairs were gone. I worked out I'd somehow ended up on the inside and runners were queueing up outside to have their bags checked as part of kit check. I'd entered other races that did kit check at the start and it was usually lip service pulling over a few random people and asking some questions. Here it looked like everyone was being checked so it was time to get outside to come back in! My kit check was very quick indeed – energy gels, waterproof trousers and a first aid kit. The checker said I had such a big bag I must have it all and didn't want to waste time on me so I quickly got back to the inside. It was now just a waiting game and I found the stage in the music venue to be the quietest spot as no-one was up there.

It was now about 30 mins to race start and the atmosphere was building with upbeat music playing on the loud speakers. Despacito by Luis Fonsi came on and at the same time a man with an alphorn came on stage and started to play along to the tune. It reminded me of travelling to the Ecotrail Paris and hearing the same tune covered by saxophone, accordion and trumpet at a metro station. He was very good at playing along but it was a little quiet and he asked me did I know if there was a microphone and I had to say I had not seen one. Undeterred he played on and at the end asked me if the speed was OK or should he have been faster. It was now time to get off the stage and in to the holding pen. Over the years I've noticed most people start too far forward and this can be a real nuisance if you are fast as you end up being stuck behind slower people but it is really hard to judge as you are using all your prejudices in looking at others. In this race virtually everyone looked to be lighter and smaller than me so both of these factors meant they would be faster. However not everyone had trail shoes on so there were some people doing this sort of thing for the first time. Based on all of this I decided to start in the middle of the field. The minutes passed quickly and at 07:12 they put on their official race song, Highway to Hell by AC/DC, and encouraged a sing-along. 07:15 came quickly and we were off. Only not really as we shuffled forward and the gantry clock ticked away. It was 2 minutes before I'd covered the 20 metres to get there and I could see the reason for the delay. A traditional looking German alpine band was walking at the front of the field (I assume) playing a tune. They pulled in to the side and we were off. Nearly. Only this time we stopped at the level crossing as a train was coming. After a short delay we were off for real. The first few kms were relatively functional and boring – at least wide enough for people to pass. It wasn't long before we hit the single track and the next few kms can best be described as 'elbowy'. Lots of people jostling for position on the twisty trails in the forest. One runner had a dog, which was very much against the rules, the dog and lead presenting a real hazard to people getting past. Eventually things levelled off a little and we were back on forest roads so there was plenty of space for everyone to find their position as we headed down to the first CP at the Eibsee. Here the food on offer was strudel, bits of fruit and what, to my untrained eye, looked like small pancakes with sun dried blueberries on them. I filled up my water bottles with 'lime and ginger sports drink', and picked up a piece of strudel and a pancake. I thought I'd eat the pancake first but quickly discovered it was some salty meat concoction so, as a pescatarian, I left it behind.

With 9.5k (D+ 840m) to the next CP we all continued on in the heat. This part of the course was quite fast and it was not long before we passed below the Ehrwald-Obermoos Zugsptizbahn, the aerial tramway from Austria to Zugspitze, then down a road to a place that had a feel for a CP location but, alas, it was further on. The sun was now getting really warm as we sweated our way up a long grassy slope to pop out at the top of a ski run which had a long path zig-zagging its way down. Some runners took a more direct straight line but I decided to be pure and keep to the markers and before long I was at CP2. The cut-off here was 12:30 and I arrived about 10:30 so this bode well for not getting timed out on the course. After guzzling down some cheese on bread, strudel and fruit it was time to top up my bottles then push on for CP3 (1617m). The route from CP2 to CP3 was very scenic looking to the Austrian mountains to the right. Slowly but surely, we gained height passing through various bits of ski infrastructure with day trippers out for short walks. The heat was really building now and at CP3 it was time to eat/drink a lot before starting on the real adventure, the high mountains on the way to CP5.

The climb was relatively easy – as we got higher it got slightly cooler with a mild breeze blowing. The path eventually levelled off as we were on the crest of a shoulder and there was a small rise ahead with a sign saying 'dangerous path' so there had to be something exciting ahead. Turning the corner this was it - the highlight of the race and what I'd come for. I could see the path traversing a cambered scree slope (this would be the danger) then drop down out of sight then go along a mighty ridge to keep going further up to the right. This was the mountain section from the on-line videos. The scree traverse wasn't really that hazardous – if it had been in a more adventurous race like UTMR it would not have got a mention – this hazard was very runnable. To the left a very narrow path left the trail and climbed steeply to cross the ridgeline and would lead back to the summit of Zugspitze – this looked so tempting for another day – another exciting looking path to add to the long mental list of things to do in life. Our route went up a shoulder with a gradient beyond 20% and quickly rose to a peak. This shoulder was a visual highlight but I wish it had been longer as it would have been more impressive – the joy of having the view down to my left and right lasted for only 10 minutes. It was now time to head along a flattish path for a few kilometres before coming to the next rise and an interesting descent. Up ahead was a snow-slope that was about 100m long and dropping about 20m. The snow was about 10cm thick and there was one rope attached at the top of the slope and anchored in three places on the way down giving four 25m sections. On each section the rope started and finished on the ground but was longer than the gap so for most of the 25m it could be held on to when walking normally.

The runner in front of me grabbed the rope and stepped back to make it taught – he was perpendicular to the rope facing it and shuffling left foot first whilst heading down the hill. Ideally there would never be more than one person on each section but the route was busy so I gave the man in front about a 5m head start then grabbed the rope and descended in the same fashion. Behind me a tourist was holding on to the rope and glissading on his bottom in delight and came crashing down and knocked me over. I wasn't happy with this but he said sorry so I stood up and carried on. About 30s later he did the same thing and crashed in to me – feet first going in to my right calf and knocked me over. I said 'if you are coming down like that you have to either let go of the rope or give me space as it is not fair what you are doing'. My worry was I'd take a fall and get injured and it would be race over for me. I headed off and again he came sliding down this time stopping about 1m away from me but pulling the rope so it was about 30cm off the ground. Somehow, I stayed on it bent forward then got up and carried on without it, feeling quite pleased to be off the rope after a minute or two. I did grumble a bit to the runner in front who pointed out the person behind me was 'just having fun' and I took this as a coded way of saying 'stop whining and let's talk about something else' so I did. We ran together for the next 30 mins and talked about various races we had done – it turned out we had both done the Transylvania 50 in 2017 – it is a small world!

The path now dropped down, crossed a rocky river, and headed up on a narrow trail - my new-found friend fell behind but I thought he would catch me so I pushed on. I was later to find out he would stop at CP4 (1417m). I was pleased to reach CP4 but the mood amongst my fellow runners was subdued at best. It was now quite hot/humid and everyone knew there was a large climb to come. Furthermore, we had only covered about 1/3 of the official distance. I say official as the distance slowly but surely grew as we went along if the various GPS watches are to be believed. I took on my water and looked at the food that had lots of big flies on it. It was calculation time. I wanted the cheese but the large flies on it may have laid some eggs that may make me sick. I knew I'd be finished in about 10-12 hrs and started to think about how long it would take to get sick and decided it was not for 4-5 hrs (based on nothing but a hunch) and thought it best to take the food as it would get me along the trail. I left CP4 and in the whole time I had been there no-one had moved – all looking in silence at the ground.

It was tough looking ahead as the path had to cross the mountains on the high alpine pasture in the distance. This had a forest in front of it with a zig-zag path on the edge of the trees in the baking sun. There was nothing to do but to start climbing and, slowly but surely, I passed the trees to start on the pasture to now realise the pasture was not the top as there was a rocky section beyond this. Having done UTMR, and Ut4M, I was used to long hot hills so this one wasn't that bad as it topped out at 2048m. The view over the other side was so different – a descending valley heading in a NE direction with high cliff lined mountains on the left and right – truly beautiful. It was along here I first came across Anton. He approached me from behind and I pulled over to let him through as he was faster and he didn't say 'thank you' or anything like that so I, in a loud passive-aggressive style, said 'thank you' and nothing came of it. Further on he was slow going up-hill so I passed him at a wide section and said 'thank you'. A little later he came steaming past and with his right elbow flicked my left elbow and cut in right in front of me so I had to stop. He was now, officially, my race nemesis and I would do what I could to beat him. As we were about 50k in and even paced it was anyone's guess who would win but I'd give it my best shot. He disappeared off and it would be a long time before we would meet again.

CP5 was down at road side and looked very busy. As I arrived, I was sent through a funnel that had some medics sitting on a raised platform on the left. This was the medical check that had been promised at CP8 in the race literature pre-race which, on the day before the race had moved to CP5/8 so I thought we would see the medics twice. They asked me how I was and I said 'absolutely fine' and gave a big smile. They asked if had been eating and drinking and I replied with 'my pee is between clear and straw coloured and I've been enjoying the fine range of snacks on offer'. For good measure I pointed to my bag and said 'if it rains, I have lots of clothes in here so I'll be nice and warm and dry'. For some reason I added 'I've never felt better'. I don't know why I went over enthusiastic at the question but I did. The medic said 'you seem absolutely fine so please continue, have a good race'. I thanked them and moved forward to see a runner in a foil blanket on a bed. I turned a corner and another runner was asleep on a bed. I exited the first aid area to the CP proper and took on some food and saw a fellow runner with a map. To save getting my own map out I asked could I have a quick look and he said 'sure' quickly followed by 'you may keep it if you want'. Puzzled I asked 'why?'. He said he was stopping. I asked if he was injured and he said no he was just tired. Every runner I spoke to in that CP was withdrawing as there was a big shiny white air-conditioned coach that was about to start boarding and was heading to the finish. They seemed puzzled I would continue in the heat knowing the course ahead which was 30k of flat followed by 20k of hills. Whilst it would have been tempting to stop, I knew if I did this it would put TDS in jeopardy as I had to be able to operate in tough conditions and to stop would be instant pleasure closely followed by a lifetime of regret. I wished them well and headed out of the CP. Now the route was very lonely with no-one visible up ahead. After a few mins I looked back and there was no-one behind. Navigation was now going to be really important right to the end.

It was becoming clear that the sun would be going down in a few hours so this next section was where distance had to be covered as quickly as possible as everything slows down at night. The trail was very flat so I got in to my powerwalking zone and kept moving forward seeing the obvious pass in the mountains that was coming up. A few runners passed me on this section and, by now, most runners were acknowledging each other in a friendly way as we all knew we were going to be entering a long night and may need the help of others if something went wrong. The route joined the road at the village of Burgraben and I could see one of the runners who had passed me standing facing a building in an odd posture – it was if he were waiting for something. As I went around the building, I could see two runners buying half litres of beer at an outside bar and downing them in one. I couldn't help but laugh, as did they and gave me a 'prost!', and I went on. It wasn't long before they came past me again full of high spirits and it's great to see people having a good time in these races and not taking everything totally seriously – after all it is about having fun!

The route was now on a quiet country road, for about 1km, and up ahead I could see a marshal below a large sign, pointing that the route crossed by him and went somewhere in to the trees on the right. The large sign seemed to be a picture of a wizened man with a beard, with the body of a sperm cell, and was in a blue/white colour. I could not work out what this sign was for but it was clear the route was going the same way so I was intrigued. It turned out the picture was of a spirit ghost/guide who inhabited the next section, the path along the Leutasch gorge. This area looked great for a day out, particularly if you liked geology and metal walkways over waterfalls and along cliff edges. Our route took a more benign forest track but there were clearly more interesting paths in here. Somewhere along here we left Austria and entered Germany and I arrived at CP6. This checkpoint was quite small and had some friendly volunteers and a fellow runner there with his top off and some quite red-looking skin – the sun had not been kind to him. I quickly left CP6 as I really wanted to reach CP7 before needing my headtorch on. My target time was 21:35 and it was looking like I'd be really close to it. This section is flat and passes the Lautersee and comes to the Ferchensee and you can see the CP a good km out. The sun was setting over the water and it was truly gorgeous – the orange hues giving way to pink. I arrived at CP7 at 21:20 and set myself up for the night – getting my headtorch on and checking that I knew where my gloves etc. are should I need them. I knew my watch would not last the distance so now was the time to try a new idea out. I had a small 'lipstick' power bank so I connected this to my watch and put it in my coat pocket so it could charge up. My plan was to leave it there to the next CP so it got a good charge. As the route marking had been pretty good, I'd follow that and the light of others would guide me. I was able to leave CP7 with a little daylight so pushed on hard on the forest trails to reach the small settlement of Elmau. This had a massive building that looked like a cross between a monastery, an expensive hotel, a church, a town hall and a secure hospital. I could not work out what this massive, well lit, institution could be. I later discovered it was the Schloss Elmau, a very expensive country retreat that had been used for a recent G7 summit. It is a spectacular building in a spectacular location. Here the path disappeared in to the trees and I caught and overtook 5 runners so then I was on my own in the night. From here I could see bits of the course ahead – namely the high point between CP9 and CP10 as there was what looked like a light in a building – it looked a long way up and hours away so nothing to worry about at this point!

From eating so much at early CPs I'd not really eaten since CP5 as my stomach was a little bloated at the time and I was starting to now get tired from both the time of day, time on my feet, and lack of fuel. The path now went temptingly close to Garmisch-Partenkirchen but I knew I was going on and not quitting. At a road crossing a marshal said it was not far to CP8 and I had visions of it being just around the corner. Suddenly the path turned a corner and dropped down to the river and it was obvious there would be a climb out the other side – it was probably only about 100m vertical but with tired legs this was noticeable!

CP8 (800m) was a small CP and here things were starting to get serious for everyone. It was time to put on waterproof trousers for the cold, add a layer of clothing, get some food/fluids and focus on the big climb to come – the official climb from here was 1270m to the top – basically a Ben Nevis in the dark! I put my now fully charged watch back on and set off up the hill. Throughout the day other runners, as well as myself, thought that the actual distances were longer than the stated distances between the CPs. This could be down to many reasons but the moral of the story is to use your eyes more than the stated distances/watch distances to work out how far there is to go.

The hill was tough. It wasn't long before it was a single-track path zig-zagging relentlessly up through the forest – climbing over fallen trees, around rocks, the path forever disappearing upwards in to the sky. At about 1200m I caught a runner who said he was out of energy and was going to pull out. His watch said he had less than 1k to go to reach the next CP. He asked what distance I had on my watch and I said the same but noted it was a lot more than 1k as we were only at 1200m and the CP was at 1600m. I asked him if he had spotted that the watch distances were more and he said he had not and he was really cold. He asked how far I thought it was and I guessed 4-5k and he was really low with this and sat down. I firmly told him sitting down wasn't going to achieve anything and he should get moving as there is a lot to do and he got up and started moving slowly. After a short while I left him and pushed onwards on the relentless quest to CP9. Eventually our path joined a ski run and we carried on walking up what was a wide gravel road, seeing runners on the other side of some tape heading to CP10. It would take one, two, who knows how many hours to reach that point but not focusing on this I just pushed on up eventually reaching CP9 (1680m). Here I asked if the light I had been seeing all the way along was the top of the course and the marshal said it was. He also said it was 2km up to it, 3km to CP10 then 5km down and done. 10k to go! It was all looking good.

Leaving CP9 I carried on up and was slowing to the point I was being overtaken by a few people which is rare for me so late in a race – it was just a big hill and I was tiring! 2k turned in to 3.5k and at this point I turned to head back down. The route down is entirely on narrow paths and not down ski pistes as I had hoped for. On this descent I overtook a few backmarkers from a shorter race and slowly but surely started overtaking runners in my race. It was a new experience for me overtaking on the downs. I caught up my race nemesis and passed him. A bit later he caught me and I pulled off the trail to let him through – no 'thank you' came. I carried on after him and got to a wider point and made my move.

At CP10 (1635m) I asked how far to go and they said 4k so I went through without stopping and got a big cheer from the marshals. My nemesis had to stop for fluids so I made a gap and carried on down overtaking a few people as I did. After about 20 mins he had caught me up so my race plan now changed. I'd now try and let him through, sit about 10-20s back, and then try and take him on a final sprint. He was about 10s behind me and I thought if he gets to 5s I'll pull over but not before. We carried on down, crossing rivers, overtaking others, crossing fallen trees and he was always about 10-20s behind – perhaps playing me at my own game! Then at one point he was just gone. I looked back and no-one was behind me. I wanted a good race but didn't want him to have had a fall but could not see him at all so I pressed on. It was now starting to get to daylight and the path kept dropping and twisting in the dark woods. One runner caught me and went through and I could see another about 20s behind gaining on me. All three of us were now racing for position as we hit a '2k to go' sign and joined the road. The runner in front sped off and I had no choice but to run also as I was not going to let the runner behind get me! The trouble was it was quite tiring running fast having been on my legs for so long so now my plan was to get sufficiently far forward to get out of sight then walk as if he could not see me, he would probably stop and walk. Rounding a bend, I'd lost him to be greeted by a very enthusiastic German spectator who was sitting beside the road with a lot of empty cans of beer and I could not stop now – this spectator made me feel like I was about to get a world record – I had to go on for all the cheering he was giving me so I just kept going. I now started to think about the end and if I would spot it – I saw a lady with a dog and shouted in advance for directions and she said 'you cannot miss it – good luck!' and off I went rounding a bend then back over the railway I'd crossed 22hs previously. I looked back and could not see the runner behind me but was not sure if he would have an epic charge and overtake so I started sprinting now at what looked like 200-300m out and quickly came to the finish lane and threw myself in to the final right-hand bend and under the gantry finishing in 22:01:07. I got my medal and waited for the next runner – he came in about 90s later. Next it was time for food so I took my big red mug to get some salty soup. Beer was also on offer but I declined this – it was 05:15 on a Sunday morning! I finished my food and my nemesis had not come in – I was starting to feel a bit worried and hoped he was OK but, after about 15 mins, he arrived. I wanted to go over and say 'hello' but he was greeted by someone else and I didn't like to interrupt.

It was now time to leave and walk the 3km back to the campsite – this seemed a lot longer than it did the day before – and when I got there, I took on some more food and waited for 08:30 when I dismantled the tent and packed my bag and headed for the bus. I took the 10:37 to Garmisch and caught the 11:06 train and was in Munich just after midday. After a spot of lunch, I headed to the airport and my flight back, getting home at about 22:00. I'd been up for 43 hrs so went to bed quite tired and woke up my normal time for work the next day. The Zugspitz Ultratrail had been a most enjoyable race, great scenery, good checkpoints and friendly staff. It's a tough course though but for my TDS training it had been the right thing to do as there were both physical and mental challenges to overcome to finish. I'd recommend it to anyone who wants a warm-up race for one of the big August races in the Alps.

20 TDS 2018

Since 2009 I'd had a will I/won't I relationship with the TDS. It was always there in the background as a challenge that would be marginal for me to complete should I ever have the privilege of standing on the start line. As the summer passed the training was continuing with about 1hr hard exercise a day either on the bike or a treadmill incline. On top of this there were a number of other 'tune-up' races which I could use to assess progress on. In the week before the event, TDS sat front and centre of my mind, maps memorised along with target times and cut off times. The next few days would either realise an ambition or end in failure. I was as prepared as I could be for this attempt so I headed to Chamonix in a calm mood for what lay ahead. E and I arrived on the Tuesday afternoon and after checking in to our hotel went along to kit check and registration in the sports centre. This was followed by a light meal then heading to the centre of Chamonix to watch the YCC races.

Walking back to the hotel we talked about where the 04:30 bus would leave from the next morning to take us to the start, but we were thinking of two different places. Fortunately, we were by the race village, a selection of temporary buildings selling all manner of races and race related gear, so this seemed an obvious place to ask. Within this was an official UTMB info desk so up I went to ask the question and was told the location. The lady behind the desk asked if I knew about the delay to the start and I didn't as no text message had arrived (it would arrive later on). Due to bad weather we would start at 08:00 and all buses would be delayed by two hours. The course would have a deviation beyond Bourg for safety reasons and there may be another diversion from Bellevue near the end. With our new-found information we headed back to the hotel for a final kit check and a rest, being in bed by 22:00. Prior to races I always put my t-shirt on the night before to save time and I'd put my compression top on as normal. In the stuffiness of the hotel room it seemed to be suffocating me like a tight bandage and inhibiting a full breath so I naturally started to weigh up taking it off but decided not to, my mind racing about what was to come the next day. After a restless night I woke up with the alarm at 05:00, ate a quick breakfast and caught the 06:15 bus. As we embarked the organisers explained no buses would come back to Chamonix from the start (as the later start would put the buses in a traffic jam in the Mont Blanc tunnel and they did not want that) so every supporter would have to go clockwise round the course – this was not a problem for E but may have been for others.

In Courmayeur, somewhat annoyingly, the bus went past the bus station (near the start) and headed for the sports centre to drop us off just as it did for CCC several years ago. Every bus did this so it was obviously the plan to give everyone a 15-minute walk to the start. At the sports centre there were a number of temporary toilets (with queues) but with 'local knowledge' we pushed on back to the bus station to use the toilets there thinking they would be quiet. They were not quiet. Standing in line I realised I'd not be able to get to them before the start so abandoned my quest and rolled back from the line and headed out to meet E so we could walk up the hill to the start by the church. After a quick goodbye I headed for the start pen – I was delighted to see a row of temporary toilets with no queue so spent a few minutes there before heading in to the pen. At big races there is a big atmosphere at the start but what makes some of the ultras different is everyone knows that many will not finish so there is a measurable tension in the air. TDS does not have the same rousing music as CCC which was a disappointment as it really helps build the atmosphere. As the fateful time approached a helicopter arrived to film the start – flying above two drones that were also filming. The countdown started and we were off, many of us embarking on the biggest adventure of our lives.

I know I'm not the fastest runner so I was very focused in not getting timed out at Bourg (51k) or earlier and as we started to move forward the road narrowed and we stopped. In my time plan I was going to make the first timed CP at Lac Combal (16k) in 3hrs30 against the cut-off of 3hrs 45 so standing still was really bad news! It took 2.5 minutes to cover the first 100m and this was not good for my plan. There is a lot of mythology about getting stuck in a queue at the TDS and wasting up to 2hrs on the first big hill and getting timed out. Everyone will have heard the story and no-one wants to take a risk. As we skirted around the town, I focused on gaining some places as I wanted to be as far up the pack as possible for when we go to single-track which I expected to be around 3 or 4 kilometres in to the course. The path climbed up a ski road and the dust left an ankle-deep cloud as we ran ever upward, no-one wanting to get timed out at the top. The single-track I expected did not materialise so we carried onwards and upwards on the wide ski road. On one of the bends I looked back and saw what I thought was about 400 people behind me so I knew I was not a back-marker, and thus had no risk of being timed out, so I could settle down and enjoy the race ahead.

Col Chericout came quickly – 1hr10 against a target of 1hr25 and here the track narrowed to traverse the mountain on the way to Lac Combal (1970m). At this point I was about 800th and everyone was running so this meant I had to run also! I didn't want to overdo things but knew the weather was going to get bad so I was content to be making fast progress. To my right I could see lenticular clouds forming over the high tops – an indication of strong winds high up. Ahead I could see rain clouds building. All of this was out of my control as I approached the checkpoint at 2:45 to fill up my bottles, eat some food, then get out for the next big climb. Leaving the CP, I was ahead of my target time by 30-minutes, and one hour ahead of the cut-off, so things were going better than planned.

The climb to the Col Chavannes (2603m) was impressive. From the bottom a series of zig-zags of ever smaller people ascending in to the sky. As we got higher and higher the path occasionally got a little technical and the line stopped whilst a runner navigated a step or something tricky. There was a cry of 'Vite!' from multiple runners every time this happened as many didn't want to stop. In these situations, I'm a little more relaxed because if someone is nervous shouting at them won't make them go faster. It's far better to have a drink or a little food and use the time wisely. From the top the view back was excellent, viewing both the long line of runners ascending and the gathering storm clouds above. Here the way forward was a long descent and it looked like there was bad weather about 15-20km ahead. Looking at the clouds and the wind direction I felt if I ran this descent, I should beat the rain – I'd much rather have the bad weather lower down than high up.

The descent was beautiful, long, and runnable. Towards the end the path cut down a steep field and I was pleased it was still dry as it looked like it could be very slippy in the wet. Crossing a small bridge, the path widened and the heavens opened, gently at first. There was some indecisiveness in the pack as to when to waterproof up. I spotted a rock to the side to sort my bits out and became fully waterproof just in time for the deluge. Everyone was stopping now and getting their gear on as it looked like quite a bout of rain. It only lasted 20 minutes but was a wake-up call for what was to come. It's really important to stay dry and some runners clearly had not managed this and started to look quite miserable. The path now skirted a lake and headed up to the St Bernard Pass. The last section was steep on slippy mud with the added thrill of having some electric fences to cross. The runner two ahead erroneously grabbed the fence, got a shock, spun round and slipped in the mud. The runner behind me did the same. I managed to carefully cross the wires without getting zapped. As we crested this hill there were about 100 supporters indicating the CP was close and around the corner a large, and mostly empty, tent welcomed us in with a live band playing. The food provisions on the UTMB series of races are vast and varied. Here I enjoyed soup, bread/cheese and cake and topped my bottles up for the next leg. It was now time to decide what my race strategy should be – on the one hand I could take it easy and get around within the cut-offs as I'd built up a good buffer – on the other hand I could push on and see what I could make of the race. Everyone around me was running so the decision was almost made for me – it would be a run down to Bourg! I could see the clouds building but thought I had a fighting chance of getting to Bourg dry and thought this would be a good boost so I put the camera away and set off at a reasonably paced jog.

It's important to stay hydrated in these races, but not over-hydrated, so this time I decided to have a pee about 10 mins before each checkpoint so I could assess the situation and plan what to do. In a secluded spot before Seez I stopped and produced 20 seconds of straw-coloured fluid which was good. Whilst doing this I spotted a fellow runner who had stopped to watch. He asked if I was OK and I said yes. He stood until I had finished then moved on. I can only assume he had a thing for urination as there was no other obvious reason to stop. Seez came quickly then I eased back on the 2k to Bourg. I wanted to arrive rested so I could get my food in and be off quickly without cramping my legs. At 823m Bourg is the low point of the course and the heat was really building as it reflected off the buildings and road. I could see the CP coming up and knew that I'd meet E here and she would have to show a piece of paper to get in. We were soon in together and E pulled out the goodies to eat – 3 small pastries and a can of Red Bull (for the caffeine). E went and selected some snacks from the food area and I quickly ate a lot of food whilst I took on extra kit from the bag E had. At this point things were going pretty well so after a brief chat I went on my way to the kit check table where I had to show my waterproofs and phone to continue. This took about 2 minutes; then it was back out on to the trail. Due to the weather the 'big hill' was off the course and I was a little disappointed as I'd focused hard on treadmill inclines but understood the safety concern in bad weather. The diversion went steeply up through the houses and runners were now sitting down beside the course – indeed one runner was actually lying in a road used by cars, he was so exhausted. This lower climb sapped the energy from everyone and it wasn't long before runners were running out of water. Fortunately, there were two water troughs on the way up and I gladly refilled. All in I'd drink 2.5 litres on the climb. What was annoying was we would go up for about 10 mins then go down for about 5 and when one's legs are tired on a big hill downs are bad as it only means more up! Eventually we reached a road and the pack was now thinning out. At 19:02 there was an absolutely epic clap of thunder high on the mountain on the big hill that had been removed from the course – we were a few hundred metres below and lucky to be out of it. Our route cut down to a quiet road to the very small village of Les Chapieux. To the right of the course I could see a valley with high snowy mountains that had a sign saying 'la ville des glaciers' – it looked such a good place to explore at some point in the future, either by being there or using the internet to look at pictures and read about. The final climb to the CP at Cormet de Roseland (1967m) would be along the road. It was now starting to get dark but I was determined to get there without using my headtorch as I wanted to preserve the battery life as long as I could. Other runners had their torches on full beam making the going quite tough as I was walking in to my own monster sized shadow.

The tent at Cormet de Roseland was hectic. There was an area of drop bags for runners to collect on the left as we went in. Along the right-hand side was a long table with food with assistants behind it. In the middle was rows of benches with runners, and their belongings, scattered all over them. As I went in, I could not see a space to sit and looked around eventually finding one that was an awkward shuffle in a tight gap between two benches to get to. I went to a pasta counter and got a good helping in my big red mug. Whilst my mug is bigger than most, I feel I can get a good helping so I don't queue twice, so it's worth carrying. Part of the space problem was runners were sorting through drop bags, their bags, eating, charging watches and not leaving in a hurry as it was now dark and wet outside. It was at this point I saw the supporters who were corralled in a pen about 5 deep and 30 long shouting to their runners about this and that and trying to pass kit across. In my mind this was not great for a supporter but there were just too many people for the space. The tent would be a really easy place to pull out of the race and catch the warm, dry, inviting bus outside back to Chamonix. In my experience many 'give up' at such points and bail, not realising their true strength. The idea of quitting in the bad weather didn't cross my mind – I was here for an adventure and bad weather would only add to the experience! It takes some element of courage to head out in to a wet, dark, night on paths that are not good and where injury is a real possibility. Some may say it takes foolishness to head out but anyone who stood on the start line earlier in the day knew what they were facing. In my mind it was getting wetter outside so things would get even slippier so it was time to get going and face the weather. As I left the tent, I turned my head torch on and headed out on the very indistinct track to Col de la Sauce. The CP was at 1967m and the Col is at 2307m in 3kms time so it does not really seem like a hill in the grand scheme of things. Of course, if a ½ marathon in the UK had a 1:10 gradient for 3k everyone would be up in arms! This section was about hopping from one muddy tuft to the next in a rapidly thinning field of runners. We came to one river crossing with a river flowing right to left. To the left was a waterfall of unknown height and in the middle was a large slab of slippy rock about 1cm under the water, the rock being canted to the left at an angle of about 10 degrees. The first runner went on to the middle of the rock and slipped right to left catching his feet on a solid protrusion then jumped to the side and was on his way. The second runner similarly surfed the obstacle. In these situations, there is no time to think and it is about getting on with it so, copying the runner in front, I surfed and hopped on my way on this very technical trail as the rain really started to build. At the top of the Col it was getting harder and harder to see anything – the track, other runners and the markers. It would be really easy to have a fall up here so everyone was concentrating really hard to get off this mountain. The path descended rapidly and I found myself completely on my own –in every direction the inky black of the night. The rain was quite bad and coupled with being in the clouds the viz was really poor. The path continued through rocks crossing a river many times and I was actually loving the solitude as it had a real sense of adventure about it – high in the mountains alone at night depending on my own ability to not get injured. In these races there is usually a line of head torches to follow but not here!

I knew in advance about the rocky passage at Curé – it is said to be both haunted (4 people died making it) and hazardous (it's cut out of the side of a cliff with a drop on one side to the river) and was looking forward to it. The surface of the ground was very uneven in it and the headtorch made it hard to judge the depth of any obstacle. To my right I could hear the Gittaz river tumbling below and twice stood on the edge peering down with my 250-lumen head torch to see if I could see the river – each time nothing – the beam of light petered to a point in the deep black of the night as I looked down the abyss. My torch was starting to play up which was a bit unnerving – I had my spare in my pocket just in case but wanted to get as much out of this battery as I could – it had barely done two hours and was complaining. Slowly the CP at La Gittaz (1665m) came in to view and after more mud and water I arrived – this CP was small with a few outside tables so nowhere to shelter. It took about 5 mins to switch my battery on my main torch before heading off again into the wet night. The thick cloud was very disorientating, and it was now time to head up to Col Est de la Gittaz (2315m) via the Entre Deux Nants (2164m). For a short period, the rain lessened and it was now possible to see a line of head torches coming in to La Gittaz and heading high from it in to the sky above. Such sights are mesmerising as the line of torches seem to point skyward giving an indication of the slope ahead. For about 10 minutes the moon was visible before it was hidden by the rain clouds again. Climbing this next slope, I kept passing a fellow runner who would stop for a micro snooze of about 5 mins about every 30 mins. It seemed to work for him but I'd never have tried it due to the fear of the cold. At this point I was annoyed with myself as I could feel a blister coming and I should have treated it at the last CP but forgot. Earlier in the day someone had poled my right ankle so my foot came partially out of my shoe thus loosening the laces. I'd kept meaning to re-tighten them but had not. Having the shoe a little loose meant a blister and it could have been avoided. There was no option but to fix it in the pouring rain there and then so I got myself just off the trail and sorted it out. 5 minutes I didn't need to have wasted if I'd spent 30 seconds hours earlier. Races are always about learning.

In the bad weather the route to Col Du Joly (1989m) was hard to identify as I was still unable to see anything, and the constant twists and turns made it very hard to have an inner appreciation of general direction. I caught up to a few runners who were not sure where to go and I spotted some shoe tread marks in the mud saying this looked like the way ahead and we set off. I was a lot more confident in covering this ground than the others and slowly built a gap until, when I looked back, I could not see them at all. Normally the UTMB races are well marked but due to the bad weather and the very low visibility (less than 10m frequently) it was hard to see the markers. The CP at Col Du Joly bought some welcome relief and after a quick bite to eat it was time to head out again. Runners were now descending the hill on different paths to add to the confusion but I continued to track the shoeprints in the damp mud and this seemed to work for me. We descended quite quickly and with every 100m dropped the visibility improved, noting we were now in a wood on a cloudy wet night so it was still not great! I managed to spot a fellow Brit runner and we had a good chat on this descent, passing Notre Dame de la Gorge (1210m) not having a clue what it was as it was so dark!

The next 5k gave some respite along the valley as it was relatively flat on the way to the CP at Les Contamines-Montjoie (1170m). This was a large tent, perhaps set up for the UTMB that would pass through on Friday night. Frustratingly the food and the benches were in separate tents which meant some walking to and fro to get food. I wasn't really hungry at this stage so only ate a few light snacks. Not eating much would soon manifest itself as a poor decision. Leaving the tent just after 05:00 felt really good. The cut-off was 10:30 so now I was really thinking finishing in sub 28hrs was possible if I stayed focused and I could be in by 12:00 in Chamonix.

The next hill would seed doubts on my plan. The first point to reach was Chalets de Truc (1721m) a mere 600m higher in 3.5k. As

I set off, I could see no-one behind and no-one ahead so it looked like another solo ascent. Slowly but surely, I was running out of energy and about 6 runners overtook me. I pride myself on my ascents having trained really hard on them and rarely get overtaken – 6 in 10 minutes was a sign that I was out of energy. However, the Chalets arrived and now I could see the steeper path ahead to the Col de Tricot (2120m) – only 3.5km ahead. One of my other rules is to never stop on a hill, no matter what, but select the right pace and keep going. I could see others stopping on the hill and I knew I needed a break so broke my rule and had five minutes to eat some food. Refreshed I set off and made the top and was surprised with what I saw. I've looked at this Col from Mont Blanc many times and it always looks very narrow but when on it this is not the case – it is wide with lots of parallel paths heading through it. Having had a disappointing ascent, the descent was a little better and I started to make progress again now thinking about the bridge ahead. When I first considered TDS in 2010 the map showed a glacier crossing with 'max 2 persons' written beside it and this always excited me as to what was there. In 2015 I'd seen it was a small Himalayan bridge but now was the time to cross it. I caught up some runners who tentatively walked across, the bridge bouncing in an ungainly fashion, and then it was my turn. The glacial outfall rushed through below as I bounced my way over and off the bridge and up the jumble of rocks that is a path in the loosest sense. This next section was quite blocky and steep so not good for short legs however I found I could overtake as firstly I had long legs and secondly, I was familiar with the course to the end. Time to step on the gas again. Bellevue (1801m) came quickly and I passed through without stopping, now focused on my 28hr target and seeing if I could make it. There was a diversion from the route to get us down to Les Houches (1010m) that was quick and steep and this suited me. I filled my bottles up and realised a sub 28hr was possible if I moved quickly and I now started to think of a sub 27hr30.

From Les Houches I gave it everything – walking as fast as I could (about 7kmph). I tried running but I wasn't any quicker so decided to save my energy for the run at the end. On this section every person I passed clapped, cheered or said 'well done'. It's a really humbling experience to have this at any time, the effect being more pronounced when sleep was over 24-hrs ago. I was overtaking other runners and heavily focused on my times working my way towards Chamonix. The feeling was amazing, overtaking ordinary walkers asking how I can walk so much faster than them considering what I've done – it really does stroke the ego.

I now started to think about the end; how would it be? Would I be emotional as many are? Would I run up touching the hands of those reaching out? Would I do a jump? Would I take my shoes off and run barefoot in? Would I sprint in? I hadn't really thought about it until this point as failure was always a possibility and I didn't want to jinx it. I approached the edge of town and was directed up the main street – everyone clapping and cheering. Lots of people took my photo as I built my speed now running at about 1/2M pace passing the pubs and shops. I knew the end was just around the corner and I would either meet, or fail, my sub 27:30 target on this final section. I now sped up to a fast 5k pace and took the final left-hand bend really tight then sped up to the end as the crowd cheered and banged the hoardings. I shot over the line and an organiser shook my hand and had a little chat. I'd done it. Mission accomplished. But where was E? I could now see E coming up on the left and E took my photo by the finish arch. In my haste I had not spotted E standing near the end on the left-hand side with her arm outstretched to catch my hand on the way past – I could only see this from a video clip online later and feel slightly bad for not spotting her at the time! Leaving the pen, we headed back to the hotel, had a quick wash, then headed out for food. At this point I was surprisingly awake and feeling OK eating a sandwich as we watched fellow runners arrive.

We'd arranged to meet Neil Thubron (X-NRG race director) in Chamonix post-race at Le Pub as fellow runners passed by on their way to the end. A small group of other runners joined us, the common link being X-NRG. Of the group two had their events tomorrow – Nathan with CCC and Jamie with UTMB. Having experienced being a supporter on three Chamonix campaigns E shared advice on the buses etc. with Jamie's supporter. It was quite a pleasant way to spend the afternoon sipping beer and eating crisps in good company. Naturally they wanted to know if I was going to enter UTMB and I said no as didn't fancy two nights awake. My plan for 2019 was to get to 100 miles and I didn't think UTMB was the way to do it. Neil mentioned the 'finishers gilet' and I said I didn't have one as didn't get anything at the end. It turned out there was a tent to go and collect this from so not wanting to miss out E and I headed back to collect my rightful trophy! All in it had been a life experience, one of the best days of my life. A lot of hard work had gone into it but it had all been worthwhile.

The following day we watched the UTMB start and I've seen nothing like it for atmosphere. Slowly the idea of entering UTMB crept into my mind. Over the next few days E and I did some good hill walking which told me my legs still had something in them. We watched people finish the UTMB then headed for home on the Sunday. Over the next week various runners asked me if I would be entering UTMB in 2019 and I always said no but slowly the idea was building in my head. Why not? TDS had been enjoyable and not a trudge or a strain and I still had energy at the end. 2019 would be about completing a 100-mile race then working a plan to UTMB. Part of me feels more alive, and relaxed, than ever when in Chamonix and coming back for another race seems an eminently sensible thing to do!

Annex A Results

The finishing time was never really that important for this story, however listing the finish times for the races covered may give a feel for 'where in the pack' I was and, perhaps, put a little more context on the experiences described. With the rise of GPS watches many runners dispute the course distances (although I've yet to find someone who finds it shorter!) so the distances below are all as quoted by the organiser.

Event	Year	Distance	D+	Time	Position	Score
CCC	2010	81k	4675m	17:23:26	709/797	448
CCC	2011	92k	5100m	20:04:33	890/1591	431
UTMR	2015	106.3k	7075m	25:45:02	77/105	446
Ecotrail Oslo	2016	78.4k	2175m	12:10:35	298/329	425
Tierra Arctic Ultra	2016	120.5k	2375m	22:17:14	31/39	448
Transylvania 50	2017	50.5k	3075m	11:06:00	146/266	434
Ut4M	2017	176.1k	11975m	36:08:37	135/247	451
Ecotrail Paris	2018	79.6k	1400m	11:31:54	1078/1738	431
Transylvania 80	2018	85.9k	4850m	20:00:45	32/53	449
Zugsptiz Ultra	2018	102.5k	5491m	22:01:53	110/134 Master Men	N/A
TDS	2018	122.8k	6775M	27:29:03	662/1328	446

The ITRA groups scores in to 19 different levels. The lowest level, Starter F, is for scores under 250 and the highest level, Top Elite AAAA, is for scores above 900 (men) and 775 (women). In the races above my scores are between 400 and 450 (with one exception)

249

which puts me as an Intermediate EEE or in the 14th level from the top. Intermediate has three levels (E, EE and EEE) and if I had a score over 500 (which I've only achieved in the Lakeland 50), I'd be in the heady heights of 'Strong D'!

The ITRA also gives a World, European and nationality ranking for different lengths of races (XXL, XL, L, M, S and XS) and a General ranking overall. For XXL (e.g. Ut4M) my world ranking is 19992 compared to 50808 for L (e.g. Transylvania 80) which shows, compared to others, I'm better at long events.

To work out if a race is possible my simple equation is to take the finish time of the fastest person, multiply by 1.5 and add an hour. This gives me a reasonably accurate assessment of how long it will take me. It also shows how fast an Elite AAAA runner can move compared to me and explains why my ranking is in five digits!

Annex B Kit list

Throughout the course of this adventure over 5000 miles have been run; 2012 was a low point with only 6 miles compared to 994 miles in 2018. A lot of kit has been tried, tested, and worn out during this period. What works for me may not work for others but here is my kit list with reasons why. It's worth noting I'm 1.96m tall, weigh 70kg, and feel the cold so I tend to carry a lot to keep me warm.

- Shoes: Salomon Speedcross (£70). I use these as I've yet to find a shoe with more grip. Whilst there is little cushioning, I feel this is a price worth paying for the grip. A downside with them is the thick insole which, when wet, helps to macerate the soles of the feet. To get around this I've sometimes taken the insole out which makes the shoe even harder underfoot but can be worth doing to save the feet. Having big feet is a real challenge as I have to buy online so never get to try something on so, when I find something that works, I stick with it.

- Socks: Lightweight 1000 mile socks (£10) have been used throughout. I find the double layer helps. As the socks, and shoes, are not waterproof this means they can dry out. I put Bodyglide lubricant on my feet pre-race and try and not touch them at all during an event. Back in 2009 I used to get blisters but in more recent years a blister has been a rarity.

- Calfguards and Quadguards: I use Compressport products (£60 for both) and find them to be really beneficial as I do not cramp up when wearing these items of compression clothing.

- Shorts: I have some cheap Nike lycra shorts (£15) I've had for years that work. They are lightweight so don't hold much moisture when wet. I owned two pairs since the late 1990s which have been used for all training and racing throughout.

- Base layer: I use a Skins compression top (£40). I use this as it helps support the lower back so helps with pain management. I use a full-length sleeve version as it keeps me out of the sun a little.

- Windproof gilet: This is a very lightweight piece of kit from Decathlon (£20) that lets me thermoregulate easily as can zip it up if a little cold. In bad weather it also serves as another layer to be wearing making an air pocket of warmth.

- Waterproof coat: Mammut Kento (£130) which has a hydrostatic head of 20000mm and vapor permeability of 15000 $g/m^2/24h$. These are quite large values to find in a jacket (about double of some competitors) and in TDS in 2018 this coat managed to keep me nice and dry.

- Waterproof trousers: Berghaus Gore-Tex (£80) as they are really light and can be bought in different waist/leg length combinations.

- Down coat: Montane Featherlite Down (£100). A good bit of kit to carry for when things get cold. Also provides some cushioning against the spine when in the rucksack.

- Fleece: Any light weight fleece (£60) with zipped pockets. I go for fleeces that have a grid pattern as they are lighter, weigh less when wet, will dry quicker when wet and the gridding provides another layer of air pockets to promote warmth.

- Gloves: I've taken a multi-glove approach as without gloves I'm nothing. I carry light weight hand warmers to put in gloves (£1), lightweight surgical gloves (50p), Sealskinz gloves (£25), Gore-Tex overgloves (£15) and Montane mountain gloves (£60). To many this seems overkill but as someone who feels the cold, I need to be able to keep my hands dry and warm.

Annex B Kit list

- Hat: If wet/cold I'd take a wool hat with a Gore-Tex lining (£15). If dry I'd take a Salomon Sahara hat that covers the neck.

- Bag: I've tried several and currently have a Raidlight vest bag (£80) that weighs 350g and can take up to 20 litres. I use my various items of clothing to pad out the spine. Unlike a conventional rucksack it sits high on the body which means it doesn't bounce on my lower back and cause disc pain.

- Fluids: When I started out, I used to use a bladder but have gone off this for a number of reasons. Firstly, it was always time consuming to fill as I'd have to empty my bag to get it in/out. Secondly it is weight on my back and I'd rather have weight on my front to try and balance things out a little. Now I use 2 500ml Lucozade bottles carried on the front of the bag. These are really easy to use and refill. If it looks like I'll need more water I add extra bottles in side pockets so can carry 2 litres.

- Food: I use a mixture of gels, energy bars, jelly chews and solid food at checkpoints. I find mixing it up is best.

- Walking poles: Black Diamond z-poles (£100) that fold in to three with a fourth section that pulls out – they sit on the front of my bag so are really easy to access. They can be a bit fiddly when hands are cold as there is a small clip to push to lock them out. Compared to traditional three-part poles they are so much more convenient to carry.

- Head torch: When I started racing, I used a 100 lumens torch that just wasn't that good in the dark. I then bought a Petzl NAO which is great – the best light out there but the trouble is it is quite bulky and uses a lot of batteries. I've since changed to taking a Petzl 350 lumens torch with a Petzl 250 lumens torch as a spare. Both of these take the same rechargeable battery – for a long event I'd carry 5 batteries.

- Survival blanket: Instead of a foil blanket I take a lightweight SOL emergency bivvy bag (£15) that packs down to about the size of a 250ml bottle of water. Having used it twice it is definitely far better than a blanket and the extra weight/bulk is definitely worthwhile. In the time when I had to use this in the mountains (not covered in this book) I discovered it only came up to my shoulders. To make my night out a little more enjoyable I emptied my rucksack, ripped the bottom of the bivvy open (to make a tube) and with my feet in my bag found I could now pull the 'tube bivvy' up to cover my body and wrap around my head. It was very heavy rain so I hung my Gore-Tex overgloves up to collect drinking water which worked rather well.

- Watch: Suunto Ambit 3 Peak (£240). This watch has been a highly effective purchase useful in races and in training. The watch life can be adjusted from a computer in advance to last for either 20, 30 or 200hrs. It does this by adjusting how often it updates its position, being 1, 5 or 60 seconds respectively. My experience with the 20hr setting is that it lasts 14-16hrs depending on the weather, the colder it is the shorter the time. With the 200-hr setting it tends to underestimate distances by about 10% but this is fine as all I need to do is add 10% on to any distance it is quoting. In any race over 50 miles I have it set to 200hrs to ensure it will last.

All of the above, including 1-litre of fluids, weighs around 7kg. This will be more compared to most but as someone who feels the cold a lot, I need my layers.

Outdoor kit can be expensive so I tend to shop around online and buy only when something is reduced. I've ordered from several shops in Spain and whilst it may take 3 weeks to arrive it is far cheaper than the UK so worth the wait. Often, I get my kit ideas from seeing what works for others in races and talking to fellow competitors about kit – this is really the best source of information.

ACKNOWLEDGEMENTS

I'd like to thank all of those who believed in me, in various ways, throughout the course of this adventure. At times TDS seemed a distant dream that was unlikely to be fulfilled so your support is greatly appreciated.

I'd also like to thank those who laid on such races as without these I would not have got to see so many amazing places and find something that truly makes me happy.

In developing this book, a number of people gave review comments, at various depths and times and all of these have been helpful in various ways. It would not do justice to one reviewer to provide a short list of names, as his name would be lost in the list. Throughout the two years it took to write this one person, DJ Alf, always stuck by the project and I'm highly grateful for the detailed review comments received. Having nothing to do with the sport made for a perfect reviewer as everything had to make sense to the lay reader. In an early draft I mentioned bagging Wainwrights and the comment that came back was what did alcohol have to do with it! (At this point I'm assuming the reader has read the book so hopefully this makes sense.)

When writing a book, it is very easy to think you can do everything. I had several ideas for what the cover would look like and somehow thought I could draw it. Before even starting I had a reality check and, around the same time, Hannah Coxon (https://www.instagram.com/raptorous.design/) offered to produce the cover. The final result is of a standard way beyond whatever I could have achieved and I'm very pleased with the result.

Finally, I'd like to thank E for being supportive throughout and waiting around at some of the races at odd times of the day or night – it does make a difference you being there!

David Byrne (runningthroughthenight@yahoo.com)

Printed by Amazon Italia Logistica S.r.l.
Torrazza Piemonte (TO), Italy